NATIONAL SECURITY AND MILITARY LAW
IN A NUTSHELL

By

CHARLES A. SHANOR
Professor of Law
Emory University

L. LYNN HOGUE
Professor of Law
Georgia State University

THOMSON
—————★—————™
WEST

Mat #40041402

COPYRIGHT © 1980 WEST PUBLISHING CO.
COPYRIGHT © 1996 By WEST PUBLISHING CO.
COPYRIGHT © 2003 By West, a Thomson business
        610 Opperman Drive
        P.O. Box 64526
        St. Paul, MN 55164–0526
        1–800–328–9352

ISBN 0–314–26357–8

TEXT IS PRINTED ON 10% POST
CONSUMER RECYCLED PAPER

1st Reprint — 2009

To
Our Families
With Love and Appreciation

To
Our Families
With Love and Appreciation

PREFACE

——————

This is the third edition of MILITARY LAW IN A NUTSHELL, a book that attempts to integrate the jurisprudence of the military, "a society apart from civilian society," into an analytical framework comprehensible to civilian lawyers as well as those having an intimate knowledge of the armed services. However, as the new title, NATIONAL SECURITY AND MILITARY LAW IN A NUTSHELL, indicates, it is a book that has evolved in important ways from the first two editions. The attacks of September 11 and the aftermath of those attacks led us to reevaluate the book's original scope and to add a lengthy new chapter entitled "National Security Law" to supplement the "National Security Constitution" framework set out in the first chapter of all three editions.

In keeping with the Nutshell series format, we have avoided extensive citations while presenting a systematic but generalized treatment of the law. The primary audience for this volume includes, in addition to law students in specialized courses on national security law, military law and constitutional law, practicing lawyers seeking a succinct overview of military law, cadets at the military academies and in college R.O.T.C. programs, and lawyers preparing to enter the Army, Navy, or Air Force Judge Advocate General's Corps. For those who seek perspective on media reports about the War on Terrorism, it provides a useful overview of the national security

V

law framework that is shaping, and being shaped by, this distinctive twenty-first century conflict.

The primary sources in this Nutshell are very ecumenical (the Constitution, treaties, federal statutes, executive orders, civilian regulations, federal court decisions, military regulations, and the decisions of courts specializing in military criminal law matters). Because of its breadth, this volume necessarily sacrifices depth. We have attempted to compensate for limited treatment of individual topics through references to collateral readings.

Growth in and addition to the basic framework chapters led us to delete the treatment of veteran's benefits contained in earlier editions.

We are indebted to Lt. Col. Rodger A. Drew, Jr., USAF, Deputy Chief Trial Judge of the Air Force Legal Services Agency, for carefully reviewing and commenting on the revised "Military Criminal Justice System" chapter. We also thank our research assistants, our students in National Security Law, Military Law, and Law and Terrorism classes, and two law students who read and commented on the new National Security Law chapter (Athanasios Agelakopoulos and Grant Harris).

Our special thanks go to Rhonda Heermans at Emory Law School for formatting and assembling this manuscript, creating the outline and the tables of authorities, and formatting the index. Any errors of substance or style that remain are, of course, ours alone.

CHARLES A. SHANOR
Professor of Law
Emory University

L. LYNN HOGUE
Professor of Law
Georgia State University
Lt. Col., U.S. Army Reserve, Judge Advocate General's Corps (Ret.)

Atlanta, Georgia

OUTLINE

TABLE OF CASES

References are to Pages

TABLE OF CASES

TABLE OF CASES

TABLE OF CASES

CHAPTER 1

THE CONSTITUTION AND
NATIONAL SECURITY

A. ORIGINS OF THE NATIONAL SECURITY CONSTITUTION

The drafters of the federal Constitution approached their task with perceived abuses of British military authority fresh in mind. They were wary of a standing army and the potential for domestic tyranny inherent in the creation of a national military force. They were also well aware that the American Revolution would not have succeeded without military force. The debate over the military components of the Constitution was shaped by the figure of General George Washington, the military leader who successfully led the fight to throw off the yoke of British rule, and who, it was widely assumed, would become the first President and Commander in Chief of the military. Washington's character and temper may have made this fusion of civilian and military roles palatable.

When the process of debate and compromise ended, the Constitutional Congress did not elect to abolish the armed forces during peacetime and rely solely on state militias. Rather, it sought to institute checks which would cabin the potentially dangerous national military force. Major limits included confining appropriations for the Army to two-year intervals, thereby requiring the Congress to review its power frequently. Art. I, § 8, cl. 12. Responsibility for the military was divided between the Congress and the President. Compare Art. I, § 8, cl. 11–16 with Art. II, § 2, cl. 1. States retained their own armed forces, the militias, in case the national government threatened popular freedoms. Responsibility for the militias was split between the central government and the states, Art. I, § 8, cl. 16, and the Bill of Rights recognized "the right of the people to keep and bear arms." U.S. Const. Amend. 2. In order that state militias would have access to weapons, each militia member would bring his own, and, since each would know how to use his own firearm, that would help assure adequate training.

B. TEXT AND DOCTRINE

A careful review of the constitutional text confirms the truth of Justice Burton's assertion that "we have a fighting constitution." Lichter v. United States (S.Ct.1948). Indeed, the *Preamble* of the Constitution lists the goal of "providing for the common defense" as one of six purposes for the 1787 Constitution that replaced the Articles of Confederation. Chief Justice Charles Evans Hughes wrote that the war power of the national government is not only the power to fight, but "the power to wage war successfully." Hughes, "War Powers Under the Constitution," 42 A.B.A. Rep. 232, 238 (1917) quoted in Hirabayashi v. United States (S.Ct.1943).

The federal Constitution contains numerous provisions which bear directly on the power to declare war as well as to establish, maintain and control a national security infrastructure comprised principally of the armed forces. Allocations of powers and responsibilities governing national security are not set out in the Constitution in any compact or unified way. Powers overlap, and a definitive resolution of important issues is lacking. Even so, it is the fundamental legal authority for protecting and defending the nation as well as for protecting American interests abroad.

Civilian control over the military is asserted through a variety of constitutional devices. The Supreme Court has recognized that both the Congress and the President have explicit powers traceable to the Constitution as well as non-textual powers. This division of authority has not functioned without complications, but it has succeeded in its intended purpose of preventing either the legislative or executive branches from using the military to wrest power from the people. It has likewise prevented the military from escaping its subordination to civilian authority and displacing legitimate governmental powers.

1. POWERS OF CONGRESS

The Congressional Vestiture Clause, Article I, § 1, assigns "[a]ll legislative powers herein granted" to the Congress. Under the federal Constitution, Congress clearly has lawmaking authority. What is not clear from the text of the Constitution is whether that power is exclusive or shared with the President. At issue, for example, is whether in matters of national security the nation is limited to steps Congress wishes to take, or whether the President also has some "lawmaking" powers which he can exercise. In Youngstown Sheet & Tube Co. v. Sawyer (S.Ct.1952), Justice Black's plurality opinion interpreted this provision as conferring all lawmaking powers on Congress: "The Founders of this Nation entrusted the lawmaking power to the Congress alone in both good and bad times * * * the President's power to see that the laws are faithfully executed refutes the idea that he is to be a law-maker." The restrictive language of the Congressional Vestiture Clause, however, easily lends itself to a contrary view that outside the range of legislative powers "herein granted," the President may independently exercise unassigned national security lawmaking powers as Commander in Chief of the Army and Navy. Art. II, § 2.

The Secret Journal Clause, Article I, § 5, allows Congress to keep secret portions of its journal, the record of its proceedings. Secrecy, although an impediment to the efficient functioning of a democratic government, is essential to the successful conduct of military and other national security operations. The full implications of the secret journal provision are not clear. Is Congress impliedly given a role in the secret side of national security since it has express constitutional authority to keep secrets? Whatever powers, if any, the clause confers upon Congress, historical practice primarily involves the executive branch taking an active role with respect to military and diplomatic secrets. United States v. Curtiss–Wright Export Corp. (S.Ct.1936).

The Spending Clause, Article I, § 8, cl. 1, implements the common defense objective. This power, along with the power to incur debt conferred in clause 2, is an important foundation of national security. Wars, as well as lesser military operations, are costly affairs. Unresolved is the relationship between such expenditures and the degree of control intended for Congress as a result of the appropriations process. Congress can exercise a kind of ultimate superintending control over national security activities simply by declining to fund them. This power is rarely resorted to since the consequence would be the politically unpalatable one of placing troops and other military assets in harm's way. Such a provision, however, was included in the appropriation for Vietnam-related activities in 1973: "[O]n or after August 15, 1973, no funds herein or heretofore appropriated may be obligated or expended to finance directly or indirectly combat activities by United States military forces in or over or from off the shores of North Vietnam, South Vietnam, Laos or Cambodia." See Holtzman v. Schlesinger (2d Cir.1973) (military activity approved until effective date of the cutoff) (dictum).

In the post-Vietnam era, Congress has exerted its power over the national purse strings to assert a role in controlling specific secret military operations. Examples include the 1976 Clark–Tunney Amendment to the Arms Export Control Act (banning covert activities in Angola), the 1974 Hughes–Ryan Amendment to the Foreign Assistance Act (limiting expenditures for operations in foreign countries to intelligence gathering unless the President certifies to Congress the operation's importance to national security), and the 1982 Boland Amendments (limiting covert activities in Nicaragua). These expressions of the checking function of Congress' appropriations power have seldom been litigated because of the limited role courts have in the national security area. Sanchez–Espinoza v. Reagan (D.D.C.1983).

Article I, § 8, cl. 10 grants Congress a role in the enforcement and perhaps in the formation of international law by allowing Congress to define and punish the crime of piracy and other violations of the law of nations, which includes the law of war. This congressional role should not be exaggerated, however, for international law may be binding as American law even without congressional action. For example, the Geneva Conventions (1949) were accepted and applied as customary international law even prior to their formal ratification by the U.S. in 1956. Department of the Army, FM 27–10: *The Law of Land Warfare* ¶¶ 505–508, pp. 180–182 (1956) (Customary international law part of U.S. law and enforceable by U.S. courts). See The Paquete Habana (S.Ct.1900).

Article I, § 8, cl. 11, grants Congress the power to declare war, to grant letters of marque and reprisal, and to make rules concerning captured property on land and water. Of these three provisions, the power to declare war is the most significant. Yet, modern circumstances and changes in the nature of warfare have affected these provisions. With the adoption of the Charter of the United Nations, the nations of the world outlawed aggressive war. U.N. Charter Article 2(4). The Charter, however, preserved the right of self-defense. U.N. Charter Article 51. As a consequence, nations are unlikely to declare war in a formal way at the commencement of hostilities. Past practice has been to declare war as the United States did in the five wars fought prior to the entry into force of the U.N. Charter: the War of 1812, 2 Stat. 755 (1812); the Mexican War, 9 Stat. 9 (1846); the Spanish–American War, 30 Stat. 364 (1898); World War I, 40 Stat. 1 (1917); and World War II, 55 Stat. 795, 796, 797 (1941).

Nations now usually go to war for purposes authorized either by the U.N. Charter directly or by the U.N. Security Council. E.g., Authorization for Use of Military Force Against Iraq Resolution, 50 U.S.C.A. § 1541, 105 Stat. 3; Authorization to use military force in Afghanistan, 50 U.S.C.A. § 1541. When recently facing a probable denial of U.N. authorization for military action in Iraq, the United States and other willing nations withdrew their proposed resolution, and instead relied upon past U.N. resolutions for the approval to attack. Most prominent was U.N. Resolution 1441, which recalled earlier authorization for "Member States to use **all necessary means** to uphold and implement" earlier resolutions.

Even if developments in international law limit Congress from moving to secure national security objectives by declaring war, Congress can still authorize war-making that falls short of declared or "perfect" war and can authorize undeclared or "imperfect" war. Bas v. Tingy (S.Ct.1800).

The importance of the power of Congress to grant private authority to make war under the marque and reprisal clause, authorizing private individuals to engage in military activity, has no doubt diminished with the decline of eighteenth century modes of conducting war on the cheap. Its persisting significance, though, lies in the vesting in Congress of the power to undertake imperfect war, or war that falls short of accepted international definitions of war. Military activity that does not rise to the level of war has been part of our national history since the beginning. The quasi-war with France was an early example. Little v. Barreme (S.Ct.1804). Also, limited hostilities are commenced without a declaration of war to fulfill such purposes as rescuing U.S. citizens. For example, in October 1983, President Reagan sent troops into Grenada ostensibly to rescue several hundred American medical students at St. George's Medical School there who were in danger from a local coup aided by Cuban communists. In the course of the humanitarian rescue effort, eighteen American soldiers were killed and 59 wounded as well as 69 Grenadians and Cubans who were killed and 396 wounded.

The Armies Clause, Article I, § 8, cl. 12, imposes limits on the general power to tax and spend for the common defense. The two-year limitation on appropriations specifically applicable to the Army has its roots in bitter pre-Revolutionary experience. This provision was described by James Madison as "the best possible precaution against danger from standing armies." The Federalist No. 41. For example, the Declaration of Independence complains that King George III "kept among us, in times of peace, standing armies, without the consent of our legislatures."

The Navy Clause, Article I, § 8, cl. 13, authorizes the creation and maintenance of a navy. The Navy Clause contains no time limit on appropriations, acknowledging that long-range planning is appropriate for the Navy. While neither clause 12 nor 13 refers to the Marines or, of course, the Air Force, Congress' constitutional authority to authorize national security forces that reflect such strategic and technological evolution is undisputed.

The Government and Regulation Clause, Article I, § 8, cl. 14, allows Congress to make rules for the governance of the land and naval forces. Authority under this provision includes providing for disciplinary regulations and administrative procedures applicable to the uniformed services, but it does not include the power to command, which belongs to the President as Commander in Chief. Ex parte Milligan (S.Ct.1866) (dictum) (opinion of Chase, C.J. and Justices Wayne, Swayne, and Miller, concurring); Swaim v. United States (Ct.Cl.1893) (dictum) ("Congress can not in the disguise of 'rules for the government' of the Army impair the authority of the President as commander in chief.").

The Militia Clauses, Article I, § 8, cl. 15–16, allow Congress "to provide for calling forth the Militia" to execute federal laws, suppress insurrections, and repel invasions. Under these clauses, the militias remain under state control until called into federal service. Congress is responsible for their organization, arming and discipline. Gilligan v. Morgan (S.Ct.1973)(Kent State student slayings); and Perpich v. Department of Defense (S.Ct.1990) (National Guard Unit called to active duty for training in Central America). While their officers are appointed pursuant to state authority, such militias are trained according to congressionally prescribed standards and are under federal control when "employed in the Service of the United States."

The Seat of the Government Clause, Article I, § 8, cl. 17, grants Congress exclusive legislative jurisdiction over federal enclaves such as the District of Columbia as well as "all Places purchased by the Consent of the Legislature of the State in which the Same shall be, for the Erection of Forts, Magazines, Arsenals, dock-Yards, and other needful Buildings * * * ." Once a state has ceded authority to the federal government, federal law applies in the enclave.

The Necessary and Proper Clause, Article I, § 8, cl. 18, allows Congress to act fully on the powers granted to it. McCulloch v. Maryland (S.Ct.1819). It does not allow legislative restraints on the national security powers granted to the President. Youngstown Sheet & Tube Co. v. Sawyer (S.Ct.1942) (Jackson,J., concurring) (Although "only Congress can provide [the President] with an army and navy to command [,] Congress cannot deprive the President of the command of [them].")

The Habeas Corpus Clause, Article I, § 9, cl. 2, protects access to the Great Writ inherited from

English common law to test, in a court of law, the legality and authority for one's detention except "when in Cases of Rebellion or Invasion the public Safety may require it." The text is silent on the important question of who may suspend the writ in circumstances when the national security is imperiled. Placement of this power among those granted to Congress implies that Congress initially determines when circumstances dictate its suspension. During the Civil War, President Lincoln suspended the writ, an action Congress subsequently approved. Ex parte Milligan (S.Ct.1866).

The Appropriations Clause, Article I, § 9, cl. 7, prevents spending by the executive branch unless Congress has appropriated the money. This power is described above in connection with the spending power. The text offers no guidance with respect to constitutional deadlocks which could occur if, for example, Congress failed to appropriate funds to permit the President to carry out express constitutional duties that touch on the executive role in international law, such as receiving ambassadors.

The Statement and Account Clause, Article I, § 9, cl. 7, provides for the publication "from time to time" of "all" public expenditures. This provision works in obvious tension with the practice of concealing sensitive national security information such as the budget of the Central Intelligence Agency or expenditures on secret weapons programs such as the Manhattan Project which created the atomic bomb, the stealth fighter program and other "skunk works." Disclosure to

Congress in executive session would hardly seem to satisfy the publication requirement; however, the generality of the clause may mean that past congressional practice sufficiently satisfies the requirement. For example, Congress has placed the budget of the Central Intelligence Agency within appropriations for other agencies such as the armed forces in order to conceal it.

Article I, § 10, cl. 3, provides for limited war-making power by the states in the event they are "actually invaded, or in such imminent danger as will not admit of delay." Otherwise, they are precluded from keeping troops or warships in peacetime or allying with other states or foreign nations without congressional authorization. There is a question as to whether this specific constitutional provision together with the habeas corpus suspension provision exhausts the instances when emergency powers may be invoked, and rebuts the existence of a general emergency power exercisable either by Congress or the President existing outside of the explicit provisions of the constitutional text. The existence of emergency powers has been conceded by the federal Supreme Court from time to time. For example, "[T]he President's independent power to act depends upon the gravity of the situation confronting the nation." Youngstown Sheet & Tube Co. v. Sawyer (S.Ct.1952) (Clark, J. concurring). Indeed, a careful review of the various opinions in Youngstown reveals that in rejecting the constitutionality of President Truman's action in this specific instance, six justices endorsed some sort of inherent emergency power in the President depending on the gravity of the emergency and whether Congress legislated in the area.

The Supreme Court has recognized that Congress also has non-textual sources of power to regulate foreign affairs. "Although there is in the Constitution no specific grant to Congress of power to enact legislation for the effective regulation of foreign affairs, there can be no doubt of the existence of this power in the [Congress]." Perez v. Brownell (S.Ct.1958), overruled on other grounds, Afroyim v. Rusk (S.Ct.1967).

2. POWERS OF THE PRESIDENT

The Executive Vestiture Clause, Article II, § 1, cl. 1, unlike the comparable Article I clause which vests in Congress only "[a]ll legislative Powers herein granted," confers on the President all "executive Power." The President has a special role in foreign affairs and matters of national security, quite apart from a specific constitutional grant. "[T]he power to make such international agreements as do not constitute treaties in the constitutional sense, which is [not] expressly affirmed by the Constitution * * * [is warranted] not in the provisions of the Constitution, but in the law of nations * * * [T]he President alone has the power to speak or listen as a representative of the nation." United States v. Curtiss–Wright Export Corp. (S.Ct.1936).

The Oath of Office Clause, Article II, § 1, cl. 7, specifically obligates the President to "defend" the Constitution. Only the President's oath is prescribed. Other officials are only required to "be bound by Oath or Affirmation, to support this Constitution." Even though the presidential oath includes an obligation to defend the Constitution, the President's special undertaking, in and of itself, probably gives him no special national security responsibility or authority.

The Commander in Chief Clause, Article II, § 2, cl. 1, is a major source of the President's national security authority and a potent source of the ambiguity over national security authority which emerges from the division of authority between the power of Congress to declare war and the power of the President to conduct war. Unanswered questions exist about (1) the President's responsibilities when an enemy attacks and (2) the power of the President to take provocative military actions short of war which carry the power to precipitate war. Contemporary examples include humanitarian rescue missions, such as the abortive rescue attempt of the Iranian hostages under President Carter or the American raid on Libya under President Reagan in response to the killing of American armed services personnel in Germany.

On October 3, 1993, in response to vicious militia attacks on U.N. peacekeepers, U.S. soldiers entered Mogadishu, Somalia on President Clinton's order. During a failed attempt to capture militia leaders responsible for attacks on U.N. peacekeepers, a U.S. Black Hawk helicopter went down and soldiers were left helpless in the field. A rescue effort launched by U.S. military forces would eventually see the loss of another Black

Hawk, and the deaths of 18 soldiers, with 84 wounded.

The Treaty Clause, Article II, § 2, cl. 2, grants the President the power "by and with the Advice and Consent of the Senate, to make Treaties, provided two thirds of the Senators present concur." The distinction between a treaty and an agreement is not sharply defined and is based in part on whether the executive branch sought Senate involvement. International agreements which "do not constitute treaties in the constitutional sense" do not require the participation by the Senate called for in this clause. In these instances, "[t]he President alone has the power to speak or listen as a representative of the nation. He *makes* the treaties with the advice and consent of the Senate; but he alone negotiates. Into the field of negotiation the Senate cannot intrude; and Congress itself is powerless to invade it." United States v. Curtiss–Wright Export Corp. (S.Ct.1936). An example of such an agreement is the Litvinov assignment to the United States of all Soviet claims against Americans holding funds of Russian companies seized after the Russian Revolution. United States v. Belmont (S.Ct.1937). The President has power to conclude agreements which affect national security. Dames & Moore v. Regan (S.Ct.1981) (Iranian hostage release negotiations).

The Appointments Clause, Article II, § 2, cl. 2, provides that "The President * * * shall nominate, and by and with the Advice and Consent of the Senate, shall appoint * * * Officers of the United States, whose Appointments * * * shall be established by Law; but the Congress may by Law vest the Appointment of such inferior Officers, as they think proper, in the President alone * * * or in the Heads of Departments." Officers of the armed forces are officers within the meaning of the Appointments Clause, either as "Officers of the United States" or "inferior Officers." United States v. Corson (S.Ct.1885). However, detailing of an officer to a different position, such as to that of a military judge, does not constitute a new appointment requiring Senate confirmation. (____ (S.Ct. ____). The differentiation between these two classifications of officers is established by the clause based on whether they are appointed with the advice and consent of the Senate, or appointed by the President or by the Head of one of the military departments alone.

The State of the Union Clause, Article II, § 3, requires disclosure to Congress of information about "the State of the Union." The clause does not indicate to what extent sensitive national security information should be revealed. The longstanding practice is for classified information to remain confidential.

The Ambassadors Clause, Article II, § 3, gives the President authority to "receive Ambassadors and other public Ministers." The president's power to enter into diplomatic relations has been said to be a consequence of the United States' membership in "the family of nations" with international powers and obligations "inherently inseparable from the conception of nationality" and not of constitutional origin. United States v. Curtiss–Wright Export Corp. (S.Ct.1936). To the extent that reception of diplomatic personnel implies recognition under international law, the President has an implied power to recognize foreign governments. This power, in turn, can have significant national security implications: recognition can confer status in the community of nations and can also trigger obligations which could draw the nation into hostile relations with other countries. The President also has the power to terminate treaties without Senate involvement. Goldwater v. Carter (S.Ct.1979) (withdrawal of recognition of the Republic of China [Taiwan] and termination of the Mutual Defense Treaty of 1955 with Taiwan).

The Take Care Clause, Article II, § 3, requires the President to "take Care that the Laws be faithfully executed." The meaning of this obligation was at issue in Youngstown Sheet & Tube Co. v. Sawyer (S.Ct.1952). During the Korean War, labor negotiations between the nation's steel companies and their employees came to an impasse. When efforts to settle the dispute failed, the Steelworkers' Union gave notice of a nation-wide strike in April of 1952. Because steel is an essential ingredient of virtually all weapons and weapons systems, President Truman feared the strike would endanger national security and issued an Executive Order seizing the mills to keep them in production. The steel companies challenged President Truman's authority to seize the nation's steel mills. The Court held that the seizure was not within the President's national security powers, a decision viewed by many, including Truman himself, as a defeat for the power to act "at all times to meet any sudden threat to the nation's security." H. Truman, 2 Memoirs: Years of Trial and Hope 478 (1956).

The government's brief in Youngstown argued on Truman's behalf that the President had an "obligation to insure the military security of the United States and its armed forces by maintaining steel production, [as well as to] carry out the national stabilization policy expressed in the Defense Production Act by seizing and operating the steel mills." This argument was accepted by three dissenting Justices: "[T]he President is a constitutional officer charged with taking care that a 'mass of legislation' be executed. Flexibility as to mode of execution to meet critical situations is a matter of practical necessity." The argument was rejected by the remaining justices. Justice Black opined: "[T]he President's power to see that the laws are faithfully executed refutes the idea that he is to be a lawmaker." What remains unanswered is the nature of the President's enforcement obligation, particularly with respect to laws which have diverse themes or are ambiguous.

Apart from the specific powers listed in Article II, does the President possess any emergency powers that do not derive from the text of the Constitution? Justice Clark, in an opinion concurring in the judgment in Youngstown, took the view that "the Constitution does grant to the President extensive authority in times of grave and imperative national emergency [indeed], such a grant may well be necessary to the very existence of the Constitution itself." Youngstown Sheet &

Tube Co. v. Sawyer (S.Ct.1952). Clark supported his position with the example of President Lincoln: "measures otherwise unconstitutional might become lawful by becoming indispensable to the preservation of the Constitution through the preservation of the nation." He also drew upon President Theodore Roosevelt's stewardship model: "[the President is] a steward of the people bound actively and affirmatively to do all he could for the people. [It is] not only his right but his duty to do anything that the needs of the Nation demand, unless such action [is] forbidden by the Constitution or the law." Theodore Roosevelt, Autobiography 372 (1914). This model has not met with general judicial acceptance and instances for its invocation have been few.

A major theme of Youngstown is the interplay of the powers of the President and the Congress in the area of national security, and particularly the use of military force. See generally M. Marcus, Truman and the Steel Seizure Case (1977). Two concurring opinions in the case, those respectively of Justices Frankfurter and Jackson, have provided important models for allocating national security powers among the President and the Congress.

Justice Frankfurter's concurring opinion pictured the Constitution as a framework whose content can be glossed by executive action:

Deeply embedded traditional ways of conducting government cannot supplant the Constitution or legislation, but they give meaning to the words of a text or supply them. It is an inadmissibly narrow conception of American constitutional law to confine it to the words of the Constitution and to disregard the gloss which life has written upon them. [A] systematic, unbroken, executive practice, long pursued to the knowledge of the Congress and never before questioned, engaged in by Presidents who have also sworn to uphold the Constitution, making as it were such exercise of power part of the structure of our government, may be treated as gloss on "executive Power" vested in the [President].

Although for Justice Frankfurter the prior instances of Executive Branch seizures cited by the government did not support President Truman's action in Youngstown, Frankfurter's opinion provided support for President Carter's suspension of all claims pending against Iran as part of his Executive Agreement to secure release of American hostages held there. Dames & Moore v. Regan (S.Ct.1981).

Justice Jackson's concurring opinion posits a three-part model: (1) A zenith of presidential authority when he "acts pursuant to an express or implied authorization of Congress [E.g., United States v. Curtiss–Wright Export Corp. (S.Ct.1936)]" merging all inherent executive power with whatever Congress can delegate; (2) A constitutional middle ground when the President acts without congressional legislation either authorizing the action or forbidding it, a "zone of twilight in which he and Congress may have concurrent authority, or in which its distribution is uncertain. [Here] congressional inertia, indifference or acquiescence may sometimes * * * enable, if not invite, measures on independent presidential responsibility"; and (3) "When the President takes measures incompatible with the expressed or implied will of Congress, his power is at its lowest ebb, for then he can rely only upon his own constitutional powers minus any constitutional powers of Congress over the matter."

Both these models have judicial and scholarly support. See Chemerinsky, "Controlling Inherent Presidential Power: Providing a Framework for Judicial Review," 58 S. Cal. L. Rev. 863 (1983). How the balance between the national security powers of the President and the Congress should be struck remains controversial along with the question of the proper role of the courts. For example, Professor Harold Koh argues that concerning national security, the Constitution is "premised on the balanced institutional participation of all three governmental branches." "Although the National Security constitution has assigned the President the predominant role in making foreign policy decisions, it has granted him only limited *exclusive* powers. Thus, the constitution directs most governmental decisions regarding foreign affairs into a sphere of concurrent authority, under presidential management, but bounded by the checks provided by congressional consultation and judicial review." Harold Koh, *The National Security Constitution: Sharing Power After Iran–Contra Affair* (1990).

3. THE WAR POWERS RESOLUTION

In the wake of the Untied States experience in Vietnam and the extension of that conflict into Cambodia and Laos in 1970–71 without Congress' knowledge or approval, Congress enacted the War Powers Resolution, 50 U.S.C.A. §§ 1541–1548, over President Nixon's veto. Nixon's veto message cited two constitutional infirmities. The first was the requirement that armed forces be withdrawn from a conflict after sixty days unless their further use is authorized by Congress. Nixon opposed this as a legislative abridgment of the President's constitutional authority as Commander-in-Chief. Second, the Resolution allows Congress to direct the withdrawal of forces from extra-territorial hostilities by concurrent resolution. § 1544(c). This President Nixon characterized as a violation of the Presentment Clauses, Art. I, § 7, cl. 2 and 3. Years later, the Supreme Court decision in INS v. Chadha (S.Ct.1983) adopted this rationale as the court rejected a provision in the Immigration and Nationality Act that allowed one House of Congress, by resolution, to invalidate an immigration decision of the Executive Branch. Frank, The Return of Humpty Dumpty: Foreign Relations Law After the Chadha Case, 78 Am. J. Int'l L. 912 (1985).

Neither Nixon nor any other President has conceded the constitutionality of the Resolution or ever fully complied with it. Instances of partial compliance with the Resolution appear when required to coax Congress into providing required support for a large action such as Operation Desert

Storm in the Persian Gulf. E.g., Authorization for Use of Military Force Against Iraq Resolution, 50 U.S.C.A. § 1541(2)(c)("Consistent with section 8(a)(1) of the War Powers Resolution, the Congress declares that this section is intended to constitute specific statutory authorization within the meaning of section 5(b) of the War Powers Resolution.")

4. POWERS OF THE COURTS

In two hundred years, remarkably few court challenges have arisen to the creation and operation of the armed forces. By and large, those which have arisen have been resolved in favor of military power. For instance, in The Selective Draft Law Cases (S.Ct.1918), the Supreme Court repudiated a wide range of challenges to Congressional creation of military forces. The Court held that (1) citizens could be compelled into military service against their wills, (2) state militia personnel may be called upon to fight against foreign enemies, not merely to engage in their normal duties of executing federal law, suppressing insurrections, and repelling invasions, (3) military service is not "involuntary servitude" prohibited by the Thirteenth Amendment, and (4) the power "to raise and support Armies" in Art. I, § 8, cl. 12 is independent of, and broader than, the power to call forth the militia in Art. I, § 8, cl. 15. The power to utilize state militia personnel has been affirmed subsequently. Johnson v. Powell (5th Cir.1969) (National Guard unit called to active duty in Vietnam); Perpich v. Department of

Defense (S.Ct.1990) (National Guard unit called to active duty for training in Central America).

Article III, § 2, provides the foundation for the exercise of federal judicial power over cases with national security implications. It extends federal jurisdiction to cases "arising under" federal constitutional and statutory law and treaties, cases involving diplomatic personnel, and admiralty and maritime cases, including prize cases involving captured vessels. Prize Cases (S.Ct.1863). While there are no apparent textual limits on jurisdiction with respect to national security cases, judicial review has been very restrained with respect to such cases. For example, the Supreme Court has consistently claimed for itself a limited role which defers to the President and the Congress:

Since the Constitution commits to the Executive and to Congress the exercise of the war power in all the vicissitudes and conditions of warfare, it has necessarily given them wide scope for the exercise of judgment and discretion in determining the nature and extent of the threatened injury or danger and in the selection of the means for resisting it * * * . [I]t is not for any court to sit in review of the wisdom of their action or substitute its judgment for theirs.

Hirabayashi v. United States (S.Ct.1943) (upholding conviction for violating a curfew based on Executive Order No. 9066).

Likewise, clear judicial boundaries exist when the relief sought by a claimant would draw the court into micro-managing the military:

[I]t is difficult to conceive of an area of governmental activity in which the courts have less competence. The complex, subtle, and professional decisions as to the composition, training, equipping, and control of a military force are essentially professional military judgments, subject always to civilian control of the Legislative and Executive Branches.

Gilligan v. Morgan, 413 U.S. 1, 10 (1973). Accord, Orloff v. Willoughby, 345 U.S. 83, 93–94 (1953) ("[J]udges are not given the task of running the Army [;] we have found no cases where this Court has assumed to revise duty orders as to one lawfully in the service.").

Judicial abstention in national security cases is supported by doctrines of judicial limitation such as the political question doctrine. E.g., Mora v. McNamara (D.C.Cir.1967) (Vietnam); McArthur v. Clifford (4th Cir.1968) (same); Massachusetts v. Laird (S.Ct.1972) (same); DaCosta v. Laird (2d Cir.1971) (same); Crockett v. Reagan (D.D.C.1982) (El Salvador); compare Orlando v. Laird (2d Cir.1971) (claims justifiable). The standing doctrine has also limited judicial review of military action, as has the ripeness requirement. Schlesinger v. Reservists to Stop the War (1974) (challenge to military Reserve membership of certain members of Congress); United States v. Richardson (1974) (failure to publish CIA expenditures). Similarly, comity and respect for the autonomous military judicial system created by Congress that governs the military requires that civilian courts honor "the separation-of-powers doctrine and * * * the needs of the military" even in habeas corpus proceedings by those entitled to discharge. Parisi v. Davidson (1972).

The Treason Clauses, Article III, § 3, set out a constitutional definition of what constitutes the crime of treason: only levying war against the United States, adhering to its enemies, or giving enemies aid and comfort is considered treason. The Founding Fathers were concerned with the misuse of treason as a catchall. The clauses also set forth an explicit evidentiary standard for treason cases, the testimony of two witnesses to the same overt act or confession by the accused in open court. Haupt v. United States (S.Ct.1947).

C. OTHER PROVISIONS

The Guarantee Clause, Article IV, § 4, requires the United States to protect the states against invasion and allows the state legislature or the executive, in the event the legislature cannot be convened, to apply for federal help in suppressing domestic violence.

The Supremacy Clause, Article VI, cl. 2, makes all treaties made either under the Articles of Confederation or the federal Constitution part of the "supreme Law of the Land." Questions persist about the scope of the treaty power in relation to other federal powers. For example, can a treaty supersede the constitutional ordering of national security powers? The Supreme Court held that executive agreements, such as status of forces agreements (SOFAs), could not provide for military jurisdiction over civilian dependents of American armed service personnel overseas thereby depriving them of constitutional criminal procedure protections secured by the Bill of Rights. "[N]o agreement with a foreign nation can confer power on the Congress, or on any other branch of Government, which is free from the restraints of the Constitution." Reid v. Covert (S.Ct.1957).

The First Amendment provides protection for speech, press and religion—prohibiting the establishment of a particular religion or requirement of faith or belief, and protecting the free exercise of religion. With respect to speech and press, national security interests have figured prominently in the development of the case law of the First Amendment. The Supreme Court began the task of developing First Amendment doctrine in a series of cases decided in the wake of World War I. The defendants asserted that their writings and spoken words were protected by the speech clause against the government's prosecution for violation of the 1917 Espionage Act or its 1918 amendments, The Espionage Act criminalized false reports or statements during wartime which interfered with the military, or caused or attempted to cause insubordination, disloyalty or mutiny, or obstructed recruiting or enlistment activities. Convictions in all the cases were upheld. Schenck v. United States (S.Ct.1919) (origin of Justice Holmes's "clear and present danger" standard); Frohwerk v. United States (S.Ct.1919); Debs v. United States (S.Ct.1919); Abrams v. United States (S.Ct.1919). Laws against criminal syndicalism and later communism provided the grist for continued doctrinal development of the First Amendment. This process culminated in the replacement of the Holmes's "clear and present danger" test with one closer to Judge Learned Hand's formulation in Masses Publishing Co. v. Patten (S.D.N.Y.1917). Speech may be punished only when it incites "imminent lawless action." Brandenburg v. Ohio (S.Ct.1969).

Any larger exposition of the development of First Amendment doctrine is beyond the scope of this work. However, specific restraints on the publication of information with actual or supposed national security implications have been attempted with varying degrees of success. For example, the Supreme Court has shown hostility toward prior restraints on publications, yet conceded that "no one would question but that a government might prevent actual obstruction to its recruiting service or the publication of the sailing dates of [military] transports or the number and location of troops." Near v. Minnesota (S.Ct.1931) (dictum). In order to come within Near's national security exception to the presumption against prior restraints, the claimed national security interest must be real, e.g., "information that would set in motion a nuclear holocaust," and not intended merely for the "suppression of embarrassing [historical] information." New York Times Co. v. United States (S.Ct.1971). Ground rules for press coverage of Operation Desert Shield/Storm were upheld even though they involved requirements for the use of press pools, restrictions on press mobility and prior submission requirements for review by military authorities. Nation Magazine v. United States Dept. of Defense (S.D.N.Y. 1991).

With respect to religion, Congress can provide for the religious needs of members of the armed forces through governmentally owned places of worship on military posts and the employment of a corps of chaplains to minister to their needs without violating the Establishment Clause. School Dist. of Abington Tp. v. Schempp (S.Ct.1963) (dictum) (Brennan, J., concurring).

The First Amendment rights of members of the armed services and their limitations in comparison with others in American society are discussed in Chapter 3.

The Second Amendment revisits the provisioning of the state militias, a topic dealt with earlier under the powers of Congress (Article I, § 8, cl. 15 and 16). The heart of the amendment is "the right of the people to keep and bear Arms." Most would agree that this amendment reflects a deep-seated suspicion of federal military power. Beyond this narrow common understanding, however, the meaning of the Second Amendment is controversial. The 5th Circuit, in *U.S. v. Emerson* (5th Cir. 2001), reviewed three interpretations of the Amendment. The *collective rights* view, adopted in four Circuits, argues that the Framers' intent was only to preserve the States' ability to raise militias, thereby allaying their fear that the Federal Government might amass a concentration of military power. In this view, there is no corresponding right of any individual to "bear arms." The *sophisticated collective rights* view, also adopted by several U.S. Circuits, recognizes a "limited species of individual right" to keep firearms. The right of an individual to keep arms extends only to those involved in an organized militia, and even then, "only if the federal and state governments fail to provide the firearms necessary for such militia service." The 5th Circuit, after completing an historical analysis of the text, favored the third interpretation, the *individual rights* view of the Second Amendment. The Court held that the Second Amendment "protects the right of individuals, including those not then actually a member of any militia or engaged in active military service, to privately possess and bear their own firearms," subject, of course, to reasonable regulations. While the Supreme Court has refused to decide the issue, the Department of Justice has issued a memorandum to its attorneys favoring the individual rights view. See <u>Memorandum From the Attorney General To All United States Attorneys; Re: United States v. Emerson</u>, Nov. 9, 2001.

The Third Amendment responds to a pre-Revolutionary grievance referred to in the Declaration of Independence—the quartering of troops in private homes. The amendment, largely bounded by history, forbids the practice except according to a law adopted by Congress.

The Fifth Amendment excepts from the criminal procedures of presentment or grand jury indictment "cases arising in the land or naval forces, or in the Militia when in actual service in time of War or public danger." The importance of the provision lies in its acknowledgment of national emergencies and in its express exemption of military law cases from some aspects of constitutional control. The implications of this differential treatment of service persons under military law are explored in Chapter 4.

D. PEACETIME AND WARTIME

It is clear that constitutional restrictions on the government are relaxed in wartime. What is controversial is the extent of that relaxation, a topic discussed in more detail in Chapter 2. Of course, the line between "wartime" and "peacetime" is far from clear. Declarations of war and treaties of peace may be some indication, but they do not control the characterizations which courts will give to a particular moment in time. For example, post-World War II price controls on rental housing were justified on the ground that "the war power does not necessarily end with the cessation of hostilities." Woods v. Cloyd W. Miller Co. (S.Ct.1948). The ascertainment of wartime is crucial to the operation of several provisions of the UCMJ. For example, authority to try civilians under military jurisdiction depends on its exercise "[i]n time of war." UCMJ, Art. 2(a)(10), 10 U.S.C.A. § 802(a)(10). The former Court of Military Appeals (now the United States Court of Appeals for the Armed Forces) has held that wartime in some instances required a formal declaration of war by Congress. Compare United States v. Averette (C.M.A.1970) (no jurisdiction to try civilians accompanying the armed forces in Vietnam under Article 2(a)(10), 10 U.S.C.A. § 802(a)(10) in absence of formal declaration of war by Congress) with United States v. Anderson (C.M.A.1968) (Vietnam conflict was in "time of war" for statute of limitation purposes under the UCMJ).

Traditional rights of American citizens to trial in civilian courts or to personal mobility may also be suspended in wartime. For example, the Constitution explicitly permits suspension of the writ of habeas corpus during times of "Rebellion or Invasion." Art. I, § 9, cl. 2. The trial of civilians by military commission instead of a civilian court is allowed when law enforcement has broken down and civilian courts are not functioning. Ex parte Milligan (S.Ct.1866). The federal Supreme Court upheld the wartime trial of German saboteurs by a military commission within the United States during a period when civilian courts were functioning and despite the claim of one of the defendants, Herbert Hans Haupt, to American citizenship. Ex parte Quirin (S.Ct.1942). Quirin was tried for violating the law of war, however, not domestic law. Finally, the Japanese internment cases illustrate the potential scope of wartime restrictions on the freedoms of citizens.

Shortly after the Japanese attack on Pearl Harbor on December 7, 1941, President Roosevelt issued Executive Order No. 9066, intended to protect "against espionage [and] against sabotage" and providing that certain military commanders might designate "military areas" in the United States "from which any or all persons may be excluded, and with respect to which the right of any person to enter, remain in, or leave shall be subject to whatever restrictions" the "Military Commander may impose in his discretion." The West Coast program established curfews, detention in relocation centers, and exclusion from areas of the West Coast for persons of Japanese ancestry.

In Hirabayashi v. United States (S.Ct.1943), the Supreme court upheld the military commander's curfew on persons of Japanese ancestry. Citing the need for security, the danger of espionage, and the potential for disloyalty by Japanese Americans out of devotion to their ancestral homeland, the Court sanctioned this wartime restriction on liberty which would have violated the equal protection clause if imposed during peacetime. Korematsu v. United States (S.Ct.1944) went even further in condoning exclusion of all persons of Japanese ancestry from prescribed areas along the Pacific Coast.

Only when the Court has found that Congress did not authorize particular "wartime necessity" actions has it struck down such restrictions upon normal civilian rights. For example, it refused to sanction further detention of a concededly loyal Japanese American during World War II at a camp on the West Coast. The Court did not say that such detention was unlawful *per se*, but that Congress' approval of relocation centers to guard against espionage and sabotage by persons of Japanese origin extended solely to use of the centers for evacuation, not detention. Further, it concluded that concededly loyal citizens could not even be evacuated under the congressional authorization of relocation centers. Ex parte Endo (S.Ct.1944).

Hirabayashi and Korematsu have proven controversial. Fred Korematsu's conviction was later vacated, Korematsu v. United States

(N.D.Cal.1984) as was Gordon Hirabayashi's, Hirabayashi v. United States (9th Cir.1987). In 1988, following a study of the internment program, Congress enacted the American–Japanese Evacuation Claims Act, which apologized for the program and provided reparations. 50 U.S.C.A. App. §§ 1981–1987. Despite these palliative steps directed toward the correction of administrative abuses of these programs, the case of Korematsu v. U.S. survives in our constitutional law. It continues to stand for the proposition that even though disadvantaging racial classifications are subject to the "most rigid scrutiny," deference to wartime necessities can satisfy that high standard and permit restrictions on citizens' freedoms that would not be allowed in peacetime.

CHAPTER 2

NATIONAL SECURITY LAW

This chapter focuses primarily on United States law concerning national security, leaving the field of military law, including the law of armed conflict, for later chapters. One caveat to this chapter is necessary: the domain of national security law is not well-defined and one could argue for inclusion of much additional material beyond the matters discussed here. For example, discussion of financial interdiction of terrorist organization funds could be discussed in much more depth, and economic sanctions, including restrictions on transfer of militarily sensitive technology, are clearly important to maintaining national security. In order to focus the chapter on those elements of national security law that most closely relate to the military law matters addressed in the remainder of the book, we do not explore these interesting and vital topics.

Section A provides a bird's-eye-view of the allocation of responsibilities for various aspects of national security. Section B presents substantive national security crimes and the processes for identifying internal threats, detaining those suspected of threatening national security, and trying such individuals. Section C outlines the law applicable to controlling our national borders.

Section D discusses secrecy in national security matters: shielding security-sensitive information from public scrutiny in our democratic society and conducting clandestine operations. Finally, Section E describes restrictions on use of military forces to deal with domestic disturbances.

A. OVERVIEW OF NATIONAL SECURITY

1. RESPONSIBILITY FOR NATIONAL SECURITY

Federal statutes have organized the national security apparatus of the United States so that responsibility is divided among executive branch officers who report to the President. The National Security Act of 1947, PL 80-253, reorganized U.S. military forces dramatically after World War II in an effort to provide civilian oversight over all the uniformed services. The Department of Defense (DOD) was established with leadership entrusted to a Cabinet-level officer, the Secretary of Defense. This legislation also coordinated various aspects of national security through the National Security Council, which included the Secretary of State, the Secretary of Defense and other officials. Finally, this legislation sought to further coordinate the operations of the military services through formal organization of the Joint Chiefs of Staff. Various aspects of the legal framework surrounding the DOD, including entry into the service, internal regulation of the uniformed forces through the Uniform Code of Military Justice, and restrictions on the law of armed conflict, are treated in later chapters of this book.

Despite the 1947 efforts to coordinate myriad foreign and domestic considerations under the National Security Council framework, security responsibilities within the United States' borders were fragmented into numerous uncoordinated federal agencies. The terrorist attacks of September 11, 2001 vividly demonstrated the need for enhanced security within the United States and better coordination of internal security efforts. The Homeland Security Act of 2002 (HSA), Pub. L. No. 107-296, 116 Stat. 2135, the largest government reorganization since creation of the DOD, created the Department of Homeland Security (DHS) headed by a Cabinet-level civilian, the Secretary of Homeland Security. DOD thus has responsibility for deployment of military forces; DHS oversees and coordinates security issues within the United States.

Protection of national security by DHS is divided into five areas of responsibility, each overseen by an Under Secretary. Together, they provide a snapshot of the scope of homeland security concerns:

- Information Analysis/ Infra-structure Protection: analyzes intelligence on possible terrorist attack and infrastructure vulnerability.
- Science and Technology: orchestrates scientific and technological counter-measures against terrorist threats.

- Border and Transportation Security: protects United States borders and transportation systems; responsibility for immigration.
- Emergency Preparedness/ Response: prepares for and responds to terrorist attacks.
- Management: handles grants, material resources, assistance management programs, and reorganization of agencies and programs required by HSA.

The preceding picture of the DOD and HSA serving as the military and internal security leads reporting to the President within the National Security Council framework still fails to give a full picture of how the national security apparatus of the United States operates. The roles of several key components of this apparatus not within DOD or HAS are not yet given their due.

First, the Department of State is the lead agency for maintaining diplomatic relations with other nations, relations which often determine the need for, and constraints upon, the use of military force through the DOD. Second, the Central Intelligence Agency (CIA), which reports to the National Security Council, has major responsibilities for obtaining and analyzing information that affects the use of military force abroad and security efforts within the United States. Third, the Attorney General has primary investigative responsibility for all federal terrorism offenses. The Federal Bureau of Investigation (FBI), conducts these investigations on behalf of the Department of Justice (DOJ). Finally, state and local officials, including many thousands of police and firefighters, have functions critical to homeland defense efforts. Indeed, they will often be the "first responders" to breaches of homeland security, just as they were in the terrorist attacks of September 11.

Finally, the United States is a party to many international treaties and is a member of the North Atlantic Treaty Organization (NATO). It is also a permanent member of the United Nations Security Council with veto authority over United Nations Security Council resolutions. The United States' NATO representative is a high-ranking military officer who reports to the Secretary of Defense. The United States Ambassador to the United Nations reports to the Secretary of State and, ultimately, the President.

2. SCOPE OF THE USA PATRIOT ACT

The scope of the Uniting and Strengthening America Providing Appropriate Tools Required to Intercept and Obstruct Terrorism Act of 2001, 115 Stat. 272 , (USA PATRIOT Act) mirrors the coverage of much of the remainder of this chapter. Enacted a scant six weeks after the September 11 attacks with little debate and virtually no dissent, the Act altered a number of provisions of then-existing national security law to provide the federal government broader powers to locate, detain, and punish terrorists. Detailed examination of this important statute may be found in Congressional Research Service Report to Congress RL 31377, "The USA Patriot Act: A Legal Analysis," by Charles Doyle. Later chapter references are to provisions of the U.S. Code as amended by this legislation; this overview refers to USA PATRIOT Act provisions directly so they may be examined by readers who are so inclined.

First, the USA PATRIOT Act addresses national security crimes and criminal investigations, covered below in Section B. It defines new federal crimes [e.g. terrorist attacks on mass transit facilities (§801), possession of biological weapons materials (§817), harboring terrorists (§ 803), affording support to terrorists (§805), and money laundering (§§ 315, 329, 353, 374-76)], enhances penalties for acts of terrorism and crimes terrorists might commit (§§810-12, 814, 1011), expands federal property forfeiture powers (e.g. §§106, 806), increases awards that may be paid to combat terrorism (§§101, 501, 502), and provides a fund for compensating victims of terrorism (§§ 421-27). The Act provides new powers to track and gather criminal communications [e.g. email pen register and trap and trace devices (§216), nationwide orders for electronic communications (§§ 210, 220)]. It also eases restrictions on foreign intelligence gathering and sharing of information between intelligence and criminal prosecution authorities (e.g. §§203, 207).

Second, the Act contains a number of provisions dealing with border control and immigration, covered in Section C. It dramatically increases money available for border patrol and customs inspections, funds development of biometric scanning systems to identify aliens entering the U.S. (§1007), provides for monitoring student visas more carefully (§ 416), expands the grounds for excluding and deporting aliens (§§ 411), and provides new authority to detain aliens (§ 412).

The USA PATRIOT Act does not directly address the issues of openness and secrecy treated in Section D but does, in subtle ways, expand the range of information available to government officials while reducing privacy protections of citizens and aliens. Finally, the Act leaves virtually unchanged the Posse Comitatus Act's restrictions on using the military to quell internal disorders, the topic covered in Section E.

B. NATIONAL SECURITY CRIMES AND PROCESSES

National security criminal processes differ from other criminal processes in two critical ways. First, there is an important legal maxim that has shaped the whole of this area of the law. Second, there are two competing and interrelated paradigms for dealing with national security issues. Each deserves brief exploration before we look sequentially at national security crimes and their processes in greater detail.

The Maxim. The Roman maxim *Inter arma silent leges* (During war, the law is silent) has shaped all aspects of national security law. The underpinning of the maxim was aptly captured by Abraham Lincoln when he responded to criticisms over limitations on civil liberties that he had imposed during the Civil War. Would you have me enforce all the laws but one (the law of necessity), he asked. If the state is not preserved, said Lincoln, the remainder of the laws, including those protective of civil liberty, will be rendered null and void.

Three aspects of the difference between law in wartime and in times of peace are summarized by Chief Justice William Rehnquist in his book ALL THE LAWS BUT ONE: CIVIL LIBERTIES IN WARTIME (1998), at 224-225. First, "in time of war the government's authority to restrict civil liberty is greater than in peacetime." Second, wartime presidents may "act in ways that push their legal authority to the maximum, if not beyond." Third, the timing of judicial decisions about the exercise of wartime power is important: "If the decision is made after hostilities have ceased, it is more likely to favor civil liberty than if made while hostilities continue." In conclusion, Chief Justice Rehnquist states that "[i]t is neither desirable nor is it remotely likely that civil liberty will occupy as favored a position in wartime as it does in peacetime. But it is both desirable and likely that more careful attention will be paid by the courts to the basis for the government's claims of necessity as a basis for curtailing civil liberty. The laws will thus not be silent in time of war, but they will speak with a somewhat different voice."

Chief Justice Rehnquist's observations make the issue of when the nation is at war important in many legal contexts. The maxim presumably would apply when a national security emergency short of war existed. In addition to having broad wartime powers, the President has constitutional authority to declare national emergencies, a power that might permit seizure of property, institution of martial law, control over transportation and communications, and the like. The reach of these powers and the extent to which they are subject to control by Congress have never been tested. One statute purporting to regulate the President's "emergency powers," with which Presidents have complied rather than testing their constitutionality, is the International Emergency Economic Powers Act (IEEPA).

The powers specified under IEEPA, 50 U.S.C. §1701 et. seq., are conditioned on more than just a proclamation of national emergency. IEEPA is only available during a national emergency declared in responsible to a threat "which has its source in whole or substantial part outside the United States." When applicable, IEEPA delegates to the President authority over all property involved in foreign exchange in the United States' jurisdiction, except personal communications, humanitarian donations, and information materials. IEEPA requires the President to consult Congress before invoking these powers whenever possible. Moreover, the President's authority under IEEPA is subject to Congressional review. See The National Emergencies Act, 50 U.S.C. §1601 et. seq..

The Paradigms. The conceptual problem involves drawing a line between national security breaches as matters to be dealt with by criminal law and the protection of national security as an aspect of the war powers set forth in Chapter 1. Though these paradigms are not mutually exclusive and indeed may work in conjunction, it is helpful to examine them separately.

The nation's response to the terrorist attacks of September 11 created a fork in the road for President Bush. Should he seek to prosecute those who aided and abetted or conspired in the suicide attacks? Or should he mount a military response against the probable perpetrators? The former route would have involved criminal investigative processes, arrests and charges, extradition or rendition of suspects from other countries, and trials in federal or perhaps international tribunals. This was the traditional way that terrorism had been countered, as in United States v. Rahman (2d Cir. 1999), which upheld the convictions of ten defendants for "seditious conspiracy and other offenses arising out of a wide-ranging plot to conduct a campaign of urban terrorism," including the 1993 bombing of the World Trade Center.

The United States Constitution requires, in criminal proceedings, that an individual be advised of certain rights upon arrest, charged or indicted of a specific crime promptly, afforded counsel of one's choice or at public expense, given a hearing where reasonable bail is set or bail is denied, and provided a speedy trial before a jury replete with procedural protections and proof of guilt "beyond a reasonable doubt." See U.S. CONST. AMEND. V, VI, and VIII. How these and other aspects of criminal procedure work will not be explored here, though comparable processes in courts-martial proceedings are explored in a later chapter.

The alternative paradigm seeks to root out terrorist organizations and those who support and harbor them worldwide primarily through use of military and diplomatic means. Waging war does not, for the most part, implicate the protections, constitutional and otherwise, inherent in criminal processes. One tries and punishes criminals; a nation at war kills and incapacitates its enemies. Criminal law processes are generally secondary and after-the-fact aspects of war, as were the Nuremberg trials after World War II.

President Bush has chosen war as the primary tool for fighting organized international terrorism, and the courts thus far have been responsive to his approach. They have treated the War on Terrorism as a state of armed conflict despite the absence of a declaration of war, a traditional sovereign state enemy, and any likelihood of termination of hostilities (in part due to the absence of any hierarchical organization that could surrender on behalf of all terrorist organizations).

In Hamdi v. Rumsfeld, (4th Cir. 2003), for example, the court said "neither the absence of set-piece battles nor the intervals of calm between terrorist assaults suffice to nullify the war making authority entrusted to the executive and legislative branches.*** The executive branch is also in the best position to appraise the status of a conflict, and the cessation of hostilities would seem no less a matter of political competence than the initiation of them." In Padilla v. Bush (SDNY 2002) the court accepted as the "legal predicate" for the government's case (1) the President's declaration of a national emergency September 18, 2001 and (2) Pub. L. No 107-40, 115 Stat. 224 (Sept. 18, 2001), authorizing the President to use "all necessary and appropriate force *** to prevent any future acts of international terrorism against the United States by such nations, organizations, or persons."

1. NATIONAL SECURITY CRIMES

A brief survey of what might be called "national security crimes" will provide context to subsequent issues concerning the processes for identifying, capturing, detaining, and trying particular defendants. This section will focus on treason-related crimes and the crime of terrorism. Later portions of this chapter and the chapter on the Law of Armed Conflict provide insight into other crimes that, in a broad sense, might be called national security offenses.

a. Treason and Related Crimes

Treason was the original national security crime. Article III, §3 of the Constitution says: "Treason against the United States shall consist only in levying War against them, or in adhering to their Enemies, giving them Aid and Comfort." It further requires that "No person shall be convicted of Treason unless on the Testimony of two Witnesses to the same overt Act, or on Confession in open Court." As codified, treason applies only to those "owing allegiance to the United States," applies "in the United States or elsewhere," and carries penalties up to death or as little as five years imprisonment (plus a fine of up to $10,000 and bar from holding office). 18 U.S.C. § 2381.

Many offenses have grown up over time which relate to, but are differently defined than, treason and often carry different penalties. These Offenses include misprision of treason, rebellion or insurrection, seditious conspiracy, and advocating overthrow of the government. 18 U.S.C. §§ 2382-2385. To the extent there is an overlap among these crimes, does the constitutional two witnesses requirement for treason apply? To the extent that these statutes involve communicative planning activity (conspiracy) or advocacy (advocating overthrow), do they infringe on protected First Amendment rights?

An illustrative recent case dealing with both issues is United States v. Rahman (2d Cir. 1999), which involved defendants convicted of seditious conspiracy (18 U.S.C. § 2384) for their roles in the World Trade Center bombing of 1993. A number of defendants argued that to the extent that treason included levying war and seditious conspiracy punishes conspiracy to levy war, the two witness requirement was mandatory. Not so, responded the court; the two have different "elements and punishment," including treason's element of "owing allegiance" to the United States.

As for the claim that seditious conspiracy prosecution violates the First Amendment, the court rejected it, citing Dennis v. United States (S.Ct. 1951). In Dennis, the Court upheld the Smith Act (now 18 U.S.C. § 2385), which made it a crime to advocate or conspire to advocate the overthrow of the U.S. government. Acknowledging that application of the Smith Act warranted careful scrutiny, the Dennis Court concluded that it did not impermissibly burden protected speech because it was "directed at advocacy [of overthrow of the government by force], not discussion."

Dennis was later narrowed by Brandenburg v. Ohio (S.Ct. 1969) and other cases to encompass only advocacy directed towards and likely to result in "imminent lawless action."

The Rahman court held that since section 2384 requires a conspiracy "to *use* force, not just *advocate* the use of force *** [it] passes the test of constitutionality." The court also rejected First Amendment arguments of overbreadth, vagueness, and persecution for religious beliefs.

b. Terrorism and Support of Terrorist Organizations

The difficulties of defining terrorism are legion. The adage "one man's terrorist is another man's freedom fighter" identifies, but does not assist in resolving, the problem. International treaty discussions have progressed for decades without resolving the difficulty. Numerous U.S. statutes punish various types of crimes that, in lay terms, involve terrorist activities. These statutes lack a common definition of what terrorism is and the elements of the different crimes might (or might not) criminalize actions that a layman would consider to be terrorism. Moreover, various state laws define and punish terrorism in ways broader than federal law. See generally Norman Abrams, ANTI-TERRORISM AND CRIMINAL ENFORCEMENT (West 2003), pp. 34-81. Here, we will look at a couple of areas of "terrorism" offenses without trying to cover them all.

"International terrorism" is defined in 18 U.S.C. § 2331 to include "violent acts or acts dangerous to human life" that "appear to be intended to intimidate or coerce a civilian population," "influence the policy of a government by intimidation or coercion," or "affect the conduct of a government by assassination or kidnapping" and are outside the US or transcend national boundaries. Elsewhere, the US Code allows the Secretary of State to specify organizations engaged in "terrorist activities" defined as activities that threaten the "national defense, foreign relations, or economic interests of the United States." 8 U.S.C. § 1189(c)(2). Funds of such organizations may be blocked, members of the organization may be prohibited from entering the United States, and individuals contributing "material support or resources" to such organizations may be severely punished. 18 U.S.C. § 2339B(a)(1).

Does this last provision, prohibiting contributions of material support to foreign terrorist organizations, violate the First Amendment? In Humanitarian Law Project v. Reno (9th Cir. 2000), several organizations and citizens wanted to give money to two such organizations "to aid only the nonviolent humanitarian and political activities of the designated organizations." They claimed, primarily, that the statute infringed their First Amendment associational rights, but the court held otherwise. It did not impose "guilt by association, for they could be members of the targeted groups so long as they did not donate money." Moreover, the ban on financial support was appropriate because, unlike advocacy or affiliation "material support given to a terrorist organization can be used to promote the organization's unlawful activities, regardless of donor intent."

Does this same provision violate the Fifth Amendment prohibition on deprivation of "life, liberty, or property, without due process of law?" In National Council of Resistance of Iran v. Dep't of State (DCCir. 2001), the court examined petitioners' claims that they had been designated as terrorist organizations without due process. First, the court found that, even if it is arguable that some foreign terrorist organizations lack a substantial enough connection to this country to even raise a due process claim, these organizations had substantial connections (not mentioned in the opinion for national security reasons). Second, the court found a deprivation of liberty interests (labeling them as terrorist was "more than mere stigmatization") and property interests (freezing bank accounts). Finally, the court held that there was not enough process given at an appropriate time to meet minimal constitutional standards. The case was remanded to the Secretary of State to provide an opportunity for him to make the designation by "showing of particularized need" that foreclosed any opportunity to contest that designation in advance.

2. IDENTIFICATION OF NATIONAL SECURITY THREATS: FISA

Electronic surveillance and physical searches are regular tools used to fight ordinary crime as well as to identify and pursue those who pose threats to national security. Surveillance and searches are both subject to the Fourth Amendment:

> The right of the people to be secure in their persons, houses, papers, and effects, against unreasonable searches and seizures shall not be violated, and no Warrants shall issue, but upon probable cause, supported by Oath or affirmation, and particularly describing the place to be searched, and the persons or things to be seized."

National security searches and surveillances involve standards and processes different from those applicable in ordinary domestic police work. In connection with ordinary police work, the police must generally obtain a warrant unless a specific judicially-crafted "exception" to the Fourth Amendment applies. Katz v. United States (S.Ct. 1967). Exceptions recognized to date include searches incident to arrest, auto, boat, and airplane searches, "stop and frisk" searches, and searches of people and things at the United States' borders.

In addition, efforts by the FBI or other agencies concerning apprehension of aliens outside the country suspected of criminal activity in the United States or against United States citizens are not constrained by the Fourth Amendment. As the Supreme Court said in United States v. Verdugo-Urquidez (S.Ct. 1990):

> For better or worse, we live in a world of nation-states in which our government must be able to function effectively *** Some who violate our laws may live outside our borders under a

regime quite different from that which obtains in this country. *** Situations threatening to important American interests may arise halfway around the globe [that] require an American response with armed force. If there are to be restrictions on searches and seizures which occur incident to such American action, they must be imposed by the political branches through diplomatic understanding, treaty, or legislation.

In United States v. Bin Laden (SDNY 2000), the court found that no warrant was necessary because of the President's foreign affairs powers, the costs of imposing a warrant requirement, and the absence of a statutory basis for obtaining warrants abroad.

Is there a "national security" exception to the Fourth Amendment warrant requirement even when the target of surveillance is within the United States? In United States v. United States District Court (Keith) (S.Ct., 1972), the Court implied that a warrant should not be required if it would "unduly frustrate" the President's exercise of foreign affairs responsibilities. United States v. Truong Dinh Hung (4th Cir. 1980), interpreting Keith, held that executive competence as well as a need for "stealth, speed, and secrecy" justified a limited exception. Truong opined that searches should only be allowed without warrants when foreign intelligence surveillance was the "primary purpose" of the surveillance.

To provide a more detailed framework for regulating national security wiretaps and other surveillance, Congress passed a statute, the

Foreign Intelligence Surveillance Act of 1978 (FISA), 50 U.S.C. §1801 et seq. This section will examine how FISA works, compare FISA to federal law enforcement searches under Title III of the Omnibus Crime Control and Safe Streets Act of 1986, 18 U.S.C. §§ 2510-2522, and explore the constitutionality of the FISA process.

FISA regulates collection of "foreign intelligence" (counterintelligence) information within the U.S., whether or not there has been a probable violation of any law. Foreign intelligence information "relates to" protection against possible hostile acts, sabotage or terrorism, or clandestine intelligence activities by a "foreign power" or its "agents." §1801(e)(1). The "agent" may be an alien or a US citizen, and "foreign power" is broad enough to include factions of nations (e.g. the Irish Republican Army or the African National Congress) as well as "any group engaged in international terrorism" (e.g. al Qaeda). Additional FISA restrictions exist concerning United States citizens and permanent residents: the person must be about to violate U.S. law, cannot be targeted "solely on the basis of activities" that are protected speech under the First Amendment, and the information must be "necessary to" U.S. national security, national defense, or foreign affairs.

The scope of FISA has grown substantially over the years. Originally, FISA was limited to electronic surveillance. A 1994 amendment expanded the statute to permit covert physical entries, a 1998 amendment added authority to obtain pen/trap orders and certain business records, and a 2001 amendment allowed "roving wiretaps" of any phone the surveillance target may use. The number of surveillance orders has grown apace, from 199 in 1979 to 934 in 2001; over this same time period, the number of ordinary crime electronic surveillance warrants under Title III increased from 466 to 1,491.   In 2002, FISA warrants jumped by another 30%, to 1228.

FISA authorized creation of two secret courts, the Foreign Intelligence Surveillance Court (FISC) and the Foreign Intelligence Surveillance Court of Review (FISCR).   FISC is comprised of eleven federal judges appointed by the Chief Justice; FISCR has three members similarly appointed. Both courts meet in secret, and both involve ex parte proceedings; the Attorney General requests a surveillance order about which the target of the request is ignorant and is unrepresented.

FISC judges have only once denied surveillance in over 13,000 requests, and they generally do not write or publish opinions granting surveillance. Challenges to surveillance orders generally occur only when the government later prosecutes a surveillance target.   See e.g. United States v. Duggan   (2d   Cir.   1984).   The   appropriate relationship between national security surveillance and the use of information obtained through such surveillance to prosecute crime has been a matter of substantial concern over many years.   The only instance in which the FISC and the FISCR have published written opinions dealt with this issue. In re   All   Matters   Submitted   to   the   Foreign Intelligence Court (FISC 2002), rev'd by In re Sealed Case No. 02-001 (FISCR 2002).

The background for these opinions requires an understanding of the "minimization procedures" which FISA required the Attorney General to adopt and the FISA judges to follow in order to "minimize the acquisition and retention, and prohibit the dissemination" of nonpublic information concerning U.S. persons. Beginning in 1995, the Attorney General's procedures called for erection of a "wall" between the FBI and the Criminal Division of the DOJ in FISA surveillance cases. This "wall" avoided a potential constitutional problem: if the standards for national security surveillance do not meet Fourth Amendment minimums, may a defendant exclude evidence at trial obtained in the course of FISA surveillance?

Three matters brought this issue to a head. First, the Department of Justice disclosed to the FISC in September 2000 that in over 75 cases, the "wall" had been breached; prosecutors had been provided access to raw national security intercepts. Second, the USA PATRIOT Act, passed October 26, 2001, changed the FISA framework to enhance national security after September 11. Congress abandoned Truong's "primary purpose" test to allow surveillance whenever national security information was "a significant purpose" of the surveillance. It also permitted intelligence officers to "consult" with federal law enforcement officers to "coordinate efforts to investigate or protect against" threats to national security. Third, the Attorney General issued a memorandum to the Director of the FBI on March 6, 2002 requiring, inter alia, that all FISA-obtained information concerning "any crime which has been, is being, or is about to be committed" must be turned over to the DOJ for potential prosecution.

On May 17, 2002, the FISC, sitting en banc, disapproved this last portion of the Attorney General's new minimization procedures on the ground that they were "designed to amend the law and substitute the FISA for Title III electronic surveillances and Rule 41 searches." The court imposed a variety of requirements designed to restore much of the "wall" between FISA activities and criminal prosecutions. When the FISC thereafter required modification of surveillance in a specific case, the Attorney General appealed to the FISCR. Reversing, the FISCR held 1) that the minimization procedures did not require a "wall" between intelligence and criminal prosecutions, 2) that the FISC had impermissibly intruded into the executive branch operations, 3) that the USA PATRIOT Act was intended in part to break down the wall, and 4) that FISA intelligence used in criminal prosecutions was constitutionally permissible so long as the surveillance was not primarily conducted to enhance ordinary criminal prosecutions. In re Sealed Case No. 02-001 (FISCR 2002). The FISCR was impressed that, when the provisions of FISA and Title III were compared, a FISA order "comes close to meeting Title III, [which] bears on its reasonableness under the Fourth Amendment." The chart below, drawn from the briefs and opinion of the FISCR, summarizes the comparisons:

Comparison of electronic surveillance under Title III and FISA

	TITLE III	**FISA**

Application to judge must include:	- "Full and complete statement" of the facts and circumstances relied upon, including:
	
	  • details of offense
	
	  • description and location of facilities surveilled
	
	  • description of type of communication to be intercepted
	
	  • identity of the person committing the offense, if known
	
	- "Full and complete statement" that other investigative procedures have been tried and failed or appear unlikely to succeed
	
	- Dep. Asst. Atty. Gen. approval
		- Statement of facts and circumstance to justify:
		
		• targeting a foreign power or agent; and
		• targeting facility (must be used or about to be used by foreign power or agent)
		
		- Certification that **significant purpose** is to obtain foreign intelligence information
		
		- Statement of proposed minimization procedures
		
		- Certification, and statement of basis therefore, that information cannot reasonably be obtained by normal investigative techniques
		
		- FBI Directory/Atty. Gen. or Deputy Atty. Gen. certification

Order granted if judge finds:	- **Probable cause to believe target has committed, is committing, or is about to commit enumerated crime** - Probable cause to believe facilities to be surveilled are being used in connection with the offense - Probable cause to believe communications concerning the offense will be obtained by surveillance - Normal investigative techniques have been tried and failed, or appear unlikely to succeed if tried	- **Probable cause to believe target is a foreign power or agent** - Probable cause to believe that facility at which surveillance is directed is used or about to be used by foreign power or agent - Proposed minimization procedures meet statute's requirements - Information sought probably can't be obtained by normal investigative techniques
Duration	Up to 30 days	Up to 90 or 120 days, or one year, depending on nature of target
Notice	At end of surveillance period	Only if communications introduced in criminal proceeding
Suppression	Yes	No, so long as government moves for *ex parte* and *in camera* consideration
Sealing	Yes	No
Other	Annual report with "general description" of surveillance	Keep Congressional Intelligence Committee "fully informed"

The bottom line to the FISCR was that these differences are based on different purposes behind national security surveillances and criminal prosecutions. The purpose of the former is to prevent acts of terror, sabotage, and the like; the purpose of the latter is to punish the wrongdoer and deter others from engaging in criminal acts. As the FISCR noted, punishment of the September 11 hijackers "is a moot point." In other words, FISA surveillance and searches are special needs cases for Fourth Amendment warrant purposes. Therefore, no warrant based on probable cause is required as a prerequisite to surveillance. If this decision is upheld by courts in which the targets of FISA surveillance are tried for violations of federal law, the Fourth Amendment will provide no defense to the use of FISA-obtained information at trial.

3. MATERIAL WITNESSES, EXTRADITION AND RENDITION

A person suspected of terrorist acts or another national security crime may be arrested and charged with that crime. But an individual detained as a material witness or captured as an enemy need not be charged with a crime. As set forth in this and the following subsection, such individuals may be detained outside the operation of the criminal processes.

a. Material Witnesses

An individual may be held as a "material witness" to matters relating to national security, in which case there is detention neither through criminal arrest nor military capture. Such a person may be held as long as there is probable cause that he or she has material evidence regarding a criminal offense.

Detention of material witnesses dates back at least to the 1500s in England, and was authorized in the Judiciary Act of 1789. The current statute concerning arrest of material witnesses, 18 U.S.C. § 3144, enacted as part of the Bail Reform Act of 1984, reads as follows:

> If it appears from an affidavit filed by a party that the testimony of a person is material in a criminal proceeding, and if it is shown that it may become impracticable to secure the presence of the person by subpena [sic], a judicial officer may order the arrest of the person and [order him detained].

To encourage individuals to be more cooperative as material witnesses, the courts not infrequently provide for alternatives to incarceration, such as recording the witness' testimony in a deposition.

Material witnesses run two substantial risks. First, the designation as a material witness may be a mere way station on the road to being a co-conspirator defendant in a national security prosecution. For example, Terry Nichols, first arrested as a material witness in the bombing of the Murrah Federal Building in Oklahoma City, later became a co-defendant. See In re Material Witness Warrant (Nichols) (10th Cir. 1996). Second, a material witness questioned before a grand jury who does not cooperate fully may later be prosecuted for perjury or obstruction of justice.

In re Grand Jury Subpoena of Ali, No. M-11-188 (RPP) (SDNY 1999) (civil contempt order followed refusal to testify about the bombings of the U.S. embassies in Kenya and Tanzania).

Shortly after the attacks of September 11, the FBI, operating at the direction of the Attorney General, confined numerous individuals as "material witnesses," almost all of whom were Muslim male aliens from middle-eastern countries. When "[t]he government refused to make public the number of people arrested, their names, their lawyers, the reasons for their detention, and other information relating to their whereabouts and circumstances," suit was filed by the Center for National Security Studies to obtain this information. This suit, brought under the Freedom of Information Act, largely successful before the District Court, was overturned on appeal. Center for National Security Studies v. United States Department of Justice (DCCir. 2003). The court majority cited the need to defer to executive officials in such cases, the possibility that terrorists would be assisted if they knew which of their colleagues had been compromised, and the privacy of the individuals detained.

In June, 2003, the Office of the Inspector General released a lengthy report critical of the detention of up to 762 illegal immigrants on the months after the September 11, 2001 attacks. Most of those arrested were in New York (491); the leading countries of origin were Pakistan (254) and Egypt (111); the detainees were held for varying but often substantial periods of time (220 held 51-100 days, 174 held 101-150 days, 151 held over 151 days); none were charged with terrorism. DOJ "makes no apologies" for the detentions, but reportedly DOJ and DHS are planning a number of structural changes to develop a better system for classifying and releasing detainees in the event of any future major terrorist event.

b. Extradition

Pursuit of fugitives from justice, whether terrorists connected to September 11 or other perpetrators of heinous acts against this country or its citizens, is a vital component of our national security. When the United States desires to prosecute an individual located in a foreign country, it may proceed through extradition processes established by treaty or by the less formal and sometimes controversial processes of rendition.

Extradition occurs when a person suspected of criminal activity in one country (the requesting country) who is found in another country (the host country) is surrendered through diplomatic channels for trial and punishment in the requesting country. For our purposes, we will treat the United States as the requesting country, although the shoe sometimes is on the other foot, in which case our obligations to extradite to another country are enforceable in United States courts. A list of extradition treaties to which the United States is a party are contained in the table following 18 U.S.C. § 3181.

Several components of extradition treaties are noteworthy. First, these treaties operate on the basis of reciprocity: the extraditable offense must be a criminal offense in both countries. Second, some countries, including Israel, Mexico, and many European countries, refuse to extradite their own citizens. Third, some countries, including Canada and Mexico, refuse to extradite fugitives who could receive the death penalty for their crimes in the requesting country. Mexico even applies this principle where the penalty could be a life penalty without parole. Fourth, there is a "political offense exception" to most extradition treaties that sometimes frustrates United States efforts to extradite individuals who argue their crimes were political. See Quinn v. Robinson (9th Cir. 1986), in which an IRA terrorist claimed his extradition on murder charges fell within the political offense loophole.

Finally, the "doctrine of specialty," as a part of customary international law, demands that the extradited person be tried only on the charges set forth in the documentation provided in support of the extradition. For example, United States v. Rauscher (S.Ct. 1886) held that the defendant could confine the prosecution to murder on the high seas under the 1842 Webster-Ashburton Treaty with England when he had been extradited for that offense alone. The doctrine of specialty is not inflexible, however, and may be "waived" by the host country. U.S Department of Justice, U.S. Attorney's Manual 9-15.500.

c. Rendition

Self-help may occur in the absence of a treaty, because the host country lacks the will to extradite a fugitive, or because extradition would be too time-consuming (perhaps leading to the escape of the fugitive). Such self-help, euphemistically, is called irregular rendition.   Techniques of rendition include (from the least to the most controversial) informal surrender by the host nation, luring the suspect by subterfuge or deception, forcible kidnapping, and military rendition.

Examples of these various techniques are fascinating and notorious. *Informal surrender* occurred when Pakistanis turned Ramzi Ahmed Yousef, the mastermind of the 1993 World Trade Center bombing, over to United States agents, who transported him to the United States the next day without extradition processes or protest. As a *lure*, the FBI and CIA in 1987 enticed suspected terrorist Fawaz Yunis onto a ship in international waters off the coast of Cyprus on the pretext of engaging in a drug deal, arrested him on the spot, and returned him to the United States. His challenge to the court's jurisdiction based on trickery was rejected.   United States v. Yunis (DCCir. 1988).   One example of United States *forcible abduction* is the retrieval of John Surratt, accused in the Lincoln assignation conspiracy, from Alexandria, Egypt.   Another was the 1960 kidnapping by Israeli agents of Adolph Eichmann, a notorious participant in Hitler's extermination of Jews in Europe.   Though Argentina protested vigorously to this "violation of its sovereignty" and the United Nations passed a resolution condemning such tactics, Eichmann was tried, convicted, and executed in Israel. Finally, *military rendition*, sometimes called "gunboat diplomacy," has been increasingly used in recent years by the

United States in cases involving terrorism and narcotics. Three examples are the 1985 diversion by military fighter jets to Italy of an Egyptian plane carrying the Achillo Lauro highjackers away from the crime scene, the 1989 dispatch of troops to Panama to extract General Manuel Antonio Noriega after they took control of Panama City, and application of military force in Afghanistan to deal with al Qaeda members implicated in the September 11 attacks and the Taliban government that refused to surrender them voluntarily.

Can a defendant prosecuted in the United States object to trial here on the ground that he or she was forcibly abducted without the permission of the host country? The Supreme Court in two cases, Ker v. Illinois (S.Ct. 1886) and Frisbee v. Collins (S.Ct. 1952) held that the legality of the abduction was not a defense to federal court jurisdiction. This proposition, known as the Ker-Frisbee doctrine, was found subject to an exception for "shocking governmental misconduct" (torture during prolonged interrogation) in US v. Toscanino (2d Cir. 1974), but this exception was rejected by another circuit court in Matta-Ballesteros v. Henman (7th Cir. 1990). Most recently, the Supreme Court held that the US-Mexico Extradition Treaty provided only one of several means for obtaining jurisdiction over a fugitive, even if the kidnapping was "shocking" to the host country. In doing so, it allowed the repatriation by force of an individual implicated in the kidnapping, torture, and murder of a DEA special agent in Mexico. As for the defense that the kidnapping violated international law, the Court said that even if it did, the Ker-Frisbee doctrine permitted trial of the defendant. United States v. Alvarez-Machain (S.Ct. 1992).

4. NATIONAL SECURITY DETENTION

What legal protections apply to those detained either as "material witnesses" or as alleged threats to national security? Do individuals detained as enemies of the United States but not charged (at least for now) with specific criminal activities have any legal protections? The discussion below shows that the place of detention is of critical importance to aliens: if detained outside the sovereign territory of the United States, they do not have access to the United States courts. Similarly-detained citizens fare better in obtaining access to civilian courts, but have generally been unsuccessful in obtaining the rights of criminal defendants.

a. Detention of Aliens

Johnson v. Eisentrager (S.Ct. 1950) involved twenty-one German nationals convicted of violating the laws of war in World War II. They had been repatriated to Germany to serve their sentences. The detainees filed writs of habeas corpus in the United States District Court for the District of Columbia alleging that their convictions and imprisonment were unconstitutional. The Supreme Court denied the petitions and held the Fifth Amendment ("No person shall be *** deprived of life, liberty, or property, without due process of law") inapplicable to enemy aliens held outside the territorial United States. In the Court's words, "these prisoners at no relevant time were within any territory over which the United States is sovereign, and the scenes of their offense, their capture, their trial and their punishment were all beyond the territorial jurisdiction of any court of the United States." See also Verdugo-Urquidez (S.Ct. 1990) (Fourth Amendment does not protect nonresident aliens against unreasonable searches and seizures conducted outside sovereign territory of the United States).

Johnson v. Eisentrager has been applied to deny habeas petitions filed by aliens held in the detention facility at the United States Naval Base at Guantanamo Bay, Cuba. In Al Odah v. United States (DCCir. 2003), the court said it was immaterial that the petitioners, unlike those in Johnson, had not been charged with any crime. Moreover, jurisdiction was lacking even though the US military exercises control over Guantanamo Bay, and despite the fact that no court anywhere would have jurisdiction over such petitions. The United States' perpetual lease over Guantanamo Bay recognizes "the ultimate sovereignty of the Republic of Cuba" over the base; sovereignty, rather than control, determines whether there is federal court jurisdiction over aliens. See also Coalition of Clergy v. Bush (9th Cir 2002) (appeals court said Johnson a "formidable obstacle" to Guantanamo detainees but did not reach this issue); and Gherebi v. Bush (C.D.Cal 2003) (applies Johnson but laments that unless it and other cases are "disregarded or rejected," detainees have no remedy).

Al Odah demonstrates the accuracy of Defense Secretary Rumsfeld's description of Guantanamo

Bay as "the least worst" place to detain aliens captured in the War on Terrorism. These detentions have been subject to criticisms by international human rights groups and various international organizations, but those detained remain in U.S. custody.

b. Detention of Citizens

Citizenship is an independent basis for federal court jurisdiction in an action against the United States. 28 U.S.C. § 1346(a)(2). Thus, the federal courts would appear to have jurisdiction over claims by United States citizens held at Guantanamo Bay or elsewhere outside United States sovereign territory. This explains why the military has not sought to detain citizens in the War on Terrorism outside the United States, but has brought them to military brigs in this country.

What are the legal rights, if any, of citizens held in the United States as enemy combatants? Must the government charge or release such individuals? May such citizens be detained indefinitely? Are they entitled to meet with counsel while detained? Two recent cases provide some guidance on these questions.

Hamdi v. Rumsfeld (4th Cir. 2003) involved a United States citizen captured in a combat zone (Afghanistan) and held without charges in the Norfolk Naval Brig. Hamdi complained that he was being held in violation of 18 U.S.C. § 4001(a) and Article 5 of the Geneva Convention. The United States statute says "no citizen shall be imprisoned or otherwise detained except pursuant to an Act of Congress," and Hamdi argued there was no such statute. The court held, however, that Congress authorized the President to use "all necessary and appropriate force" in Pub. L. No 107-40, 115 Stat. 224 (Sept. 18, 2001) including capturing and detaining enemy combatants. Moreover, the court noted that Congress had appropriated funds to detain such prisoners. As for the Geneva Convention claim that Hamdi was entitled to a formal determination of his status as an enemy combatant "by a competent tribunal," the court held that this convention did not provide Hamdi with a private right to sue. Such treaty violations "are vindicated by diplomatic means and reciprocity," not by the courts.

Hamdi claimed also that he was wrongly detained as an enemy combatant, and the court explored the extent to which it could examine this issue. After noting that the ordinary habeas petition "naturally contemplates the prospect of factual development," it found that "[t]o transfer the instinctive skepticism, so laudable in the defense of criminal charges, to the review of *** military determinations made in the field" was inappropriate. The District Court had erred in examining a declaration "line by line" that portrayed Hamdi as an enemy combatant captured with the Taliban while carrying an AK-47 rifle. The courts owe substantial deference to the military in the conduct of overseas combat operations, said the court.

Finally, the court rejected Hamdi's claim that "even if his detention was at one time lawful, it is no longer so because the relevant hostilities have reached an end." Though skeptical about judicial competence to decide when hostilities have ended in a war, the court found it unnecessary to reach this issue because "troops are still on the ground in Afghanistan."

The second case, Padilla v. Bush (SDNY 2002), reached many of the same conclusions as the Hamdi decision. Padilla, a United States citizen, was taken into custody in Chicago on May 8, 2002 upon his return from Pakistan. Though initially detained as a "material witness" who might have knowledge of terrorist activities, Padilla was charged by President Bush on June 9, 2002 with "preparation for acts of international terrorism." It was later alleged that he planned to detonate a "dirty bomb" designed to disperse radioactive material in the United States. Rather than charging Padilla with any crime, however, the President directed that he be detained as an enemy combatant. Moreover, as an "unlawful combatant" rather than a POW under the Geneva Conventions, Padilla could be interrogated during his detention.

Padilla claimed that the Constitution prohibited his indefinite detention without trial. The court rejected this claim. It held that the President had the authority to detain Padilla even though there was no declaration of war in the War on Terrorism. Padilla was not a "battlefield combatant," but the court found that he could be detained so long as the government had "some evidence" of his enemy combatant status. The court found that Congress had sufficiently authorized the detention ordered by the President and that it need not decide "when the conflict with al Qaeda may end."

Padilla did decide one issue adverse to the government which has been certified for appeal along with the other questions in the case. The government argued that Padilla should not be provided consultation time with counsel to develop factual responses to the government's treatment of him. Though the court found the Sixth Amendment right to counsel inapplicable because Padilla had not been charged with a crime, it held that consultation should be allowed "under such conditions as the parties may agree to or, absent agreement, such conditions as the court may direct so as to foreclose, as far as possible, the danger that Padilla will use his attorneys for the purpose of conveying information to others." On appeal, DOJ argues that allowing a lawyer access to Padilla would interfere with interrogation and might enable Padilla to pass information through the attorney to other terrorists.

5. NATIONAL SECURITY TRIALS

Terrorists and others who pose a threat to national security may be tried for criminal acts. While much could be said about such trials, two matters unique to such situations will be addressed here. First, if such a case is brought in federal court, how can information be handled that might compromise national security interests? Secondly, can such trials be handled by military tribunals and if so, what processes govern such tribunals?

a. Secret Information

Lowering the "wall" between FISA surveillance and criminal prosecutions, discussed above, will provide more opportunities for the government to introduce surveillance information into criminal trials. Will such information be available to the defendant? If not, can the Constitution's guarantees to defendants of public trials and an opportunity to question witnesses be satisfied? What if the defendant has security-sensitive information? Can the defendant compromise national security by presenting such evidence in open court?

When secret information is essential to a criminal prosecution, the government often must make a tough choice: proceed with the prosecution and allow the information to become public, or drop the prosecution in order to keep the information confidential. If the government tries to have its cake and eat it too by prosecuting and withholding the information, it risks having the prosecution dismissed on due process grounds. See, e.g. American-Arab Anti-Defamation League v. Reno (9th Cir. 1995).

But there may be a middle ground. Could the government present to the judge for in camera inspection a statement of detailed and relevant facts allegedly proven by security-sensitive information, allowing the judge to question and seek verification of the information? If satisfied, the judge would let trial continue with the statement substituting for the sensitive information; if not satisfied, the judge could pose the alternative to the government of dismissal of its case or release of the information to the defendant for cross-examination in open court.

This possible middle ground is similar to that contained in the Classified Information Procedures Act (CIPA), 18 U.S.C. app. III §§ 1-16, which provides a pretrial procedure for the defense to describe in advance any classified information that it "reasonably expects to disclose or cause the disclosure of" at trial. Here is an explanation of that procedure from a case, United States v. Lee (DCNM 2000), in which the defendant argued that the CIPA process was unconstitutional as applied to his case:

Under CIPA procedures, the defense must file a notice briefly describing any classified information that it "reasonably expects to disclose or to cause the disclosure of" at trial. Thereafter, the prosecution may request an in camera hearing for a determination of the "use, relevance and admissibility" of the proposed defense evidence. If the Court finds the evidence admissible, the government may move for, and the Court may authorize, the substitution of unclassified facts or a summary of the information in the form of an admission by the government. Such a motion may be granted if the Court finds that the statement or summary will provide the defendant with "substantially the same ability to make his defense as would disclosure of the specific classified information. However... if the government prevents a defendant from disclosing classified information at trial, the court may: (A) dismiss the entire indictment or specific counts, (B) find against the prosecution on any issue to which the excluded information relates, or (C) strike or preclude the testimony of particular government witnesses. Finally, CIPA requires that the government provide the defendant with any evidence it will use to rebut the defendant's revealed classified information evidence. (references deleted)

The court found the procedure constitutional. It did not violate the defendant's Fifth Amendment right against self-incrimination by forcing him to reveal portions of his proposed testimony on the ground that, even after disclosure, the defendant could choose not to testify on the matter. Nor did it violate his Sixth Amendment right to confront and cross-examine witnesses because the Constitution "does not guarantee the right to undiminished surprise with respect to cross-examination of prosecutorial witnesses." Finally, CIPA did not deny the defendant due process because the statute balanced duties of the defendant with "reciprocal duties" of the prosecution.

Two recent federal prosecutions ended with no significant secret evidence problems or national security concerns. On October 4, 2002, John Walker Lindh, the "American Taliban," entered a guilty plea in which he stated "I have never supported terrorism in any form and never would" in exchange for a 20 year sentence. The second, British subject Richard Reid, the "shoe bomber," pleaded guilty on the same day. Unrepentant for his acts, Reid was given a life sentence in prison.

One federal prosecution still in progress as this book goes to press is that involving Zacharias

Moussaoui, originally discussed in the media as the "20th Hijacker" in the September 11 attacks. Moussaoui, a French citizen who has been detained since August 2001, admits membership in al Qaeda but denies any advance knowledge of or involvement in the attacks. The pretrial issues relating to Moussaoui vividly demonstrate some of the problems for the parties to such a proceeding.

First, the government, obligated to produce documents to the defendant, inadvertently produced a number of classified documents which it then had to seek permission to retrieve from Moussaoui. Second, Moussaoui demanded access to witnesses, including at least one al Qaeda prisoner held by the United States. He claimed such witnesses would exonerate him from involvement in the September 11 attacks. Third, there is a motion by various news media seeking release of pleadings and other records in the case that have to date been sealed. At present, it appears that the government may dismiss its prosecution in federal court, moving Moussaoui's trial to a military tribunal.

b. Military Tribunals

An alternative for dealing with sensitive information is to try the defendant before a court that, unlike an Article III federal court, has secret proceedings. One such forum might be the Alien Terrorist Removal Court, created by the 1996 Anti-Terrorism and Effective Death Penalty Act, 8 U.S.C. §§ 1531-1537. But this court has never been convened, perhaps because in cases involving removal of alleged alien terrorists, the government has come up with another and better option (see section C infra), or because the government does not wish to test the constitutionality of this court.

A broader option for secret proceedings that will preserve sensitive information is to convene a military tribunal to try the defendant. Two important issues with such proceedings are (1) when they may be used and (2) what processes they will utilize in lieu of standard criminal processes.

Military tribunals were implicitly recognized in the Articles of War, the relevant provisions of which were later codified in Articles 18 and 21 of the Uniform Code of Military Justice, 10 U.S.C. § 821. Congress has delegated to the President the authority to set the rules of procedure for such tribunals. 10 U.S.C. §836. Though Congress has not specified the offenses that may be tried by such tribunals, two statutory offenses for which tribunals may be convened are aiding the enemy, 10 U.S.C. § 904, and spying, 10 U.S.C. § 906. In addition, there are cases, some of which will be discussed below, that suggest such forums are appropriate to try war crimes. But before we discuss current issues surrounding military tribunals, a brief history of their use is appropriate.

The United States' earliest "war courts" date to the Revolutionary War, where they were called courts-martial. The terms "councils of war" and "military commissions" were apparently introduced in the war with Mexico in the 1840's, when General Winfield Scott used them to try Mexican citizens accused of violating the laws of war, such as by using guerrilla tactics or enticing American soldiers to desert. These commissions were not sanctioned by Congress; General Scott relied on his authority as occupier of the territory in which the trials were conducted. In the Civil War, by Act of March 3, 1863, Congress suspended the writ of habeas corpus and, "as a necessary means for suppressing...all rebels and insurgents, their aiders and abettors," made such persons "liable to trial and punishment by courts-martial or military commission." In April 1863, Union Army General Order Number 100 announced the appropriateness of military commissions to try cases in cases not covered by statute according to the common law of war, and more than 2,000 cases were so tried during the Civil War and Reconstruction. Such commissions were not used by President Wilson during World War I, in part because Wilson's Attorney General had doubts about their constitutionality, but they were reinstituted by President Roosevelt in World War II. Following the capture of eight German saboteurs (two of whom were American citizens), Roosevelt issued Proclamation 2561 on July 2, 1942 entitled "Denying Certain Enemies Access to the Courts of the United States." Concurrently, Roosevelt issued a Military Order appointing a commission of seven general officers to try the defendants for "offenses against the law of war and the Articles of War." The trials resulting from this order were upheld by the Supreme Court in Ex Parte Quirin (S.Ct. 1942).

Against this backdrop, President George W. Bush issued a Military Order on November 13,

2001, in response to the attacks of September 11. The order recites Congress' authorization to use "all necessary and appropriate force" against those involved in or supportive of the September 11 attacks as well as the UCMJ provisions that envision use of military commissions. It applies to non-citizen (including resident alien) members of al Qaeda, participants or conspirators in "acts of international terrorism," and those who harbor international terrorists. Such defendants shall be tried for "any and all offenses triable by military commission." The order specifies that such commissions shall have "exclusive jurisdiction" over such offenses with no remedy in the courts of the U.S., any state, any foreign nation, or any international tribunal. Further rules for such proceedings were left for promulgation by the Secretary of Defense.

On March 21, 2002, Defense Secretary Rumsfeld promulgated Military Commission Order No. 1, which provided substantial additional details concerning the prospective application of military commission trials to international terrorists. This order details the number of members (3-7), the composition of the commissions (commissioned officers including reservists), the credentials for the presiding officer (a judge advocate), the credentials of Chief Prosecutor and Chief Defense Counsel, the rules concerning choice of defense counsel by the accused, the procedures accorded the accused (including discovery rights), and trial conduct details. The trial conduct matters are particularly significant, for they include "a full and fair trial," "open proceedings" absent "grounds for closure," use of "evidence [having] probative value to a reasonable person," direct and cross-examination of witnesses, and processes for safeguarding national security information. Commission members are to vote for a finding of Guilty concerning an offense if and only if the member is convinced beyond a reasonable doubt. A two-thirds vote is required for conviction, and a unanimous vote is specified for imposition of the death penalty. Following trial, the order provides for review by a military review panel, by the Secretary of Defense, and the President. No appeal to any civilian court is contemplated, but the writ of habeas corpus appears to be available to challenge the legality of a particular conviction. See Ex Parte Quirin (S.Ct. 1942).

There are many issues concerning the precise language of Military Commission Order No. 1 and there are some divergences from both civilian criminal processes and court-martial processes. See Generally NATIONAL INSTITUTE OF MILITARY JUSTICE, ANNOTATED GUIDE: PROCEDURES FOR TRIALS BY MILITARY COMMISSION OF CERTAIN NON-UNITED STATES CITIZENS IN THE WAR AGAINST TERRORISM (LexisNexis 2002). Most of these are matters that might be changed or further articulated by later orders, or that remain hypothetical in the absence of any trials to date under these procedures. One divergence between the President's Military Order and Military Commission Order No. 1 is troubling: the former says that death sentences shall require a 2/3 vote, while the latter requires unanimity for such sentences. This conflict would probably be resolved in favor of the 2/3 rule, because Military

Commission Order No. 1 states that "[i]n the event of any inconsisten *** the provisions of the President's Military Order shall govern."

On April 30, 2003, the DOD issued eight Military Commission Instructions that further flesh out the future operation of these military tribunals. Instruction No. 1 sets forth some basic parameters of the remaining instructions including that failure to adhere to the instructions does not create a private cause of action and that the instructions do not otherwise limit other DOD authority. Commission Instruction No. 2 lays out the crimes triable by military tribunal. Preliminarily, this instruction defines some terms in ways consistent with the views of the administration and the courts in the War on Terrorism. For example, "combatant immunity" is extended only to "lawful combatants," "enemy" is defined to explicitly include "any organization of terrorists with international reach, and "armed conflict" is defined to include single but severe hostile acts. The list of crimes triable includes willful killing of protected persons, attacking civilians, attacking civilian objects, attacking protected property (such as "buildings dedicated to religion, education, art, science, charitable purposes, historic monuments, hospitals," etc.), pillaging, rape, denying quarter, taking hostages, employing poison and analogous weapons, using protected persons as shields, using protected property as shields, torture, causing serious injury, mutilation or maiming, use of treachery or perfidy, improper use of flag of truce, improper use of protective emblems, and degrading treatment of a dead body. Other offenses that "should be separately charged" include hijacking or hazarding a vessel or aircraft, terrorism, murder by an unprivileged belligerent, destruction of property by an unprivileged belligerent, aiding the enemy, spying, perjury or false testimony, and obstruction of justice related to military commissions.

Commission Instructions 3-8 set forth the responsibilities of the prosecutor and defense counsel, qualifications of civilian defense counsel, reporting relationships, sentencing, and various administrative procedures.

As this book goes to press, no case has yet been tried in a military tribunal under President Bush's Military Order, Secretary Rumsfeld's Military Commission Order No. 1, and the DOD Commission Instructions.

C. BORDER CONTROL AND NATIONAL SECURITY

Immigration is the essential ingredient to America's melting pot of cultures, a vital furnace for creativity and productivity. Our nation of immigrants continues to draw scientific and other talent from around the globe, as witnessed by the fact that a third of America's Nobel Prize laureates have been first-generation immigrants and more than 50 of the world leaders joining the War on Terrorism studied in or were official visitors to the United States. At the same time, undesirables from other parts of the world may pose terrorist threats or foist unwanted problems on America. The September 11 terrorists, mainly in this country under expired and unmonitored student visas, took advantage of America's lax immigration policy to destroy lives and property. While it is less well-known, nearly one-fourth of those incarcerated in America's federal prisoners are aliens. The cost of incarceration of these aliens was estimated at $724 million in 1990, and these individuals foreclose immigration opportunities to others who would be productive citizens.

The balance between openness to immigration and closure of our borders for security reasons has shifted over the course of American history. Indeed, major changes in that balance have recently occurred and others are anticipated. We cannot hope to be definitive about this nation's immigration policies (that is a task for other books) and must offer the caveat that much of what is said here is in flux; nevertheless, we will attempt to organize the current strands of legal rules into a coherent framework. Three components seem worthy of exploration: (1) the rules about who may enter the country, (2) the restrictions upon and tracking of those who are allowed to enter, and (3) the processes for dealing with aliens who are deportable.

Before we look at these issues seriatim, two fundamental premises of immigration law should be put on the table. First, "In the exercise of its broad power over naturalization and immigration, Congress regularly makes rules that would be unacceptable if applied to citizens." Mathews v. Diaz (S.Ct. 1976). Second, "any policy toward aliens is vitally and intricately interwoven with contemporaneous policies in regard to the conduct of foreign relations, the war power, and the maintenance of a republican form of government." Harisiades v. Shaughnessy (S.Ct. 1952).

1. ENTRY OF ALIENS

Legal immigrants into the United States in 2001 numbered approximately a million, and about 30 million noncitizens enter the United States each year, mainly as tourists, students, and business visitors. Additionally, an unknown number of illegal aliens, mostly from Mexico, enter the country each year, generally in search of better employment opportunities than they have at home. The 2000 census data suggests that there are currently about 8 million foreigners in the United States without proper authorization.

Under United States law, illegal immigrants may be summarily stopped at the nation's borders and returned to their country of origin. As the Supreme Court has held, no due process is owed such excluded aliens. The Chinese Exclusion Case (S.Ct. 1889); see also Zadvydas v. Davis (S.Ct. 2001). The main problem in excluding illegal immigrants is therefore one of resources, not law. Beefed-up resources to the Border Patrol and the Coast Guard, provided by the USA PATRIOT Act and the Homeland Security Act, are a partial answer to this concern.

Legal immigrants, on the other hand, are dealt with under a complex set of visa categories, including a variety of student and work visas. Recently, the main effort has been to monitor those issued such visas and the organizations to which they are attached more carefully than in the past. For example, the new Student and Exchange Visitor Information System (SEVIS) program requires colleges and universities to engage in reporting with respect to foreign students enrolled at their institutions. Employers, under the Immigration Reform and Control Act of 1986 (IRCA), are held responsible for ensuring that their workers possess proof of citizenship or appropriate work authorization (usually a "green card"). Not surprisingly, the tightening up on visas has led to significant delays in granting of visas and in some instances has probably deterred prospective students or employees from coming to this country.

As this book goes to press, fingerprinting has begun for entrants into the country from specific "high-risk" countries. In addition, new high-tech systems for identifying entrants at border crossings and international airports are in progress. The purpose of these systems is to cross-check fingerprints or other biodata on the entrant against databases of those issued visas and those on terrorist watch lists. Challenges to such systems, on privacy or perhaps equal protection grounds, are anticipated.

One special group of immigrants consists of those who seek asylum in this country, often based on allegations of torture or likely political punishment in their native lands. Until very recently, asylum-seekers were permitted to be released, generally to the custody of relatives in the United States, pending a decision whether to accept their petitions (which were backlogged by many months). The standard used by immigration judges was whether the individual posed a risk of flight or a danger to the community. Very recently, the Attorney General reversed an immigration judge's decision to release an asylum-seeker from Haiti that used the traditional criteria. The reasons for the reversal given by the Attorney General were (1) to discourage the migration of vast numbers of Haitians to the United States and (2) that Haiti was a "staging area" for terrorists from Arab and Muslim nations. Presumably the latter of these criteria would apply to any asylum-seeker from Saudi Arabia (home to 15 of the 19 September 11 hijackers) or Afghanistan (when the Taliban ruled), even though the asylum-seeker asserted he was victimized by these regimes.

Entry of goods into this country, though it implicates the balance between international trade and interdiction of security-threatening materials such as weapons of mass destruction, will not be covered here.

2. TRACKING OF ALIENS

An estimated 8 million illegal aliens live and work in the United States under the radar of law enforcement and immigration authorities. Indeed, it is estimated that approximately 300,000 noncitizens in the United States subject to final orders for their removal are hiding out avoiding deportation. These "absconders" have recently been prioritized and enforcement agencies have been working to find and deport those who are males from certain Arab and Muslim countries.

The Department of Homeland Security is attempting to create computerized databases on those in the country on temporary visas and it has tightened up on those who overstay their visas. Additionally, male noncitizens from specific (mainly Muslim and mid-eastern) countries have been required to register with federal authorities. Of 82,000 who registered as required, some 13,000 as of June 2003 have been ordered to appear in immigration court for deportation hearings. Many of these have wives holding green cards and children born in the U.S. (who are therefore U.S. citizens).

Proposals for a national ID card have been rejected by Congress, but state drivers' licenses are becoming more standardized and access to information concerning such licenses is becoming more available to law enforcement officials nationally.

In times of crisis, aliens in the United States have sometimes been targeted for arrest or detention for criminal actions to which their primary or only connection was their ethnicity. For example, in the Palmer Raids of 1919, the government rounded up thousands of immigrants suspected loosely of being involved in a number of small bombings in the U.S. thought to be tied to radicalism and the Russian Revolution. During World War II, those viewed as "alien" because of Japanese origins were incarcerated in detention camps on the west coast. And mid-eastern male aliens bore the brunt of the post-September 11 detentions. In such crisis moments, government authorities, who would "rather be safe than sorry," have sometimes not adhered to civil liberties norms that this country cherishes. The cases dealing with the Japanese detentions are covered in Chapter 1.

3. REMOVAL OF ALIENS

The point at which the legal "rubber meets the road" is in the deportation or removal process. The Immigration and Nationality Act (INA), which has undergone numerous revisions, provides for a process of hearings before special Article II tribunals. The Immigration Judges who decide these cases may be reversed upon order of the Attorney General. Indeed, until the Supreme Court ruled it unconstitutional on separation of powers grounds, the law once provided that Congress could exercise a "legislative veto" over the Attorney General's decisions. INS v. Chadha (S.Ct. 1983).

The Fifth Amendment due process clause applies to deportation processes, and aliens held in detention may seek release using the writ or habeas corpus, 28 U.S.C. § 2241, even though provisions of the INA preclude direct judicial review over decisions of the Attorney General. But neither the Constitution's applicability nor the availability of habeas corpus review affords those involved the same rights afforded criminal defendants. Two recent Supreme Court decisions are instructive.

In Zadvydas v. Davis (S.Ct. 2001), the Court
construed INA § 1231 not to allow indefinite
detention of an alien following a final order of
removal. It held that detention for 90 days was
presumptively lawful and that further detention
for an additional period of time "reasonably
necessary to secure the alien's removal" was
permissible. This construction, far from obvious
from the statutory language, avoided a serious
constitutional question: Is indefinite detention a
permissible deprivation of liberty under the due
process clause of the Fifth Amendment?

Even more recently, the Court considered
whether an alien could be detained during the
period of his removal proceedings. Demore v. Kim
(S.Ct. 2003). The Court held that this was
permissible, distinguishing Zadvydas on two
grounds. First, while Zadvydas was an alien for
whom removal was "no longer practically
attainable," so that detention did not serve an
immigration purpose, the detention of Kim served
the purpose of preventing his flight prior to or
during the proceedings. The Court noted that 20%
to 25 % of those detained in circumstances like
Kim's did not show up for their removal
proceedings. Second, while Zadvydas' detention
was "indefinite," and "potentially permanent,"
Kim's detention had a definite termination point
(decision of his case), a period of time generally
less than the 90 days presumed reasonable in
Zadvydas. The Court noted that removal
proceedings are completed in an average time of 47
days and a median time of 30 days.

Some questions remain open after these decisions. Perhaps most importantly, it is unclear how these rulings will apply to asylum-seekers pending determination of their petitions (see above).

D. OPENNESS, SECRECY, AND NATIONAL SECURITY

Open government is a central premise of democratic governance: without disclosure of what the government is doing, how can the citizenry reward those who work diligently and punish those who are venial, deceptive, or lazy? At the same time, secrecy with respect to national security matters is often necessary, lest enemies of the United States use information about our vulnerabilities to injure us. As a general matter, we the public agree to forego access to some sensitive information, allowing certain elected leaders access to that information as our proxies. What is the proper balance between openness and secrecy concerning national security? And who makes decisions concerning where to establish the balance in particular cases?

1. ACCESS TO INFORMATION

The Freedom of Information Act of 1966 (FOIA), 5 U.S.C. § 552, is the starting point for answering these questions. Under this statute, "agencies" are responsible for providing "records" "reasonably described" in a "request" made by "any person." FOIA permits but does not require withholding of classified data. In the more turgid language of the statute, there is an exemption for "matters that are (A) specifically authorized under criteria established by an Executive order to be kept secret in the interest of national defense or foreign policy and (B) are in fact properly classified pursuant to such Executive order."

Thus, the availability of national security information through FOIA requests is in large part a function of the classification system put in place by specific presidential orders. The Supreme Court held in connection with an earlier version of this exemption that courts should not review the propriety of such classifications as evidenced in agency affidavits saying the classification was proper. EPA v. Mink (S.Ct. 1973). Congress, in response to this interpretation, granted courts the power to engage in *de novo* review of such classifications. While the lower court standards for judicial review are divergently stated and the Supreme Court has not spoken on the issue, there is a strong tendency for the courts to deny access to information classified on a "reasonable basis" by the agency.

President Reagan's 1982 guidance, Executive Order No. 12,356, listed categories of information that could be kept secret followed by a catch-all provision of "other categories of information that are related to national security and that require protection against unauthorized disclosure." The Reagan order also provided that documents "shall" be classified if disclosure "reasonably could be expected to cause damage to the national security." The presumption, in short, favored classification and hence nondisclosure of materials that might have national security ramifications.

In 1995, President Clinton issued Executive Order No. 12,958 to establish a less restrictive system for "classifying, safeguarding, and declassifying national security information." The premise of this order was that "[i]f there is significant doubt about the need to classify information, it shall not be classified." Section 1.2(b). To that end, E.O. 12,958 limits national security information to a list that includes military plans, foreign government information, intelligence activities, foreign relations or activities (including confidential sources), "scientific, technological, or economic matters relating to national security," nuclear materials and facilities information, and "vulnerabilities or capabilities of systems, installations, projects or plans relating to the national security." Section 1.5. The Reagan catch-all clause was deleted. Additionally, the new order allowed (but did not mandate) classification when disclosure "reasonably could be expected to result in damage to the national security *and the original classification authority is able to identify or describe the damage.*" Section 1.2(a)(4)(emphasis added). No such identification or description was required under the Reagan order.

The Clinton order also established a "sunset" provision for declassification of classified national security information 10 years after the date of the original classification decision, subject to exceptions where the information's release would have specific, adverse, and foreseeable consequences. E.O. 12,958 provided for broad declassification of materials over 25 years old, with rare exceptions.

Since September 11, the balance between disclosure and nondisclosure has shifted back toward the approach taken by the Reagan administration. A memorandum dated October 12, 2001 from Attorney General Ashcroft to Heads of All Federal Departments and Agencies instructed agencies that they could "carefully consider FOIA requests and decide to withhold records, in whole or in part" and that the Department of Justice would "defend your decisions unless they lack a sound legal basis." As this book is being written, it is expected that President Bush will issue a new executive order on national security classification of documents that will create more secrecy in order to protect national security.

In addition to FOIA, a citizen may occasionally prevail in asserting a common law right to know where FOIA does not apply, such as to congressional records. Schwartz v. US DOJ (DCCir. 1979). Additionally, there may be a limited implied right to know under the First Amendment, though its application to national security information is unclear. Compare Richmond Newspapers v. Virginia (S.Ct. 1980) with Houchins v. KQED (S.Ct. 1978); see Nation Magazine v. US DOD (SDNY 1991).

2. RESTRAINTS ON PUBLISHING DATA

How can "leaks" of sensitive national security information be restrained? First, access to such

information may be confined not only to persons
having a "need to know," but to persons having an
appropriate security classification. There are
various security clearances premised on
background investigations applicable both to
government employees and government
contractors. Second, several million people having
access to sensitive information are or have been
contractually bound not to release or disclose such
information. Violations of such agreements may
be subject to discipline including dismissal and
may form the basis for civil suit against the
employee by the government. Third, if release is
imminent despite such screening and contractual
protections, the government may seek a court
injunction against release or publication
enforceable by imprisonment of anyone who
violates the injunction. See Snepp v. United States
(S.Ct. 1980), holding a former CIA agent to a
contractual obligation to submit material intended
for publication for prior agency review and holding
proceeds from publication in constructive trust.
Finally, those who leak information claimed by the
government to be sensitive may be prosecuted for
espionage under 18 U.S.C. §§ 793-798.

The details of these restraints on release of
information are beyond the scope of this book, but
two cases are essential to understanding the
Constitution's limits upon the government's ability
to constrain release of allegedly sensitive
information.

The first is the so-called Pentagon Papers case,
New York Times Co. v. United States (S.Ct. 1971),
which dealt with the proposed publication of some

7,000 pages of a DOD study of the United States' involvement in Vietnam from 1945 to 1967, each page of which had been stamped with varying levels of secrecy classifications. On June 15, 1971, the Nixon administration, following the second installment of the Pentagon Papers in the Times, sought an injunction to suppress further publication after warning the newspaper's publisher that publication was "espionage" that would cause "irreparable injury to the defense of the United States." The provision referred to, 18 U.S.C. § 793, makes it criminal for an unauthorized possessor of any document "relating to the national defense" to "willfully communicate...that document to any person not entitled to receive it" or "willfully to retain" the document. Following hectic and inconclusive skirmishes in the lower courts, the Supreme Court granted certiorari on June 25, heard argument June 26, and issued its decision on June 30.

The Court's per curiam opinion noted that "any system of prior restraints of expression comes to this Court bearing a heavy presumption against its constitutional validity" and that the government had not met its burden in seeking to overcome that presumption. The justices explained their views in different ways. For example, Justice Black called injunction against publication "a flagrant, indefensible, and continuing violation of the First Amendment," Justice Douglas stressed the relevance of the Pentagon Papers to the ongoing public debate over the Vietnam War, Justice Brennan pointed out that the government simply hadn't made its case for restraint, and Justice Stewart opined that he could not say that publication would result in "direct, immediate, and irreparable damage to our Nation or its people." While the Times won its case, the balancing process used by the Court and the divergence of views left room for a future administration to obtain injunctive relief against publication in a proper case.

The second is United States v. The Progressive (W.D. Wis. 1979), a case involving an injunction sought by the government to prevent publication of an article concerning the details, complete with illustrations, of the trigger mechanism used in making a hydrogen bomb. Relying on provisions of the Atomic Energy Act of 1946 and fearful that a ruling favoring publication "could pave the way for thermonuclear annihilation," the court issued an injunction. The Supreme Court refused to hear an expedited appeal, and while the case was pending in the Court of Appeals, the information was published elsewhere. Seeing that the cat was out of the bag, the government withdrew from the appeal and The Progressive published the article.

3. CLANDESTINE OPERATIONS

Intelligence operations include countering terrorism, fighting international crime (including drug trafficking), and disrupting illegal financial activities. These operations are global in scope and raise legal questions including: 1) Who controls them? And 2) How are they restricted by law?

Control over covert operations is largely but not exclusively in the hands of the President. As Chapter 1 explains, the President's power may stem from his amorphous authority as inheritor of preconstitutional sovereignty, United States v. Curtiss-Wright Corp. (S.Ct. 1936), his ability to maintain secrets and confidences as an aspect of executive privilege, United States v. Nixon (S.Ct. 1974), and his "emergency powers." In re Neagle (S.Ct.1890). He also may draw upon a lengthy history of congressional deference to secret operations conducted by the Executive.

But the Congress has authority here also, including the Statement and Account Clause, which forbids permanent secrecy concerning expenditure of funds for covert operations, the Secret Journal Clause, which shows that the Framers intended to entrust Congress with sensitive information, the Marque and Reprisal Clause, which may have been intended to place control over privateers in Congress, and Congress' inherent authority to investigate current Executive operations in the exercise of its own Article I powers.

The courts have little role to play in drawing the lines between the President and Congress in this field. See United States v. Richardson (S.Ct. 1974), in which the Court found that the plaintiff lacked standing to enforce the Statement and Account clause.

The Neutrality Act of 1794, 18 U.S.C. § 960, outlawed private warfare, but did not bar unilateral military actions by the President. Moreover, it has no application other than when the nation is "at peace;" when the President engages in military actions against another country, our countries are not at peace, even when

Congress has not declared war and indeed has removed funding from related operations by the executive branch. United States v. Terrell (SDFla. 1989). See also Koohi v. United States (9th Cir. 1992) ("time of war" should be judged by "contemporary realities," not formal declarations).

Another statute of ancient vintage, the Logan Act of 1799, 18 U.S.C. § 953, criminalizes citizen actions to "influence the measures or conduct of any foreign government or of any agent thereof, in relation to any disputes with the United States." Though the Logan Act has occasionally been used to threaten private parties whose views were at odds with those of the administration, there has never been a Logan Act prosecution. Undoubtedly, that is because such a prosecution would raise serious First and Fifth Amendment questions.

The National Security Act of 1947 was the charter for the nation's intelligence operations. It created the National Security Council including the President, Vice-President, Secretary of State, and the Secretary of Defense. The NSC was charged with "effectively coordinating the policies and functions of the departments and agencies of the Government." Its duties include "assess and appraise the objectives, commitments, and risks of the United States in relation to our actual and potential military power" and "consider policies on matters of common interest to the departments and agencies of the Government concerned with the national security."

The National Security Act describes the authority of the CIA and the Director of Central

Intelligence in vague terms, including "facilitate the development of an annual budget for foreign intelligence information," "establish requirements and priorities for foreign intelligence information," "protect intelligence sources and methods," and "perform such other functions as the President or the National Security Council may direct." This final catch-all function is often referred to the CIA's "fifth function." Arguably, this "fifth function" includes covert psychological operations and paramilitary operations, at least if there is a relationship of these activities to intelligence operations. Indeed, the CIA took over numerous covert operations almost immediately in order to counter communism.

Over the course of the "cold war," the CIA engaged in numerous covert operations, some of which violated U.S. law. Concerns about such activities and the executive branch's practice of "plausibly denying" them led to congressional investigation, oversight, and regulation. In 1974, the Hughes-Ryan Amendment, 22 U.S.C. § 2422, required for the first time that the President account for covert activities and report them to Congress. Two years later, The Senate Select Committee to Study Governmental Operations with Respect to Intelligence Activities, popularly known as "The Church Committee," carefully and publicly documented these activities. S. Rept. No. 94-755, 94th Congress, 2nd session, Book I (1976). In response to the Church Committee Report, and perhaps to co-opt more far-ranging statutory restrictions, a number of executive orders were issued adding controls on covert operations. The only statute to arise from Congress' work in this era was the Intelligence Oversight Act of 1980, which required disclosure of intelligence activities to the intelligence committees of Congress.

President Reagan's 1981 Executive Order No. 12,333 was arguably the most important of the presidential initiatives to deal with control over intelligence activities. This order recited the purpose of providing for "the effective conduct of United States intelligence activities and the protection of constitutional rights." In addition to specifying some particular duties of the CIA (e.g. collecting intelligence information "not otherwise obtainable" and "intelligence on foreign aspects of narcotics production and trafficking"), the order precluded all agencies other than the CIA (other than the military in time of war) from conducting "any special activity unless the President determines that another agency is more likely to achieve a particular objective." Two provisions state that "Nothing in this Order shall be construed to" (1) "apply to or interfere with any authorized civil or criminal law enforcement responsibility" or (2) "authorize any activity in violation of the Constitution or statutes of the United States." E.O. 12,333 prohibits any "person employed by or acting on behalf of the United States Government [from] engag[ing] in, or conspir[ing] to engage in, assassination." There is no definition of assassination in the order, but it is generally agreed that it is permissible to target individual terrorists who have attacked the United States and leaders of enemy forces during war. See generally Addicott, "Proposal for a New Executive Order on Assassination," 37 U. RICH. L.

REV. 751 (2003). Finally, to assure that the order is only for presidential control of intelligence operations, it explicitly denies any intent "to confer any substantive or procedural right or privilege on any person or organization."

The controls on covert operations were tested in the 1986 Iran-Contra Affair, in which proceeds from arms sales to Iran had been diverted by the CIA to gain release of hostages held in Lebanon and to support the Contras fighting the Sandinista government of Nicaragua. The arms sales to Iran were found by a House Select Committee in 1987 to have violated the Arms Export Control Act (AECA), 22 U.S.C. §§ 2751-2796, but there were eight dissenters among the 26-member committee. Moreover, the President may have had some inherent Article II authority to trade arms for hostages, and the Hostage Act of 1868, 22 U.S.C. §1732 may have enhanced that authority. As for failing to report the arms sales to Congress, President Reagan had some "covert operations" cover under § 501 of the National Security Act. The President's advocates also argued that a 10-month delay was a report made in "timely fashion" as the statute required and that executive orders, such as E.O. 12,333, could not bind the President himself.

The support for the Contras may have violated a congressional prohibition on such aid embodied in legislation referred to as the Boland Amendments. Technical arguments against application of the Boland Amendments included (1) Congress' opposition to such aid was inconsistent (different versions of the Amendments were in effect during different time periods when aid was given to the Contras), and (2) the Boland Amendments applied only to the CIA, not members of the National Security Council, who had provided the aid. Finally, the President's advocates countered that the Boland Amendments violated the President's Article II foreign affairs powers.

Fourteen individuals, including Lt. Col. Oliver North and John M. Poindexter, were prosecuted by an independent counsel in the Iran-Contra Affair. Eleven were convicted, but were pardoned by President Bush in December 1992. The president premised the pardons on patriotism, long government service, and what he viewed as "the criminalization of policy differences." Independent Counsel Lawrence Walsh responded in a report to Congress that the President had abused his pardon power.

Reforms instituted following the Iran-Contra Affair and the pardons have been limited. The Intelligence Authorization Act of 1991 arguably beefed up presidential obligations to report covert activities, but President Bush's signing statement asserted the position that the reporting requirements were merely consistent with prior law and that the president's inherent authority entitled him to take covert actions in the interest of national security. Congress also asserted enhanced budget oversight, but there are serious questions about how effective the oversight could be and the extent to which taxpayers can demand that the President provide the public with information concerning expenditures. Richardson v. United States (S.Ct. 1974). Finally, Congress amended the Arms Export Control Act and the Hostage Act in 1989 to ban exports of munitions to terrorist nations even for humanitarian reasons. The President, however, can avoid this restriction by certifying that such a transaction is "essential to the national security interests of the United States" and "consulting" with a congressional committee.

Three fascinating cases explore legal issues that may arise from CIA covert operations. In 1964, Reinaldo Juan Lopez-Lima hijacked a plane in Florida and ordered the pilot, at gunpoint, to fly to Cuba, where he was jailed by the Castro regime. In 1989, two years after returning to the United States, Lopez-Lima was approached by the State Department for information about Cuba. When the State Department checked out his background, they discovered that Lopez-Lima had been indicted for aircraft piracy in 1969. When the government prosecuted him, Lopez-Lima's defense was that the CIA had authorized him to hijack the plane, fly it to Cuba, and work to undermine Castro. The court found that, if factually accurate, this would be a defense to the charge since, in 1964, the CIA had the power to authorize such conduct. United States v. Lopez-Lima (SDFla. 1990). Prior to trial, the government dismissed the prosecution in order to avoid disclosing classified information to which the court held the defendant was entitled.

The second case, Halkin v. Helms (DCCA 1982), involved a suit by alleged targets of CIA "dirty tricks" for violation of various constitutional rights. They showed that a CIA operation in the United States (Operation CHAOS) had compiled extensive

files on the activities of individuals and groups
engaged in anti-Vietnam War protests. The CIA
had infiltrated a number of such domestic
organizations, opened mail, collected private
information on individuals, and monitored phones,
at least for international calls. When the plaintiffs
sought through discovery to examine the files
relating to them, the government claimed that
release of the specifics would violate national
security concerns. The court held that the
information was privileged and dismissed the suit
because none of the plaintiffs could show a
personal injury on which relief could be granted.

Finally, Christopher v. Harbury (S.Ct. 2002)
shows the limits of citizen redress for even the
most personally damaging of covert operations.
Harbury alleged that U.S. officials had
intentionally deceived her by concealing
information that her husband, a Guatemalan
dissident, had been detained, tortured, and
executed by Guatemalans paid by the CIA.
Moreover, she alleged, this denial of information
kept her from being able to assert a claim in court
that might have saved her husband's life. The
Supreme Court rejected her claim, saying that
access to the courts was inextricably linked to the
specifics of a substantive remedy. Here, said the
Court, there was no substantive claim because
whatever the CIA might have done was pursuant
to the conduct of foreign relations of the United
States, about which judicial inquiry would
inappropriately breach the separation of powers.
Though Harbury could not reach the CIA and
other parts of the Executive Branch with her

denial of access to the courts claim and therefore would not have any claim that might save her husband, the Court opined that its decision did not preclude tort claims against those who tortured and killed her husband.

E. THE MILITARY AND INTERNAL DISORDERS

Domestic difficulties may run the gamut from serious insurrections to minor law enforcement activities. Federal authority with respect to domestic threats is well recognized. In re Neagle (S.Ct.1890). Disturbances too extensive to be handled by state and local police forces often lead to involvement of the National Guard, either as an agent of the state or federal government. The National Guard has been used to control riots, keep the mails moving, and render disaster relief and protection from looting. In rare situations, such as when state authorities use the National Guard to resist federal authority, the Guard may be called into federal service. This was done to integrate schools and colleges in Southern states during the 1950s era of "massive resistance" to the Supreme Court's desegregation decisions.

In some instances, units of the Army, Navy, Air Force or Marine Corps may be called upon to render aid. Military involvement in police activities is restricted, but not totally prohibited, by the Posse Comitatus Act, 18 U.S.C.A. § 1385, which provides:

Whoever, except in cases and under circumstances expressly authorized by the Constitution or Act of Congress, willfully uses any part of the Army or the Air force as a posse comitatus or otherwise to execute the laws shall be fined under this title or imprisoned not more than two years, or both.

The intent of the Act is to limit the direct, active use of federal troops for civil law enforcement. The original purpose of the law was to end the use of federal troops to police state elections in ex-Confederate states where civilian authority had been restored. Although the law is a criminal statute, there are apparently no instances of its ever being enforced. Its primary impact is its moral suasion. By its terms, the law applies to only the Army and Air Force. It does not apply to the Navy. United States v. Yunis (D.C.Cir.1991). Nor does it apply to the Coast Guard. United States v. Chaparro–Almeida (5th Cir.1982). The Navy and Marines follow the proscriptions of the Posse Comitatus Act only as a matter of policy. SECNAVINSTR. 5820.7 (May 15, 1974). Likewise, the Act does not restrict on-base military law enforcement activities against civilians who commit crimes on a fort, post or base. United States v. Banks (9th Cir.1976).

Even the Army and Air Force may act "indirectly" to counsel or advise civilian law enforcement authorities and may loan or sell military equipment to law enforcement officials for their use. United States v. Red Feather (D.S.D. 1976). Prohibited "direct" actions include arrests, seizures of evidence, searches of people or buildings, crime investigations, interviewing witnesses, pursuing escaped civilian prisoners, and the like. Permissible "indirect" actions include mere presence, preparation of contingency plans for mobilization, advice on tactics or logistics, aerial reconnaissance, and delivery and maintenance of military equipment and supplies. Bissonette v. Haig (8th Cir.1985)(occupation of Wounded Knee, South Dakota). Military involvement in disaster relief, operation of public services and transportation, assistance in safety and traffic programs, and civil defense activities do not trigger the prohibitions of the Posse Comitatus Act.

A regulation entitled "Employment of Military Resources in the Event of Civil Disturbance," 32 C.F.R. § 215.4, details two constitutional and four statutory exceptions to the Posse Comitatus Act. The constitutional exceptions are (1) emergency authority to prevent loss of life or property destruction and (2) authority to protect federal property and functions when "duly constituted local authorities are unable" to provide adequate protection.

Three of the four statutory exceptions relate to the use of federal troops to suppress insurrections. 10 U.S.C.A. §§ 331–335. In the event of an insurrection, the President must issue a proclamation calling upon insurgents to disperse and retire peaceably within a limited time. § 334. The first statutory exception authorizes the President upon request of the state governor or legislature to use the militia or federal armed forces to suppress domestic violence. § 331; U.S.

Const. Art. IV, § 4. The second authorizes use of the militia or federal armed forces when the laws of the United States cannot be enforced through conventional means. § 332. The third authorizes use of the militia or federal armed forces when people are deprived of their rights by "any insurrection, domestic violence, unlawful combination or conspiracy." § 333; U.S. Const. Art. II, § 3 and Amend. 14. The fourth statutory exception to the Posse Comitatus Act is an uncodified provision, H.J.R. 1292, June 6, 1968, P.L. 90–331, 82 Stat. 170, that directs all departments of the federal government, upon request of the Secret Service, to assist the Secret Service in carrying out its statutory duties to protect government officials and major political candidates from physical harm. See DOD Directive 3025.13, "Employment of Department of Defense Resources in Support of the United States Secret Service," July 15, 1968.

In addition to the exceptions recited in 32 C.F.R. § 215.4, Congress has facilitated the indirect or collateral use of military assets to assist in law enforcement activities such as drug interdiction, the control of illegal immigration, and tariff law enforcement. 10 U.S.C.A. §§ 371–380. The direct participation by members of the armed forces in "search, seizure, arrest or other similar activity" is forbidden. § 375. Instead, members of the armed forces can provide assistance to law enforcement though such means as providing information collected in military training activities and operations, § 371, providing military equipment and facilities, § 372, providing training and advice to civilian law enforcement officials, § 373, and operating detection and monitoring equipment, conducting aerial reconnaissance, transporting personnel and providing communications. § 374.

An unresolved issue with respect to the Posse Comitatus Act is whether it applies outside the nation's borders. Siemer & Effron, "Military Participation in United States Law Enforcement Activities Overseas: The Extraterritorial Effect of the Posse Comitatus Act," 54 St. John's L. Rev. 1 (1979). The question arose in the trial of Panamanian military leader Manuel Antonio Noriega but was not resolved. United States v. Noriega (S.D.Fla.1990) (motion to dismiss based on alleged violations of the Posse Comitatus Act withdrawn).

CHAPTER 3

ENTRY INTO THE MILITARY

Article I, § 8 of the Constitution grants Congress the power "to raise and support Armies," "to provide and maintain a Navy," and "to provide for calling forth the Militia to execute the Laws of the Union, suppress Insurrections and repel Invasions." In order to fulfill its constitutional duties, Congress has established four basic routes into military service: enlistment, officer appointment, activation of reservists, and conscription. For each route, Congress has prescribed certain qualifications for and conditions upon entry into the military. Eligibility and procedures have been further defined by the secretaries of the services, military administrative regulations, and judicial decisions.

A. ENLISTMENT

1. THE NATURE OF THE RELATIONSHIP

Enlistment in the military has characteristics of both contract and status. Bell v. United States (S.Ct.1961). The typical military enlistment agreement provides for a six-year military service obligation, generally divided between an active duty tour and a period of reserve service. The agreement recites many understandings, the most important of which are:

The Enlistee's Understandings

1. That the enlistee is subject to the Uniform Code of Military Justice (UCMJ) and may be tried by court martial;

2. That lawful orders given by authorized persons will be obeyed;

3. That, if separated from the service under less than honorable conditions, the enlistee may be detrimentally affected in seeking later employment;

4. That service in combat or other dangerous duty may be required;

5. That specific promises of benefits by the armed forces may be abrogated in the event of war;

6. That enlistments in effect at the beginning of or during a war may continue in effect until six months after the war ends; and

7. That post-enlistment changes in statutes and regulations may alter the status, compensation, or obligations of a member of the military, notwithstanding contrary agreement upon enlistment.

The Armed Forces' Understandings

1. That the enlistee will receive the pay and allowances provided by law and regulations; and,

2. That promises set forth in the enlistment agreement will be honored concerning "assignment to duty, geographical area, training, or a particular school or special program; government quarters; physical and other qualifications for assignment to a particular school, rating, or specialty; bonuses or other compensation; promotions; or transportation of and support to dependents."

2. THRESHOLD REQUIREMENTS

There are several important restrictions on who may enlist in the Armed Forces. These restrictions arise not only from the statutes and regulations, but also from the enlistment agreements signed by agents of the military and by the enlistee. A body of case law surrounding enlistment requirements has developed primarily through challenges to the validity of particular enlistment agreements and efforts to enforce obligations set forth in the agreement. The validity of enlistments has been raised both by individuals (seeking either to avoid or claim military status) and also by the military (seeking either to retain or remove persons from its ranks). In either case, enlistment agreements are generally analyzed under traditional contract law notions. Peavy v. Warner (5th Cir.1974) (serviceman entitled to cancellation of service extension if 1) Navy refused legitimate requests for cancellation and, 2) Navy through misrepresentation induced servicemember to execute 'reaffirmation' agreement). Although some courts have been reluctant to hear these cases on their merits, other courts are more open to these challenges.

a. Age Standards

A threshold requirement for enlistment is that enlistees be of appropriate age. Congress has prohibited enlistments of individuals under age 17, permitted enlistment of individuals age 17 to 18 only with parental consent, and prohibited enlistment of individuals over age 35. 10 U.S.C.A. § 978.

One person who enlisted at age 15 and allegedly went AWOL before age 16 was deemed never to have been subject to court-martial jurisdiction, since the minimum age for enlistment was 17. United States v. Blanton (C.M.A. 1957). Similarly, the enlistment by a 16–year-old who presented a birth certificate which showed his age as 17 was void for lack of parental consent to enlistment, since consent is required for enlistment of persons up to age 18. United States v. Brown (C.M.A. 1974).

A further factor in Brown was recruiter misconduct. No constructive enlistment was deemed to have occurred when a 16–year-old recruit was assisted by the recruiter in falsifying the required parental notification consent form. The court held that "[a]n opposite conclusion would give encouragement to those who would attempt fraudulently to enlist at age 16, as well as to the recruiting of such persons in the hope that, if everyone keeps silent, the fraudulent enlistment will soon mature into a constructive enlistment."

When the military reasonably believes it has obtained consent from a proper parent or guardian for a 17–year-old's enlistment, and the fraudulent enlistee, after reaching age 18, continues to accept pay and other benefits from the military, in effect ratifying the contract, a constructive enlistment will arise. United States v. Graham (C.M.A. 1972); United States v. Boone (A.C.M.R.1981).

At the other end of the age spectrum, a forty-year-old enlistee argued that his enlistment was void and therefore the military court did not have jurisdiction to court-martial him. In contrast to the under-aged enlistment cases, the Supreme Court permitted departure from the statutory rules. The Court held that the enlistment gave the enlistee the "status" of soldier, and that the maximum age limit was waived where the government accepted the enlistee's services. United States v. Grimley (S. Ct. 1890).

In general, then, the enlistment of one under age 17 is void, the enlistment of one aged 17 or 18 without proper consent of a parent or guardian is void until age 18, and enlistment of one over the maximum age for enlistment is voidable at the discretion of the military.

b. Voluntariness and Improper Recruiting

A condition precedent to the validity of any civilian contract is that it be entered into voluntarily. This is no less true in the military context. In Grimley, for instance, the Court suggested that had there been evidence of "duress, imposition, ignorance, or intoxication" when the plaintiff enlisted, it would have viewed the government's attempt to court-martial Grimley less favorably.

Several cases in this area have dealt with the enlistment of people who were given the choice between enlisting in the armed services and going to jail. In United States v. Catlow (C.M.A. 1974), the court held void the enlistment of a man who had been given the Hobson's Choice between a jail term and Army duty. Different, however, was the case of a servicemember who joined the Army in exchange for reduced charges in a civilian criminal prosecution. United States v. Bachand (A.C.M.R.1983). The Bachand court distinguished Catlow: unlike Catlow's involuntary enlistment, Bachand's decision to join the Army was not court-imposed but was made voluntarily and with the full support of his family.

c. Unwed Parents

Army Regulation 601–210, Rule G prohibits unmarried parents of children aged 18 years or younger from enlisting or remaining enlisted in the Army, since people in those circumstances are unable to maintain the flexibility necessary in the armed forces while tending to their children. This is a nonwaivable restriction. Due Process and Equal Protection challenges to that regulation have generally failed. In West v. Brown (5th Cir.1977), the Fifth Circuit refused to invalidate the regulation, finding that the plaintiff's claim was not reviewable. The court held that this regulation was a rational restriction, because the government's interests would be hurt if unmarried parents joined the armed forces. See also Mack v. Rumsfeld (2d Cir.1986).

d. Homosexuality

Military regulations state that homosexuality is "incompatible with military service." For many years, courts of appeals have accepted arguments by the military that neither equal protection nor First Amendment challenges to the regulation are viable. For example, in Ben–Shalom v. Marsh (7th Cir.1989), a Seventh Circuit panel reasoned that constitutional protections are different in the military than in civilian life. Therefore, the court deferred to the Army's opinion that the presence of gay, lesbian, or bisexual servicemembers would be detrimental to the morale of the forces. However, one court held that the distinction between gay and lesbian service members and heterosexual service members has no rational basis. Dahl v. Secretary United States Navy (E.D.Cal.1993).

This issue became hotly contested in 1993, when President Clinton announced his intention to eliminate the ban on gay men, lesbians, and bisexuals from the Armed Forces. This announcement generated substantial opposition, both by the military and in Congress, forcing the President to compromise on his original goal of fully opening the armed services to homosexuals. President Clinton's modified position became "don't ask, don't tell", which meant that the military should not inquire about sexual preferences and individuals should not disclose those preferences. This policy was incorporated in a directive by the Secretary of Defense which states that while homosexual orientation should not be a bar to military service, homosexual conduct—or a propensity to engage in homosexual conduct—would be. Guidelines annexed to the Directive created a rebuttable presumption that a servicemember who states that he or she is homosexual will engage in homosexual conduct.

The result of that debate was passage of a federal statute, 10 U.S.C.A. § 654. In general, this provision authorizes dismissal and non- enlistment of servicemembers who engage in, or attempt to engage in, homosexual acts. Section 654 also authorizes non-enlistment of servicemembers who state that they are homosexual or bisexual. The statute does not require the discharge of servicemembers who state that they are homosexual or bisexual but who do not engage in or have a propensity to engage in homosexual acts.

This sensitive political debate is unlikely to end with the present law. Several suits by servicemembers who were discharged after they claimed publicly to be homosexual but claim also never to have engaged in homosexual conduct are now proceeding through the federal courts. The first court to address the constitutionality of this Act noted the apparent contradiction between the Directive's permissiveness and the presumption described in the Act. "The message * * * appears to be not to avoid private homosexual acts but to stay in the closet and hide their orientation." *Able v. United States* (E.D.N.Y.1994). The court issued a preliminary injunction against the discharge of those soldiers until the case can be adjudicated fully.

e. Signing the Enlistment Contract

Another threshold requirement for an enlistment is for the new recruit to sign the enlistment contract in the presence of the officer administering the oath of allegiance. 10 U.S.C.A. § 502. While failure or refusal to sign generally means that there is no enlistment, a person can be inducted into the military without taking the oath under limited circumstances. Moreover, it is possible that the putative enlistee's subsequent conduct may ratify the enlistment contract by evidencing a clear desire to change his or her status voluntarily from civilian to military.

f. Other Requirements

Insane or intoxicated persons and those convicted of felony or of deserting from the armed forces are disqualified from enlistment. 10 U.S.C.A. § 504. Aliens not admitted for permanent residency are also disqualified. 10 U.S.C.A. § 3253. In addition, servicemembers can be separated and denied re-enlistment for certain UCMJ violations. See also AR 635–209 (unsuitability for further military service).

One interesting enlistment requirement, contained in Army Regulation 601–210, permits the enlistment of men, but not women, who have a General Education Diploma rather than a high school diploma. A district court analyzed this regulation under a rational basis test, and held that it was reasonably relevant and necessary to the national defense. Lewis v. United States Army (E.D.Pa.1988). A similar hiring criterion in the civilian public sector would almost certainly violate the Equal Protection Clause.

3. CONSTRUCTIVE ENLISTMENT

Many enlisted personnel who have faced court-martial for UCMJ offenses have argued their enlistments were void for failure to satisfy some standard established by Congress. This after the fact route to challenging enlistments was mostly eliminated in 1980 when Congress, in order to prevent servicemembers from using the enlistment requirements as a route to avoiding military punishment or to leave the service, added Articles 2(b) and 2(c) to the UCMJ. 10 U.S.C.A. §§ 802(b) and (c). These provisions confirmed a preexisting reluctance by the courts to permit court-martial defendants to avoid punishment by arguing that their enlistments were defective. See Lonchyna v. Brown (N.D.Ill.1980).

Article 2(b) of the UCMJ validates for jurisdictional purposes the enlistment of "any person who has the capacity to understand the significance of enlisting." Thus, even if a servicemember was too young at the time of his or her enlistment, that soldier might still be forced to face charges in a military court. Article 2(c) states that an individual who voluntarily submits to military authority is subject to the UCMJ until active duty service is terminated so long as the age and competency requirements are met, pay and benefits are accepted, and military duties are performed. The effect of Article 2(c) is that it creates a "constructive enlistment" that can "cure" an originally defective enlistment.

Following the passage of Articles 2(b) and 2(c), military courts consistently have found court martial jurisdiction where enlistees have challenged the validity of their enlistments. In United States v. Ghiglieri (A.C.M.R.1987), for example, the servicemember's original enlistment agreement was arguably void because at the time of enlistment, Ghiglieri was still on probation for a civilian criminal offense, a nonwaivable moral disqualification under Army regulations. Nevertheless, the court held that there was court-martial jurisdiction over Ghiglieri. When his probation ended, and the disqualification expired, he entered into a constructive enlistment under Article 2(c) by continuing to accept military compensation and perform military duties. See also United States v. Hirsch (A.M.C.R. 1988), which held that one who claimed to have been under the influence of marijuana at the time of signing an enlistment contract was constructively enlisted because he voluntarily submitted to military authority, performed military duties, received pay and allowances, and made no official protests.

4. JUDICIAL REVIEW OF ENLISTMENT DECISIONS

The extent to which enlistment issues are subject to judicial review is a matter of deep division within the federal courts of appeals. In Mindes v. Seaman (5th Cir.1974), the Fifth Circuit fashioned

a test for review of the constitutionality of
discretionary military decisions, saying that
judicial review was proper only if these four factors
balance in favor of review: (1) the strength of the
plaintiff's claim, (2) the potential harm to the
plaintiff if review is denied, (3) the type and degree
of anticipated interference with the military
function, and (4) the extent to which military
expertise or discretion is involved. In Rucker v.
Secretary of Army (11th Cir.1983), the Eleventh
circuit permitted judicial review of the plaintiff's
challenge to his discharge for three main reasons.
First, "Rucker would have this court determine
whether he was entitled to certain rights under
applicable regulations and to make this
determination we would have to go no further than
the regulations. Second, the appropriate regulation
was mandatory and not discretionary. Third, the
interference with military affairs in that case was
minimal. See also Lindenau v. Alexander (10th
Cir.1981) (applying Mindes, court refuses to review
military policy of not permitting enlistment of
single parents having children under 18). Wenger
v. Monroe (9th Cir.2002) (applying Mindes, court
dismisses a suit seeking the alteration of plaintiff's
permanent military record); Guerra v. Scruggs,
(4th Cir.1991) (using Mindes test, court reverses
an injunction against plaintiff's dismissal from
service as a non-justiciable suit).

Other circuits are far more open to reviewing the
validity of enlistment policies challenged on
constitutional or statutory grounds. The Third
Circuit, in Dillard v. Brown (3d Cir.1981), for
example, found constitutional and statutory
challenges to enlistment policies reviewable on

their merits, even when such a challenge "appears weak or frivolous." The Second Circuit has similarly concluded that broad review of military policy on the merits is preferable to the Mindes analysis. See, e.g. Mack v. Rumsfeld (2d Cir.1986) (reviewing policy of not enlisting single parents with children under age 18). Several courts have departed further from Mindes and "adopted a per se prohibition of damages actions brought against military officers for the violation of subordinates' civil rights." Most significantly, the Fifth Circuit itself has abandoned Mindes and adopted a per se rule with respect to damages; thus, "Mindes has been banished from its homeland." Wright v. Park (1st Cir.1993); See also Trerice v. Summons (4th Cir.1985); Mollnow v. Carlton (9th Cir.1983); Martelon v. Temple. However, the retreat by these circuits from judicial review of "internal military decisions" has been limited to suits seeking damages, leaving those seeking injunctive relief within the province of the Mindes analysis. See Wenger v. Monroe (9th Cir.2002); Meister v. Tex. Adjutant General's Dep't (5th Cir.2000); Guerra v. Scruggs (4th Cir.1991); Roig v. Puerto Rico Nat'l Guard (D.P.R.1999).

5. ENFORCING ENLISTMENT AGREEMENTS

Beginning with the seminal case of United States v. Grimley (S.Ct.1890), courts have regularly held that enlistment does not simply create a contractual duty, but also changes the new recruit's status. Remedies for breach of enlistment agreements point out the difficulties in classifying enlistment as a matter of contract or status. While personal service contracts are not normally enforceable, breach of an enlistment contract by an enlistee leads not to monetary damages but to the servicemember remaining in service or being imprisoned. Similarly, breach of an enlistment contract by the government may void the enlistment rather than merely requiring monetary compensation to make the enlistee whole. Jablon v. United States (9th. Cir.1981).

A number of cases, however, have emphasized contractual components for enlistment agreements. In Grulke v. United States (Ct.Cl. 1981), the United States Court of Claims pointed out that the United States presently uses an all-volunteer military and that the military must therefore bargain with recruits to gain bright and well-qualified enlistees. The court found that the language of enlistment agreements, which speak in terms of "guarantees" and "promises," supported a contractual approach to the enlistment process. Two courts of appeals have found enlistments void or voidable under traditional concepts of contract law. Woodrick v. Hungerford (5th Cir.1986); Cinciarelli v. Carter (D.C.Cir.1981).

Some courts have refused to apply traditional common law principles to enlistment contract disputes, preferring instead to construct a "federal common law" by interpreting relevant federal statutes. Brown v. Dunleavy (E.D.Va.1989); McCracken v. United States (D.Ct. Conn.1980). For example in a suit for payment alleged to be due a servicemember, the Court held that applicable statutes and regulations will clearly displace common law, and rejected arguments premised on the terms of an enlistment contract. United States v. Larionoff (S.Ct.1977). In another case, when a group of optometrists claimed that they were induced to enter the service by recruiters' promises of special pay and benefits, the court refused to grant them relief. The court looked to the controlling statutes in effect at the time the optometrists enlisted and determined that they had received the pay and benefits to which they were entitled. Ramey v. United States (D.D.C.1982). Similarly, in a suit by the Air Force to recover costs associated with the training of certain enlistees who did not complete their obligations, a court held that the case involved "a question of fiscal policy far too involved for simple contract principles to settle." McCullough v. Seamans (E.D.Cal.1972).

The more frequent cases involve plaintiffs seeking rescission of the enlistment contract and discharge from the service because of alleged misrepresentations and promises by recruiters. Some courts will predicate the granting of relief upon whether they find a material misrepresentation, Withum v. O'Connor (D.P.R.1981), and whether the enlistee relied on the misrepresentations, Tremblay v. Marsh (D.Mass.1984).

In Pence v. Brown (8th Cir.1980), a medical student was told by a recruiter that he would enter the Air Force as a major but he was actually commissioned as a captain. Pence was accorded relief where the court found that the recruiter's negligent misrepresentation was material and that the enlistment agreement was silent as to rank and promotion opportunities. In distinguishing Dr. Pence's case from one seeking money damages or specific performance, the court stated, "The proposition that the government cannot be held responsible for the misstatements of its agents does not extend to representations which induce a contract when the remedy sought is rescission." The court, recognizing the critical need for military doctors, gave the Air Force the option of honoring the promises made by the recruiter as an alternative to discharging Pence.

The possibility of contract rescission as a result of the existence of material misrepresentations leads almost inexorably to allegations by servicemembers that they were made promises which remain unfulfilled, and therefore they should be released from service. Some courts have looked only to the terms of the enlistment agreement itself to identify the promises made. McCracken v. United States (D.Conn.1980) (the enlistment agreement was the only contract between the Navy and the plaintiff and any misrepresentations by a recruiter created no contract). Others have looked beyond the written terms. For example, in Brown v. Dunleavy (E.D.Va.1989), the court rejected the application of the parole evidence rule, holding that "under the general principles of contract law * * * there is a well established exception allowing extrinsic evidence to show inducement to contract by fraud or misrepresentation, even if the contract has a merger clause."

Courts are generally reluctant to apply estoppel against the military where a servicemember claims misrepresentation. In McCracken, for example, the court held that estoppel would require egregious and affirmative misconduct and was limited to "cases in which a government employee or officer violated a regulation, which had the force of law, requiring him to do something." One of the few cases where the court did apply equitable estoppel against the military involved a reservist who was activated after missing one more than the allowable number of drill periods. The court there found that the Navy had engaged in affirmative misrepresentation as to the number of drill periods required. The court imposed estoppel after finding that such relief, limited to returning the plaintiff to his reserve status, would not harm the government. Santos v. Franklin (E.D.Pa.1980).

B. OFFICER APPOINTMENTS

The Appointments Clause of the Constitution, Art. II, § 2, cl. 2, provides:

"[The President] shall nominate, and by and with the Advice and Consent of the Senate, shall appoint Ambassadors, other public Ministers and Consuls, Judges of the Supreme Court, and all other Officers of the United States, whose appointments are herein otherwise provided for, and which shall be established by Law: but the Congress may by Law vest the Appointment of such inferior Officers, as they think proper, in the President alone, in the Courts of Law, or in the Heads of Departments."

By statute, members of the armed forces with Regular appointments in the grades of second lieutenant or ensign (01) through colonel or captain (06), or Reserve appointments above the rank of major, are officers of the United States appointed with Senate participation. 10 U.S.C.A. § 531. This does not mean "that each of the more than 240,000 active military officers (see Department of Defense, Military Manpower Statistics, Table 9, p. 18 (Mar. 31, 1993)) is a principal officer" within the meaning of Article II, but only that Congress has "simply declined to adopt the less onerous appointment process available for inferior officers." Weiss v. United States (S.Ct.1994) (Souter, J. concurring). Those with Reserve appointments in the grades of second lieutenant or ensign (01) through major or lieutenant commander (04) are made by the President alone. 10 U.S.C.A. § 12203. It is rare for the President to be personally involved in military appointments other than at the very highest levels and Senate confirmations of military officers are generally handled en masse rather than individually.

There are two facets to such an appointment: (1) the officer is appointed to a particular component of an armed force and (2) the officer is appointed to a rank within that component. When the officer is reassigned to another component or changes rank, a new appointment is required. Moreover, a new appointment may sometimes be constitutionally required if a commissioned officer takes on duties not germane to the original appointment. Shoemaker v. United States (S.Ct.1893) (new

appointments not required of Chief of Engineers of
the Army and the Engineer Commissioner of the
District of Columbia to serve on commission to
develop Rock Creek Parkway, since duties were
germane to their duties under preexisting military
commissions). In Weiss v. United States, supra,
the Supreme Court held that new appointments
were not required for military officers detailed to
serve as military judges. The Court found that
"[a]lthough military judges obviously perform
certain unique and important functions, all
military officers, consistent with a long tradition,
play a role in the operation of the military justice
system." The Court also pointed out that "the
position of military judge is less distinct from other
military positions than the office of a full-time
civilian judge is from other offices in civilian
society."

Despite the holding of Weiss—that commissioned
officers do not need new appointments to serve as
military judges—the armed forces do not exercise
unbridled discretion to detail any commissioned
officer to any duty, no matter how much more
powerful and different those duties are from the
officers' normal duties. Congress has required
separate appointments and confirmations for many
top-level or politically-sensitive military positions,
such as the Chairman of the Joint Chiefs of Staff,
the Commandant of the Marine Corps, the
Surgeons General of the Army, Navy, and Air
Force, and the Chief of Chaplains. Other positions,
such as the Deputy and Assistant Chiefs of Staff
for the Army, the Chief of Staff of the Marine
Corps, instructorships at the military academies,

and positions with the American Red Cross, are positions to which particular officers may be detailed.

C. ACTIVATION OF RESERVISTS

Reservists are civilians performing part-time military duty with military reserve or national guard units. Inactive (non-pay, non-duty) reservists are former active duty officers, enlistees, and draftees waiting for their terms of obligation to expire. The active reservists' basic obligations are to perform week end, or week night, and short term military duty (typically in the summer). However, reservists also have another exposure to military duty: activation or call-up for full-time military duty.

There are two basic types of activation for extended active duty: (1) call-up of individuals or entire units to meet military needs and (2) activation of individuals for failure to comply with reserve obligations.

The former is an aspect of Congress' power "to raise and support Armies" (Art. I, § 8, cl. 12); Congress is not limited to using reservists exclusively for executing laws, suppressing insurrections, and repelling invasions under its power to "[call] forth the Militia" (Art. I, § 8, cl. 15). Thus, members of the National Guard who sign dual enlistment contracts enlisting in both a state national guard and "as a Reserve of the Army with membership in the National Guard of the United States." Because of this reserve status, they may be subjected to call-up although the purpose of the call-up is not to execute laws, suppress insurrections, or repel invasions. Johnson v. Powell (5th Cir.1969). Indeed, Johnson permitted call-up of an entire unit for a full 24 months of active duty even though selective call-ups of individuals were limited by statute to 24 months less any time served previously on active duty.

Congressional power to call up reservists was challenged in the mid-eighties by several governors who threatened to withhold (or withheld) their consent to federally ordered active duty missions by their states' National Guards. After Congress enacted the Montgomery Amendment, 10 U.S.C.A. § 672(f) (Supp. IV 1986), prohibiting governors from withholding consent to active duty missions outside the United States based on location, purpose, type, or schedule of duty, Minnesota Governor Perpich filed suit in federal court alleging that the Montgomery Amendment infringed "the Authority of training the Militia" reserved for the states by the Constitution. The Supreme Court held that "the dual enlistment system, under which guard members enlist and serve in both the state National Guard and the federal National Guard of the United States, was a necessary and proper exercise of Congress' power to raise and support armies." Perpich v. Department of Defense (S.Ct.1990). See also Dukakis v. United States Dept. of Defense (D.Mass.1988).

The second type of activation is punitive. A reservist absent without acceptable excuse from five or more drills or one who refuses to abide by legal rules applicable to reservists (e.g., maximum hair length standards) is liable for involuntary activation. The military services have established very detailed procedures for handling such controversial situations, and the courts have held the services to strict compliance with their announced procedures. For example, an activation for missing drills was overturned for failure of the unit commander to check into the reasons for absences before initiating a request for activation, even though the activated reservist was given an opportunity to explain his absences after the request had been submitted. Hall v. Fry (10th Cir.1975).

D. CONSCRIPTION

Conscription, sometimes called the ultimate weapon in Congress' efforts "to raise and support Armies," has had an erratic presence in American military history. Not until World War I did Congress use the draft systematically by creating local draft boards to rule on requests for exemption from military service. While the draft was a primary method of obtaining troops for World War II, the Korean War, and the Vietnam War, it was abolished in 1972. The draft boards were placed on standby in 1976. This section will examine the constitutionality of the draft, its administrative framework, its structure of deferments from service, and judicial review of Selective Service System decisions by civilian courts.

1. CONSTITUTIONALITY

The Supreme Court has said that Congress' power to conscript Americans for military service is "beyond question." United States v. O'Brien (S.Ct.1968). In the Selective Draft Law Cases (S.Ct.1918), the Court relied upon the constitutional power of Congress to "raise and support Armies" and "to make all laws which shall be necessary and proper for carrying into execution the foregoing powers." It summarily rejected arguments that 1) federal power to draft could not be delegated to state officials; 2) administrative officers were vested with unbridled legislative discretion; 3) judicial power was unconstitutionally handed to draft authorities; 4) the draft either established a religion or interfered with the free exercise of religion; and 5) conscription constituted involuntary servitude contrary to the Thirteenth Amendment. Eligibility for the draft of men alone does not violate the equal protection rights of men or women. Rostker v. Goldberg (S.Ct.1981).

2. ADMINISTRATION

The draft operated under basic procedures established by Congress and administrative regulations enacted by the Selective Service System. These procedures attest to the tension between efficiently providing military manpower and ensuring fair treatment of each draftee's objections to service. For example, while registrants were not permitted to be represented by counsel before local boards for fear that the induction process would come to a grinding halt, the registrant was accorded (1) the right to a personal appearance before the local board at which he could present evidence and witnesses, and (2) the right to a written appeal to the State Appeal Board.

Because these processes were summary, the courts generally required procedural requirements to be strictly followed for draft evasion convictions to be upheld. Moreover, if a registrant appeared confused about his rights and his confusion was not unreasonable, the draft board had an affirmative duty to clear up the registrant's misunderstanding. United States v. Grier (5th Cir. 1975). A fortiori, the board had "an affirmative duty not to mislead and to give correct information and advice" to the registrant. United States v. Cordova (10th Cir. 1972).

In order to further the efficient operation of the induction system, local draft boards accelerated the induction of persons who either destroyed their Selective Service System registration cards or returned their cards to Selective Service System authorities, and the United States prosecuted such individuals. In United States v. O'Brien (S.Ct. 1968), the Court upheld the constitutionality of a Federal statute forbidding the destruction of draft cards. It found that destroying the card was "conduct," not "speech," and hence was not protected by the First Amendment. The Court found no Congressional authorization in the Selective Service Act to support local draft board decisions to declare registrants "delinquent" for not possessing registration certificates or for otherwise committing "transgressions that affront the local board." Gutknecht v. United States (S.Ct.1970).

3. EXEMPTIONS AND DEFERMENTS

The draft never reached all members of American society. Exemptions (permanent relief from duty so long as there is no change in the exempted condition) and deferments (temporary relief from military duty) targeted the draft primarily at healthy young men. Men under 18 and over 35 have seldom been drafted, and women have never been conscripted into military service. Resident aliens sometimes have been exempted from and at other times subjected to the draft. See Vazquez v. Attorney General (D.C.Cir.1970). Additionally, a long list of physical, mental, and moral conditions have spared many otherwise eligible draft-age men from military service. Many such conditions disqualified men from service who were able to function normally in civilian life.

a. Conscientious Objection

In addition to the exemptions above, § 6(j) of the Universal Military Training and Service Act exempts those who by reason of "religious training or belief, [are] conscientiously opposed to participation in war in any form." "Religious training and belief * * * means an individual's belief in a relation to a Supreme Being involving duties superior to those arising from any human relation, but does not include essentially political, sociological, or philosophical views or a merely personal moral code." While this exemption for conscientious objectors (COs) released very few from the reach of the draft system, it spawned considerable litigation. The two primary issues have been: 1) What is "religious training or belief?" and 2) What is "participation in war in any form?"

Two Supreme Court cases largely resolve the first question. While exemptions had readily been granted to members of recognized sects which opposed participation in war, it was not until United States v. Seeger (S.Ct.1965), that the Court faced the problem of the individual objector not affiliated with an organized religion. Seeger was brought up in a religious home and attended church, but neither belonged to nor adhered to the beliefs of any organized religious group opposed to participation in war. When filling out his exemption application, Seeger struck the words, "training and," and placed quotes around "religious" before signing the statement, "I am, by reason of my religious training and belief, conscientiously opposed to participation in war in any form." He was uncertain whether he believed in a "Supreme Being" but had strong and sincere scruples against participating in war.   The Supreme Court reversed the denial of Seeger's CO exemption, interpreting the Congressional intent of § 6(j) to encompass beliefs which, in the registrant's own scheme of things, played the role of a religion in his life.

Subsequently, the Court broadened this reading of the statute even further by applying § 6(j) to a man who struck the entire phrase "my religious training and" from the exemption form. The Court found that, despite the registrant's own refusal to characterize his beliefs as religious, his objections to war rose above mere "considerations of policy, pragmatism, or expediency." Welsh v. United States (S.Ct.1970). In an opinion which expresses the unstated reasons for the majority's interpretation of § 6(j), Justice Harlan concurred on the grounds that Congress could not distinguish between "theistic and non-theistic religious beliefs on the one hand and secular beliefs on the other" in a manner consistent with the Establishment Clause of the First Amendment.

The second, less difficult, question similarly has been resolved by the Supreme Court. In Sicurella v. United States (S.Ct.1955), a denial of exemption to a Jehovah's Witness who was opposed to all wars other than a theocratic war commanded by Jehovah was overturned. The Court found a theocratic war to be so highly abstract that it did not undermine the registrant's conscientious opposition to participation in the "real shooting wars" Congress had in mind. Conversely, Gillette v. United States (S.Ct.1971), rejected the claim of a registrant opposed to participation in the "immoral" Vietnam War when the registrant admitted being unopposed to participation in other wars. The language of § 6(j) was quite clear, and no constitutional difficulties attached to Congress' circumscribing the exemption where it did.

There is one caveat to conscientious objection: whatever the registrant's beliefs, they must be sincerely held to qualify for the exemption. While a draft board could not deny an exemption because the registrant's beliefs are unorthodox, the board had substantial discretion to disbelieve the sincerity of the objector's beliefs. No First Amendment problems are raised by the denial of an exemption for lack of sincerity.

b. Compassionate Exemptions

Congress has also established certain "compassionate exemptions." For example, § 6(o) of the Selective Service Act of 1948 provides that "where the father or one or more sons or daughters of a family were killed in action or died in line of duty while serving in The Armed Forces * * * the sole surviving son of such family shall not be inducted for service * * * " In McKart v. United States (S.Ct.1969), the Court construed this statute to exempt a registrant who had no remaining family members, his mother having died when he was already classified as a "sole surviving son." McKart's draft board had withdrawn his exemption upon his mother's death on the theory that McKart no longer was needed to provide "solace and consolation" to any remaining family member. The Supreme Court reversed, noting that Congress also intended to grant the exemption to avoid extinction of the male line of the family.

In addition to the "sole surviving son" exemption, hardship exemptions were granted to prevent substantial harm to persons dependent on the registrant. Such exemptions were not easily obtained, for the test was one of extreme hardship, not mere inconvenience or moderate difficulty. The burden of establishing extreme hardship was on the registrant, and each case varied with the facts. One court listed the following factors involved in making an ad hoc determination of extreme hardship:

1. The degree of need of the claimed dependent;

2. The nature of the need;

3. The extent of the registrant's contribution to the need;

4. The lack of a viable alternative source of contribution to the dependent's support; and

5. The degree of distress resulting to the dependent from loss of the registrant's contribution.

United States v. McGee (7th Cir.1972). For example, a prima facie case was made out by a registrant whose father was disabled, whose mother was too ill to work and had suffered a heart attack, who had a minor sister, whose family lived in a remote area, when the family's only sources of outside income were Social Security and Welfare, and when the registrant did all the heavy work for the entire family. United States v. Cate (9th Cir.1973).

c. Deferments

Most of the exemptions to conscription discussed above were designed to screen out those Congress felt would be least desirable in combat situations. Deferments, on the other hand, were generally structured to channel the manpower of the United States in certain directions. Many questions have been raised concerning the appropriateness and effectiveness of giving such temporary relief from

military duty to persons in particular lines of
endeavor. It is therefore not surprising that the
classes of deferments have changed substantially
over time. For example, educational deferments for
undergraduate   and   graduate   students   and
occupational deferments for persons engaged in
certain occupations "vital to the national interest"
were largely eliminated in 1970. In their place, a
random selection system based on birth dates was
implemented which made men with low lottery
numbers prime targets for induction in their 19th
year. Ministers, however, have remained exempt
from the draft under § 6(g) of the Selective Service
Act since 1948. This exemption was granted to
those ordained in accordance with the rituals of
their sects who taught and preached the principles
of their sects and conducted public worship in the
sects' traditions regularly and as a vocation.
Dickinson v. United States (S.Ct.1953).

4. JUDICIAL REVIEW

To avoid delaying prompt mobilization for the
national defense, review of Selective Service
System decisions by civilian courts has been
among the most narrow known to the law. The
registrant's two primary options for challenging an
induction have been (1) refuse induction, be
prosecuted for refusal to report, and raise the
wrongful classification or erroneous procedure as a
defense and (2) to submit to induction, enter the
armed forces, and then seek release through a writ
of habeas corpus. Neither option is very attractive,
for the registrant runs the risk of either a felony
conviction or time in the service. It is not

surprising, therefore, that some judicial exceptions were fashioned to the general rule against pre-induction review of Selective Service decisions.

In Oestereich v. Selective Service System Local Board No. 11 (S.Ct.1968), the Supreme Court reviewed a case involving "a clear departure by the Board from its statutory mandate." The Court held that a theological student punitively reclassified for turning in his draft card should not be forced to risk jail or military service to uphold his clear entitlement to the Selective Service Act's theological student deferment. On the other hand, the Court in a companion case rejected a registrant's appeal based on a claim of improper bias by a local board (which had denied his CO claim), on the ground that the local board had the authority to deny such claims and its action involved both determinations of fact and exercise of judgment. Clark v. Gabriel (S.Ct.1968). The Court held that, while the theological student exemption was by statute unconditional, the CO classification is by statute conditioned upon the registrant's claim being "sustained by the local board."

One collateral aspect of the narrowness of judicial review over Selective Service decisions was that the registrant usually had to exhaust all Selective Service remedies prior to seeking relief in federal court. Thus, a failure to make a personal appearance before the local board or to appeal to the proper State Appeals Board would generally result in the federal court refusing to consider the registrant's case. Similarly, when a registrant refused to document a possible deferment, he was

barred from relief for failure to exhaust his
administrative remedies. McGee v. United States
(S.Ct.1971). However, when a registrant's claim
involved a pure question of statutory construction
and no local board fact-finding, the Supreme Court
did not require the registrant to follow through on
his Selective Service review procedure. McKart v.
United States (S. Ct. 1969).

CHAPTER 4

RIGHTS OF SERVICEMEMBERS

The military services are a "society apart" from civilian society by virtue not only of function, but also by virtue of the fact that servicemembers enjoy more limited constitutional rights than American civilians. As Yale Law Professor Joseph W. Bishop, Jr. observed in Justice Under Fire: A Study of Military Law, at 114 (1974), the Supreme Court "has never to this day squarely held that a soldier has any constitutional rights when he is court-martialed, or indeed that he has any constitutional rights of any variety." His appraisal of the state of the law then was as follows: "[n]o matter what the draftsmen of the Constitution intended, and no matter what the Supreme Court may have said and done between 1791 and the Korean War, I think it safe to say that soldiers today have constitutional rights, although it would be most unsafe to dogmatize about the precise extent of those rights." Id. at 122. Subsequent developments have qualified Bishop's generalization: "The time is long past when scholars disputed the applicability of the Bill of Rights to service personnel. Instead, our premise must be 'that the Bill of Rights applies with full force to men and women in the military service unless any given protection is, expressly or by necessary implication, inapplicable * * *' "United States v. Stuckey (C.M.A.1981) (Everett, C.J.). Servicemembers also enjoy analogous (and sometimes more generous) rights secured by statute and executive order. See Gilligan, "The Bill of Rights and Service Members," The Army Lawyer, Dec. 1987, 3–11.

A. DUE PROCESS RIGHTS

In marked contrast to the due process rights of those not in the military, the due process rights of members of the armed services begin and often end with the process Congress has provided. In a civilian context, Mathews v. Eldridge (S.Ct.1976), set the standard that due process "generally requires consideration of three distinct factors: the private interest that will be affected by the official action; the risk of erroneous deprivation and the value of additional or substitute procedural safeguards; and the Government's interest in the fiscal and administrative burdens" such additional process would entail.

In place of Mathews, the Supreme Court employs a different standard to determine the due process rights of members of the armed services. In determining what process is due, courts "must give particular deference to the determination of Congress, made under its authority to regulate the land and naval forces [asking] whether the factors militating in favor of the [asserted due process right] are so extraordinarily weighty as to overcome the balance struck by Congress." Middendorf v. Henry (S.Ct.1976).

With respect to members of the armed services, early cases stated a contrary principle in stark terms: "To those in the military or naval service of the United States, the military law is due process." Reaves v. Ainsworth (S.Ct.1911). An even earlier case, Dynes v. Hoover (S.Ct.1857), concluded from Congress' power to regulate the land and naval forces (U.S. Const. Art. I, § 8) and the grand jury exception for "cases arising in the land and naval forces" (U.S. Const. Amend. 5) that Congress has more, and the courts less, constitutional authority than in civilian affairs. Dynes held that the power to prescribe rules for those in the armed services "is given without any connection between it and the 3d Article of the Constitution defining the judicial power of the United States; indeed, that the two powers are entirely independent of each other." A member of the armed services is "subject to military law and the principles of that law, as provided by Congress, [constitute] for him due process of law in a constitutional sense." United States ex rel. French v. Weeks (S.Ct.1922).

Despite strong deference shown in Dynes to the power of Congress over military personnel, however, the Supreme Court insisted on careful adherence to the law Congress made. Thus, in Runkle v. United States (S.Ct.1887), the Court held with regard to a court-martial and its review by the President that

> The trial, finding, and sentence are the solemn acts of a court organized and conducted under the authority of and according to the prescribed forms of law. It sits to pass upon the most sacred questions of human rights that are ever placed

on trial in a court of justice,--rights which, in the very nature of things, can neither be exposed to danger, nor subjected to the uncontrolled will of any man, but which must be adjudged *according to law*. And the act of the officer who reviews the proceedings of the court, whether he be the commander of the fleet or the president, and without whose approval the sentence cannot be executed, is as much a part of this judgment, according to law, as is the trial or the sentence. When the president, then, performs this duty of approving the sentence of a court-martial dismissing an officer, his act has all the solemnity and significance of the judgment of a court of law.

Runkle illustrates that, although military law may have defined the extent of due process afforded the service member, whatever principles of law Congress specified must be scrupulously adhered to.

Similarly in Rostker v. Goldberg (S.Ct.1981), the Court refused to particularize the degree of deference due to a law passed by Congress dealing with military affairs and national security, but clearly accorded such laws substantial deference:

None of this is to say that Congress is free to disregard the Constitution when it acts in the area of military affairs. In that area, as in any other, Congress remains subject to the limitations of the Due Process Clause [citations omitted], but the tests and limitations to be applied may differ because of the military context. We, of course, do not abdicate our ultimate responsibility to decide the constitutional question, but simply recognize that the Constitution requires such deference to congressional choice [citations omitted]. In deciding the question before us we must be particularly careful not to substitute our judgment of what is desirable for that of Congress, or our own evaluation of evidence for a reasonable evaluation by the Legislative Branch.

A number of lower courts have approached due process issues with insufficient sensitivity to the "different application" of constitutional protections required by the "different character of the military community." Parker v. Levy (S.Ct.1974). For example, Hagopian v. Knowlton (2d Cir.1972), held that a cadet facing dismissal from the U.S. Military Academy at West Point for excess demerits must be given a separate due process hearing at which he would have the right to appear personally and present evidence, including witnesses on his behalf, before being excluded from the Academy for excess demerits. He is not entitled to be represented by counsel at the hearing, which may be informal and nonadversarial, but must be allowed to retain counsel and seek advice to assist him in preparing his defense at the hearing. The court found the Academy procedures deficient, saying that they failed to satisfy the "minimum procedural due process [that] must be accorded a cadet before he may be separated from the Academy." See also Wasson v. Trowbridge (2d Cir.1967)(similar procedure used by the Merchant Marine Academy at Kings Point, NY. found deficient on due process grounds).

In Hagopian, the Second Circuit gave inadequate deference to the scheme of due process fashioned by those empowered by Congress to determine procedure at the Military Academy. Indeed, a footnote in a federal Supreme Court case holding that public school pupils were entitled to a due process hearing before being temporarily suspended for misconduct for up to ten days probably indicates that both Hagopian and Wasson are at bottom public school expulsion cases: "lower federal courts have uniformly held the Due Process Clause applicable to decisions made by tax-supported educational institutions to remove a student from the institution long enough for the removal to be classified as an expulsion." Goss v. Lopez (S.Ct.1975)(citing Hagopian). Hagopian thus evidences an improper eagerness to substitute judicial conclusions as to what constitutes due process for the U.S. Military Academy cadet. Hagopian has also been questioned on other grounds. Phillips v. Marsh (2d Cir.1982).

A more detailed treatment of the due process issues arising in the military justice area is presented in Chapter 6.

B. EQUAL PROTECTION RIGHTS

Equal protection principles apply to the federal government under the due process clause of the Fifth Amendment. Strict scrutiny of racial classifications, first suggested in United States v. Carolene Products (S.Ct.1938), was first applied in a case involving the internment of persons of Japanese ancestry whose disloyalty was feared at the onset of hostilities in World War II. Korematsu v. United States (S.Ct.1944). Subjection of Congress to equal protection requirements through the Fifth Amendment's "equal protection component of the due process clause" was confirmed in Bolling v. Sharpe (S.Ct.1954) and Hampton v. Mow Sun Wong (S.Ct.1976).

In weighing the equal protection interests of members of the armed services, the court looks at the determination of Congress expressed in legislation just as it does in due process inquiries. Rostker v. Goldberg (S.Ct.1981)(equal protection challenge to male only draft registration) and Schlesinger v. Ballard (S.Ct.1975)(equal protection challenge to statute granting women naval officers a longer period of commissioned service before mandatory discharge for failing to be promoted).

The Supreme Court, in Frontiero v. Richardson (S.Ct.1973), considered an equal protection challenge to a law that provided that spouses of male members of the uniformed services are dependents for purposes of obtaining increased quarters allowances and medical and dental benefits, but that spouses of female members are not dependents unless they are in fact dependent for over one-half of their support. The Court held that the different treatment of spouses of men and women violated equal protection. A plurality of the court applied "strict scrutiny," requiring that the classification be narrowly tailored to meet a compelling governmental interest. Four other members of the Court reached the same conclusions under less searching "middle tier" scrutiny, whereby the classification must be closely related to fulfilling an important governmental interest. A major component of Justice Rehnquist's lone dissent was his view that the courts should defer to Congress' policy choices in the area of military rules and regulations.

Indeed, other cases do show more deference than Frontiero to Congressional military policy. For example, in Schlesinger v. Ballard (S.Ct.1975), the Court rejected a male officer's attack on sex-based distinctions in the Navy's promotion system that granted female officers longer to achieve promotion before facing mandatory discharge:

> "[T]he different treatment of men and women naval officers under [the statute challenged] reflects, not archaic and overbroad generalizations, but instead, the demonstrable fact that male and female line officers in the Navy are not similarly situated with respect to opportunities for professional service [because of the effects of the combat restriction on women.]"

One view is that the law in Frontiero rested on "archaic and overbroad" generalizations while that in Schlesinger rested on distinctions based on real differences, thus satisfying the applicable equal protection standard for reviewing gender-based discrimination. Craig v. Boren (S.Ct.1976). Another interpretation of Schlesinger is that it (but not Frontiero) is consistent with the line of cases represented by Parker, Middendorf and Weiss (discussed supra in Chapter 1). The following excerpt from Schlesinger supports this interpretation:

> In both Reed and Frontiero the reason asserted to justify the challenged gender-based classifications was administrative convenience, and that alone. Here, on the contrary, the operation of the statutes in question results in a flow of promotions commensurate with the Navy's current needs and service to motivate qualified commissioned officers to so conduct themselves that they may realistically look forward to higher levels of command. This Court has recognized that "it is the primary business of armies and navies to fight or be ready to fight wars should the occasion arise." [citations omitted] *The responsibility for determining how best our Armed Forces shall attend to that business rests with Congress and with the President [citations omitted]. We cannot say that, in exercising its broad constitutional power here, Congress has violated the Due Process Clause of the Fifth Amendment.* [Emphasis added].

Under this view, Frontiero represents a failure by the courts appropriately to defer to congressional judgments regarding governance of the military society.

Application of the Parker–Middendorf–Weiss standard to a contemporary issue such as the constitutionality of congressional restrictions on the sexual activities of homosexual members of the armed services illustrates how the model of constitutional analysis applicable to servicemembers may produce different results than would obtain for civilians. Congress has determined that homosexual conduct is incompatible with military service. 10 U.S.C.A. § 654. The special deference due congressional determinations regulating the unique military society could outweigh the interest of homosexuals in serving in the military.

Texas v. Lawrence (S.Ct.2003) held a civilian law criminalizing consensual sodomy unconstitutional, overruling Bowers v. Hardwick (S.Ct.1986). Lawrence's effect on § 654 is unclear because service members enjoy more limited constitutional rights than civilians. But, as Justice Scalia's dissent notes, the lower courts relied on Bowers to uphold the military's ban on homosexual conduct. Will Congress remove the ban in light of Lawrence? Will courts defer to Congress and the military's judgment or not? Stay tuned for future developments.

C. FIRST AMENDMENT RIGHTS

The First Amendment provides:

> "Congress shall make no law respecting an establishment of religion, or prohibiting the free exercise thereof; or abridging the freedom of speech, or of the press; or the right of the people peaceably to assemble, and to petition the Government for a redress of grievances."

While First Amendment rights are not absolute with respect to anyone, the First Amendment rights of members of the armed services are more limited than are those of civilians. The legal basis for this distinction is the Constitution: both the First Amendment and the authority to regulate the armed services are granted by the Constitution. Some balance must be struck between the freedoms provided by the First Amendment and the demands of military life and military society. Welsh v. United States (S.Ct.1970).

1. RELIGION

The issue of freedom to hold religious beliefs rarely arises in the military context. Conscientious objectors who interpose beliefs as a bar to service have been exempt from combatant service during times of conscription. United States v. Seeger (S.Ct.1965); Welsh v. United States (S.Ct.1970); and Gillette v. United States (S.Ct.1971).

Transition to an all-volunteer force has reduced, but not eliminated, the incidence of conscientious objector claims. More frequent deployments abroad, heavier post-Vietnam reliance on reserve components, family commitments and a desire to escape from service following extensive training at government expense have equated in-service conscientious objector claims with those raised by draftees in earlier years. E.g., Lipton v. Peters (W.D. Tex. 1999) (contract with the Air Force enabled 2LT Lipton, a Baptist, to attend medical school; habeas corpus denied because facts do not support a claim of conscientious objector status).

Processing of conscientious objector claims is governed by 32 C.F.R. Part 75 and applicable service regulations. To qualify for discharge from

military service as a conscientious objector, an
applicant must establish that 1) he or she is
opposed to war in any form, Gillette v. United
States (S.Ct. 1971); 2) his or her objection is
grounded in deeply held moral, ethical, or religious
beliefs, Welsh v. United States (S.Ct. 1970); and 3)
his or her convictions are sincere, Witmer v.
United States (S.Ct. 1955). These issues are of fact
and the scope of judicial review of service findings
is among "the narrowest known to the law."
DeWalt v. Commanding Officer, Fort Benning, Ga.,
(5th Cir. 1973).

An emerging issue in conscientious objector cases
is the role of the Religious Freedom Restoration
Act of 1993 (RFRA), 42 U.S.C.A. § 2000bb. Passed
in response to Employment Div., Depart. of
Human Resources of Oregon v. Smith (S.Ct. 1990),
the RFRA's stated purposes are "(1) to restore the
compelling interest test as set forth in [Sherbert v.
Verner (S.Ct. 1963)] and to guarantee its
application in all cases where the free exercise of
religion is substantially burdened; and (2) to
provide a claim or defense to persons whose
religious exercise is substantially burdened by
government." Government burdens are prohibited
unless the government can demonstrate that the
burden "(1) is in furtherance of a compelling
governmental interest; and (2) is the least
restrictive means of furthering that . . . interest."
By its terms, it applies to any "branch,
department, agency, instrumentality, and official
(or other person acting under color of law) of the
United States"

Although RFRA was held beyond the legislative power of Congress to regulate activities by States in City of Boerne v. Flores (S.Ct. 1997), its application to the federal government has been upheld. Hartmann v. Stone (6th Cir. 1998). Issues with respect to in-service conscientious objectors arise, for example, as to whether the government's interest is sufficiently compelling to allow the religious burdening of conscientious objectors (it probably is) and whether accommodations by the service to the conscientious objector represent the least restrictive means of furthering that interest as compared with discharge. These claims are reviewed in Lipton v. Peters (W.D. Tex. 1999).

The need for order and discipline can outweigh an individual's interests in pursuing particular religious practices. Thus, religious practice cannot be raised as a defense to a refusal to obey a lawful order. For example, a soldier can be ordered to cook on his Sabbath. United States v. Burry (C.G.C.M.R. 1966); may be required to salute despite his religious objections, United States v. Cupp (A.F.C.M.R. 1957); may be forced to receive inoculations against certain diseases in violation of religious beliefs, United States v. Chadwell (M.C.C.M.R. 1965); and may be required to attend mandatory premarriage counseling for overseas servicemembers, United States v. Wheeler (N.C.M.R. 1961). Similarly, members of the armed forces can be precluded from religious practices which conflict with military regulation of such things as uniform standards. Goldman v. Weinberger (S.Ct.1986) (Air Force regulation banning the wearing of headgear indoors upheld when individual's religious belief required wearing a yarmulke). After the Goldman decision, Congress enacted a statute providing for the wearing of religious apparel while in uniform unless "the wearing of the item would interfere with the performance [of] military duties [or] the item of apparel is not neat and conservative." 10 U.S.C.A. § 774(b).

Not all military considerations, however, will override individual objections to regulations of religion. In Anderson v. Laird (D.C.Cir.1972), a federal appeals court invalidated the compulsory chapel attendance policies of the military academies at West Point, Annapolis and Colorado Springs, as a violation of the First Amendment's establishment clause. The opinion includes a dissent by Judge MacKinnon which reflects more deference to congressional and executive power to administer the military.

Goldman v. Weinberger (S.Ct. 1986) implicitly repudiated Anderson's more deferential approach to military interests:

> Our review of military regulations challenged on First Amendment grounds is far more deferential than constitutional review of similar laws or regulations designed for civilian society. The military need not encourage debate or tolerate protest to the extent that such tolerance is required of the civilian state by the First Amendment; to accomplish its mission the military must foster instinctive obedience, unity, commitment and esprit de corps. * * *
> [Therefore] when evaluating whether military needs justify a particular restriction on

religiously motivated conduct, courts must give great deference to the professional judgment of military authorities concerning the relative importance of a particular military interest.

Not every instance of military restriction on religious practice will be sustained. For example, Hartmann v. Stone (6th Cir. 1995) stuck down an Army regulation prohibiting on-base family child care (FCC) providers from having any religious practices during day care conducted in providers' homes under contracts with parents. Proscribed practices included prayer before meals and at other times, reading Bible stories, and attendance at church worship services as agreed to by the parents and the FCC. The court held that although the regulation was appropriately neutral as among religions, it was not neutral between religion and non-religion and violated the First Amendment. This lack of neutrality and general applicability prevented the regulation from being reviewed in terms of the effect of the RFRA, discussed above. Neutral, generally applicable laws of federal origin could well present issues under the RFRA.

Because these FCC regulations in Hartmann did not apply to service members, the court found that the "traditional deference owed to military judgment did not justify regulation, absent showing of necessity of restriction on religion to military's central mission of effective combat." Regulations directed at service members themselves could well produce a different result. For example and by way of comparison, Mellen v. Bunting (4th Cir. 2003) invalidated the daily "supper prayer" offered at the Virginia Military Institute (VMI) as a violation of the Establishment Clause of the First Amendment. That result turned on the fact that the practice was required by the State of Virginia, not a branch of the federal military. The court expressly noted that it was "not called upon to address whether, or to what extent, the military may incorporate religious practices into its ceremonies. The Virginia General Assembly, not the Department of Defense, controls VMI." Hence, a practice such as grace before meals at one of the service academies could well be sustained as necessary to the formation of those training for the profession of arms where it could not be required of students at a state-supported college with a military tradition such as VMI. Similar overtly religious requirements that are part of military tradition would presumably be protected as well.

2. SPEECH

In the civilian realm the First Amendment protects speech, with some exceptions, unless it is "directed to inciting or producing imminent lawless action and is likely to incite or produce such action." Brandenburg v. Ohio (S.Ct. 1969). The test in the military is a substantially lower standard. Speech loses its protection if it "interferes with or prevents the orderly accomplishment of the mission or presents a clear danger to loyalty, discipline, mission, or morale of the troops." United States v. Brown (U.S.C.A.A.F. 1996). In United States v. Hartwig (C.M.A. 1994) the court held the applicable standard to be the "clear and present danger" test of Schenck v. United States (S.Ct. 1919), a test substantially altered as to civilians in Brandenburg. Specifically, Schenck recognized that speech may be restricted to prevent the "substantive evils that Congress has a right to prevent." The Hartwig court concluded:

> In a military context, those "substantive evils" are violations of the Uniform Code of Military Justice. [For example, w]hen an alleged violation of Article 133 is based on an officer's private speech, the test is whether the officer's speech poses a "clear and present danger" that the speech will, "in dishonoring or disgracing the officer personally, seriously compromise . . . the person's standing as an officer." Para. 59c(2), Part IV, Manual for Courts-Martial, United States, 1984.

The rationale for a more limited right of free speech in the military was aptly identified early on: "An army is not a deliberative body. It is the executive arm. Its law is that of obedience. No question can be left open as to the right to command in the officer, or the duty of obedience in the soldier." In re Grimley (S.Ct. 1890).

a. Contemptuous Words

The differences between First Amendment rules for civilians and those in the armed forces is most vividly illustrated by Article 88 of the UCMJ. The UCMJ makes it a crime for "[a]ny commissioned officer [to use] contemptuous words against the President, the Vice President, Congress, the Secretary of Defense, the Secretary of a military

department, the Secretary of Transportation, or
the Governor or legislature of any State, Territory,
Commonwealth or possession in which he is on
duty * * * " Art. 88, 10 U.S.C.A. § 888. Given the
time-honored American pastime of criticizing the
government and its officials in blunt, unflattering
and often derogatory terms, this Article is a
substantial limitation on the First Amendment
freedoms of members of the military. However,
Article 88 was upheld against constitutional attack
as violating the First and Fifth Amendments in
United States v. Howe (A.C.M.R. 1966). Second
Lieutenant Howe was convicted of using
contemptuous language against President Johnson
while off-duty and in civilian clothes. At the time
of the offense, Howe was participating in an anti-
war demonstration in Texas and carrying a sign
calling the President a fascist aggressor in
Vietnam. The spirit of Article 88 is reflected in an
incident in 1993 when Air Force Major General
Harold Campbell was reprimanded and forced to
retire after a speech in which he characterized
President Clinton as "draft-dodging, pot-smoking,
womanizing, and gay-loving."

Several limitations apply to Article 88. A
purpose of Article 88 is apparently to prevent a
threat to civilian control of the military by stifling
criticism of the government by the officer corps.
By its terms, since the 1950 revision of the UCMJ,
Article 88 applies only to commissioned officers
(previously officers in the sea services were
prosecuted for this offense as conduct unbecoming
or under the general article). The textual
limitation of Article 88 to commissioned officers

necessarily excludes warrant officers, enlisted personnel, cadets, and midshipmen of the military academies who share with civilians the right to criticize the government and its leadership. Retirees subject to the UCMJ are unlikely to be prosecuted for offenses of this sort; they present none of the evil against which Article 88 is directed.

The prohibition against disrespectful criticism directed at the President or other specified civilian officials and institutions draws no distinction between contemptuous language directed against the President of other covered official in his or her official capacity or personal capacity. Under the Article, the truth or falsity of the statement is irrelevant.

Four exceptions apply to charges under Article 88. First, ordinary or even emphatic political discussion is immune from sanction so long as it is not personally contemptuous. Second, private conversations are immune from prosecution. To constitute a violation of Article 88, the contemptuous speech must become publicly known. Third, Congress has by statute (10 U.S.C. § 1034) protected the right of all military personnel to communicate with members of Congress. Otherwise contemptuous language under Article 88 would not be covered since prosecution may not be used to retaliate against service members who avail themselves of this statutory right. United States v. Schmidt (C.M.R. 1966) (Ferguson, J., concurring). Complaints pursuant to Article 138 enjoy an exemption similar to communications under 10 U.S.C. § 1034. Fourth, information submitted as part of legal proceedings is privileged and cannot be prosecuted as contemptuous under Article 88. For example, even a complaint about the President, the Commander in Chief, alleging attorney misconduct submitted as part of legal proceedings is protected. By way of illustration, consider a complaint accusing President William Jefferson Clinton, an attorney licensed in Arkansas, of lawyer misconduct because of improper activities including conduct inimical to, and destructive of, the administration of justice, such as lying, deceit, perjury, fraud, dishonesty, untrustworthiness, obstruction of justice, subornation of perjury, and witness tampering with respect to his deposition testimony of January 17, 1998, regarding sexual relations with Monica Lewinsky in the case of Paula Jones. See Jones v. Clinton (E.D.Ark. 1999) and Hogue v. Neal (E.D. Ark. 2000).

b. Disloyal Statements

UCMJ Articles 133 (conduct unbecoming) and 134 (service-discrediting conduct) are the usual bases for prosecution of disloyal statements. To be prosecuted under Article 134, the statement must be directed to the United States as a political entity, and not to a department or other agency which forms part of its administrative operation. A statement against the President, a branch of the service, or a national policy may not be prosecuted under Article 134, although it may be prosecuted under Article 88, as discussed above. Case law indicates that the statement must be made publicly and with the intent to promote disloyalty toward the United States. United States v. Gray

(M.C.C.M.R. 1970); United States v. Priest (C.M.A. 1972). Despite the inherent ambiguities concerning what constitute disloyal statements, both Articles 133 and 134 have been upheld against allegations that they are vague and overbroad. Parker v. Levy (S.Ct.1974).

c. Complaints Under Article 138

Military policy and regulations insure that all military personnel may present complaints either orally or in writing through the command structure without fear of reprisal or disciplinary action. UCMJ Article 138 provides that any member of the armed forces who is refused redress by his commanding officer may complain to any superior officer, who will then forward the complaint to the officer exercising general court-martial jurisdiction over the complainant's commanding officer.

The complaint procedure under Article 138 is an important mechanism for the resolution of grievances within the military:

The right to seek redress of wrongs is an integral part of the complex of rights granted by the Congress to those subject to military law. Those to whom an application for relief under [Article 138] is submitted may not lightly regard the right it confers, nor dispose of such application in a perfunctory manner. Its provisions should not be construed by those charged with the administration of military justice, at any level, in a manner calculated to lead anyone to believe that the right of redress of wrongs is of minor importance and one which may be disregarded entirely or perfunctorily complied with. Tuttle v. Commanding Officer, 21 U.S.C.M.A. 229, 230, 45 C.M.R. 3, 4 (C.M.A. 1972)(exhaustion of Article 138 remedy required to challenge unlawful confinement prior to seeking habeas corpus under 28 U.S.C.A. § 1651(a)).

Exhaustion of remedies is required before resort to the Article 138 complaint procedure. For example, military regulations provide for appeals of unfavorable efficiency reports, appeals of administrative reductions in grade, appeals from findings of pecuniary liability under Article 139 and appeals from administrative reprimands. These appellate routes must be pursued before an Article 138 complaint will be acted upon.

In addition, military administrative regulations also provide for complaints, grievances and requests for assistance from the Inspector General (IG) and his office. The IG investigates complaints and, if the complaint is justified, recommends corrective action. As with Article 138, available appellate remedies must be exhausted before the IG can act. One significant way in which the IG complaint procedure differs from the Article 138 procedure is that Article 138 is limited to complaints by members of the armed services, while the IG complaint procedure may be utilized by anyone, thus affording an avenue of redress to a servicemember's family or friends.

d. Political Participation

The subject of political participation is sensitive because of America's tradition of subordination of the military to civilian control and a desire to exclude the military from interference with the functioning of our democratic society. The interference of Union soldiers with Southern elections during Reconstruction was a source of friction after the Civil War. Commissioned and noncommissioned officers are specifically prohibited from attempting to influence any member of the armed forces to vote for any particular candidate for public office. 50 U.S.C.A. § 1475. Administrative regulations impose restraints on the political activities of members of the armed services. 32 C.F.R. § 53.2(a)(2).

e. Symbolic Expression

Members of the armed services can be disciplined for participating in parades and demonstrations as a means of protest. Cortright v. Resor (2d Cir.1971). Moreover, servicemembers can be required to participate in parades sponsored by organizations supporting political viewpoints with which they disagree. Jones v. United States Secretary of Defense (D.Minn.1972). This contrasts sharply with comparable rights of civilians. Hurley v. Irish–American Gay, Lesbian and Bisexual Group of Boston (S.Ct.1995)(state law requiring private citizens who organize a parade to include a group imparting a message the organizers do not wish to convey violates the First Amendment).

3. PUBLICATIONS

a. Publications by Servicemembers

Members of the armed services may publish so-called "underground" newspapers and similar materials so long as they do so off-base, on their own time, and with their own money and equipment. Unless the publication contains language otherwise punishable under federal law or the UCMJ, mere publication is not an offense and is not subject to discipline.

The services may restrict writing or speaking in an individual capacity when the subject involves military matters or foreign policy. For example, the Army requires submission to appropriate headquarters of materials, including fiction, which relate to military matters. AR 360–5. The material will be reviewed to insure that it contains no classified information and statements of policy will be reviewed for accuracy and propriety. Under the regulations, fiction is subjected to a security clearance only. All other public writings and speeches will be reviewed for conformity with Department of Defense and other government policies, and will be subjected to "constructive suggestions" on matters of accuracy and propriety.

Similar regulations were upheld in United States v. Voorhees (C.M.A. 1954). Voorhees, an Army officer, had written and published material relating to his experiences during the Korean War, including his description of a major breach of military security by the Supreme Commander of the United Nations forces, General Douglas

MacArthur. The material was published without the clearance required by Army regulations, and this led to Voorhees' court-martial. Although the Court of Military Appeals upheld the regulations, the three opinions from the court are so fragmented on the First Amendment issue that the case is of little precedential value.

b. On-base Distribution

The sale, distribution and display of publications on a military installation are subject to restraints imposed by the installation's commanding officer. Dash v. Commanding General (D.S.C. 1969) To impose a restriction, the commander must have cogent reasons supported by evidence for the restriction. The commander may not impose a restriction merely because he or she disagrees with a publication's content, finds it personally objectionable, or because it is critical of government policies or officials. Reasons could include interfering with the loyalty, discipline, or morale of troops, or the disruption of training or the performance of any military mission.

Congress has authorized the censorship of many publications through the Military Honor and Decency Act (10 U.S.C.A. § 2489a), which prohibits the sale or rental of sexually explicit material on property under the jurisdiction of the Department of Defense. The law also authorizes the Secretary of Defense to promulgate regulations enforcing the law. The Act defines "sexually explicit" material as that in which "the dominant theme of which depicts or describes nudity, including sexual or excretory activities or organs, in a lascivious way."

The law covers sales in commissaries, exchanges and ships' stores.

The Act and its implementing regulations restrict material that could not be proscribed in a civilian context because it is protected expression under the First Amendment. Obscenity, narrowly defined as "[p]atently offensive representations or descriptions of ultimate sexual acts, normal or perverted, actual or simulated, [or p]atently offensive representations or descriptions of masturbation, excretory functions and lewd exhibition of the genitals" may be banned. Miller v. California (S.Ct. 1973). Not all pornography is obscene, however; some sexually explicit (even lascivious) material is protected by the First Amendment. For example, nude depictions are protected speech. Jenkins v. Georgia S.Ct. 1974) and Erznoznik v. Jacksonville (S.Ct. 1975) including plays such as the musical "Hair" in which the actors are nude. Southeastern Promotions, Ltd. v. Conrad (S.Ct. 1975). Robert Mapplethorpe's explicit photographic depictions of homoerotic and sadomasochistic activities have been held to be protected speech as have the sexually graphic sound recording by 2 Live Crew, "As Nasty As They Wanna Be." Luke Records, Inc. v. Navarro (11th Cir. 1992). Child pornography produced with real children can be banned. New York v. Ferber (S.Ct. 1982). The Supreme Court has ruled that "virtual" child pornography in which no children are harmed by the production of sexually explicit depictions is constitutionally protected. Ashcroft v. Free Speech Coalition (S.Ct. 2002) (The Child Pornography Prevention Act of 1996 banning any image or picture that "is, or appears to be, or a minor engaging in sexually explicit conduct" reached speech that could not be proscribed.)

Although the Military Honor and Decency Act censors material that would be protected in a civilian context, it has been upheld against First Amendment challenges. PMG Intern. Div., L.L.C. v. Rumsfeld (9th Cir. 2002); General Media Communications, Inc. v. Cohen (2d Cir. 1997). The Defense Department, thus, has substantial authority to restrict sexually explicit materials.

c. On-base Civilian Activity

Civilians are subject to restrictions to protect the order, discipline and military readiness of the installation. Ethredge v. Hail (11th Cir.1995) (bumper sticker on civilian base employee's truck castigating Presidents Reagan and Bush violated a base administrative order barring "bumper stickers or other similar paraphernalia" that "embarrass or disparage" the Commander in Chief).

The federal Supreme Court has held that in instances where the military has abandoned any interest in regulating speech activities, as by leafleters, then the power to regulate is lost. Flower v. United States (S.Ct.1972). However, where the installation had never abandoned its special interest in regulating political activities, speakers and leafleters could be barred by regulation. Greer v. Spock (S.Ct.1976). Merely inviting the general public to enter a facility, as for example with an annual open house, will not transform the post into a public forum under Flower. United States v. Albertini (S.Ct.1985).

d. Servicemember Possession of Publications

Generally, a member of the armed services may possess any publication on base that he or she wishes unless the quantity on hand indicates an intent to distribute. Possession of contraband, such as child pornography, would not be protected.

United States v. Dees (A.F.C.C.A. 2002) (conviction for storing sexually explicit materials on a government computer in violation of Article 92 and possessing computer discs containing images of child pornography in violation of 18 U.S.C.A. § 2252A(a)(5)(A), a violation of Article 134).

4. ASSEMBLY

a. Demonstrations by Servicemembers

On-base demonstrations and meetings conducted by servicemembers are subject to the same prior restriction as distribution of publications. Dash v. Commanding General (D.S.C.1969). Off-base meetings or demonstrations by members of the armed services are subject to restriction when any of the following factors are present: 1) the servicemember is in uniform; 2) the servicemember is on duty; 3) the demonstration takes place in a foreign country; 4) the activity constitutes a breach of law and order; or 5) violence is likely to result. AR 600–20. These provisions of Army regulations are typical of the policies of other military departments. For example, the court-martial of a member of the Air Force for participating in a demonstration in London was upheld. Culver v. Secretary of Air Force (D.C.Cir.1977).

Just as the speech of service members can by limited by the demands of good order and discipline, so can activities such as union organizing that are ordinarily protected in the civilian realm. For example, union organizing activities by service members is forbidden by statute, 10 U.S.C.A. § 976, and can be prosecuted as a violation of the UCMJ. United States v. Brown (U.S.C.A.A.F. 1996).

b. Demonstrations by Civilians

Civilians are subject to restriction with respect to demonstrating on post. They may be excluded if they pose a threat to the military mission of the post. Greer v. Spock (S.Ct.1976). In Kiiskila v. Nichols (7th Cir.1970), the commanding officer ordered a civilian employee of the credit union permanently excluded from the base on the ground that she had distributed anti-war literature near the base and had, in an on-base conversation, given an officer a ticket to an anti-war rally for which she was the chairperson. The Seventh Circuit overturned the order on First Amendment grounds, finding that the military had failed to produce evidence that military discipline was actually affected either by the plaintiff's presence on the installation or by her extension of an invitation to participate in off-base activities.

5. COMMUNICATIONS WITH CONGRESS

Under 10 U.S.C.A. § 1034 provides that "no person may restrict any member of an armed force in communicating with any member of Congress, unless the communication is unlawful or violates a regulation necessary to the security of the United States." The statute, directed specifically to members of the armed forces, reflects the First Amendment right to petition the Government for a redress of grievance. There is no doubt that the statute protects from military scrutiny and restriction all individual letters of servicemembers to members of Congress, but issues have arisen about the circulation of petitions on base for the purpose of gathering the signatures of others. Advance approval can be required for such activities in the interest of maintaining the military commander's responsibility for morale, discipline and readiness. The servicemember's right under § 1034 is to correspond with his or her elected representative without going through official channels; Congress did not intend to protect the circulation of petitions to other members of the armed services. Brown v. Glines (S.Ct.1980).

6. ASSOCIATION

The First Amendment protection of freedom of association arose indirectly in Stapp v. Resor (S.D.N.Y.1970). The plaintiff was discharged from the Army for security reasons because he had maintained a personal association with a member of the Communist Party. The plaintiff challenged the discharge on grounds that it violated his First Amendment rights. The district court declared the discharge void because it was based on mere associations and political beliefs wholly removed from the plaintiff's military duties. The associates and political beliefs of a member of the armed services are not immune from scrutiny, but adverse actions must be based on a connection between the associations and the servicemember's military duties.

D. OTHER RIGHTS OF SERVICEMEMBERS

1. RIGHT TO VOTE

Members of the armed services have a right to vote and participate in the election of the government. Carrington v. Rash (S.Ct.1965). In his opinion in Carrington, Justice Stewart quoted with approval Georgia Governor Ellis Arnall's injunction that "[T]he uniform of our country [must not] be the badge of disfranchisement for the man or woman who wears it."

2. PRIVACY

Civilians enjoy a rather robust right of privacy that has been developed through a series of court decisions. These decisions are based on values that cannot be traced directly to constitutional text, history or structure but are a product of "substantive due process" based on an interpretations of the right to "liberty" in the Fifth or Fourteenth Amendments or "substantive equal protection" in the Fourteenth Amendment. Many of these cases deal with rights related to such interests as the family, sex, procreation and abortion. For example, Meyer v. Nebraska (S.Ct. 1923) recognized "liberty" interests in "the right of the individual to contract, to engage in any of the common occupations of life, to acquire useful knowledge, to marry, establish a home and bring up children, to worship God according to the dictates of his own conscience . . . ." Subsequent cases acknowledged "the liberty of parents and guardians to direct the upbringing and education" of their children, Pierce v. Society of Sisters (S.Ct. 1925) and Troxel v. Granville (S.Ct. 200); as well as the right to marry and procreate, Skinner v. Oklahoma (S.Ct. 1942), Loving v. Virginia (S.Ct. 1967) and Zablocki v. Redhail (S.Ct. 1978); to live together as an extended family, Moore v. East Cleveland (1977); to use contraceptives, Griswold v. Connecticut (1965); to have access to contraceptives even if unmarried, Eisenstadt v. Baird (S.Ct. 1972), or a minor, Carey v. Populations Services International (S.Ct. 1977); and to have an abortion, Roe v. Wade (S.Ct. 1973) and Planned Parenthood of Southeastern Pennsylvania v. Casey (S.Ct. 1992).

Cases such as these have given rise to a cultural mindset that favors the individual and his or her preferences over those of the community collectively expressed through governmental regulation. Bumper stickers exhort "Keep your laws off my body."

This privacy culture, supported by a caselaw-based legal regime, is at odds in many respects with the culture of the military. The federal Supreme Court has cautioned that, "The fundamental necessity for obedience, and the consequent necessity for imposition of discipline, may render permissible within the military that which would be constitutionally impermissible outside of it." Parker v. Levy (S.Ct. 1974). And lower courts have echoed similar views: "The 'expectation of privacy' . . . is different in the military than it is in civilian life . . . . The soldier cannot reasonably expect the Army barracks to be a sanctuary like his civilian home." Committee for GI Rights v. Callaway (D.C. Cir. 1975). Military culture subordinates the interests of the individual soldier, sailor, marine or airman to those of the mission and the units that will carry it out. Base and installation commanders permissibly promulgate numerous regulations that foster such values as orderliness, civility, and uniformity with the objective of fostering the overall fitness of a unit to perform its military mission that in turn result in a communal environment vastly different from that in the civilian world.

The court's description of the differences between a civilian and military home and the respective degree of privacy they afford is well captured in United States v. McCarthy (C.M.A. 1993) (warrantless search upheld):

> While the physical trappings of a modern barracks or military dormitory may be more comfortable and private than an open bay barracks, the need for discipline and readiness

has not changed. * * *   A soldier may lawfully be ordered to move from private family quarters into the barracks, for reasons related to military discipline or military readiness [or ordered to stay away from on-base family quarters] * * * While a civilian may retreat into the home and refuse the entreaties of the police to come out, a soldier may lawfully be ordered to come out of his or her quarters [or ordered to leave an off-base residence and report for duty].   In short, the threshold of a barracks/dormitory room does not provide the same sanctuary as the threshold of a private home.

Personal choice and autonomy is also limited. Again, as McCarthy notes, "[The service member] was assigned his room; he did not choose it. [He] was assigned his roommate; he did not choose him. [He] could not cook in his room, have overnight guests, or have unaccompanied underage guests. [And] he was subject to inspection to a degree not contemplated in private homes [in that] the CQ had a key to the room and was authorized to enter the room on official business.]"

Similarly, the military can prescribe grooming standards that regulate such matters as hair length and styling and can set different standards for male and female service members. United States v. Young (C.M.A. 1976).   Military uniform regulations can be just that -- uniform -- and individual variations, even for deeply held personal or political reasons, forbidden.   U.S. v. New, 55 M.J. 95 (USCAAF 2001)(upheld a conviction for failure to obey a lawful order to wear United Nations (UN) accoutrements on deployment to

Macedonia with the United Nations Preventive Deployment Force (UNPREDEP)).

Differences in military and civilian practice exist even in the area of sexual privacy. For example, a service member who has tested positive for HIV infection can lawfully be given a "safe sex" order and required to wear a condom while engaging in sexual relations, even including those with a spouse, although it might interfere with procreation. United States v. Pritchard (U.S.C.A.A.F. 1996). Compare Skinner v. Oklahoma (S.Ct. 1942) and Griswold v. Connecticut (S.Ct. 1965) cited above.

The lack of choice extends to personal medical decisions. Civilians have long been held subject to compulsory vaccination when demands of public health warrant. Jacobson v. Massachusetts (S.Ct. 1905). Military personnel may be ordered vaccinated against such agents as anthrax in order to assure mission readiness. Mazares v. Department of Navy (Fed Cir. 2002) (civilian seamen employed aboard a Navy vessel).

3. RESIDENCY AND TAX SITUS

Members of the armed forces are immunized to a certain extent from invidious treatment by states because of their status. Because they are assigned involuntarily by orders to where they will work and live the law protects their choices as to state residency and protects them against taxation of their income by states of which they are not a resident. For example, a member of the armed services is presumed to retain "the domicile which he had at the time of enlistment" unless there is "clear and unequivocal" evidence of a change of domicile. Deckers v. Kenneth W. Rose, Inc. (M.D.Fla.1984). Section 514 of the Soldiers' and Sailors' Civil Relief Act, 50 U.S.C.A. App. § 574(2)(b) expressly preserves the original, pre-enlistment residence of a servicemember for property tax and income tax purposes. Woodroffe v. Park Forest (N.D.Ill. 1952). The benefits of this protection have been lost in some states through use of expansive definitions of "domicile" and "residency." See Kisor, "Who's Defending the Defenders?: Rebuilding the Financial Protections of the Soldiers' and Sailors' Civil Relief Act," 48 Naval L. Rev. 161 (2001).

A member of the armed forces who is stationed in a state other than his or her state of residence may change residence to a new state by undertaking clear and unequivocal acts such as registering to vote, registering a motor vehicle, securing a driver's license and otherwise establishing a nexus with the new state that indicates an intention to change state citizenship.

4. SOLDIERS' AND SAILORS' CIVIL RELIEF ACT

The Soldiers' and Sailors' Civil Relief Act (SSCRA) protects members of the armed services from legal or financial disadvantage on account of their being ordered to active duty military service. 50 U.S.C.A. App. §§ 501–591. The SSCRA applies to all persons serving in the Army, Navy, Marine Corps and Air Force as well as members of the Coast Guard and all officers of the Public Health

Service detailed for duty with the Army or Navy, and members of the National Guard and Air National Guard when called into federal service. The protections of the law also extend to military dependents and to persons secondarily liable for the obligations of members of the armed services (e.g., sureties, guarantors, endorsers, accommodation makers).

The SSCRA allows servicemembers a variety of federal remedies to alleviate hardships caused by going on active duty. In some instances these remedies are available to dependents and others. The remedies include a stay of civil proceedings in any state, federal or territorial court, but not criminal actions or administrative proceedings, if participation is "materially affected by reason of military service." The stay is within the discretion of the court and servicemembers with accrued leave which would enable them to participate in the proceedings have been found not entitled to a stay. The stay may not exceed the period of active duty plus three months. Stays of execution of judgments, attachments or garnishment are available although use of this provision to avoid family support obligations runs counter to the pervasive military family support policy. See 32 C.F.R. Part 584 (Army); 32 C.F.R. Part 733 (Navy); 32 C.F.R. Part 818 (Air Force); 32 C.F.R. Part 733 (Marine Corps). Default judgments against servicemembers can be set aside and reopened, assuming the defendant has a defense to the action, so long as it is done so within 90 days of leaving active military service.

The SSCRA protects servicemembers and their families against foreclosures on real or personal property, assuming: 1) the obligation arose prior to his or her entry into active duty; 2) the servicemember owns the property subject to the security instrument; and 3) his or her ability to meet the obligation was materially affected by military service.

The requirement that the obligation must have arisen prior to the servicemember's entry onto active duty explains why the foreclosure provisions are not routinely available to members of the armed services.   Obligations incurred while on active duty are not subject to the law.   For this reason, a servicemember who is eligible for protection should be cautious about renegotiating a loan and losing the law's protection.

The SSCRA caps interest rates at six percent on obligations incurred prior to entry onto active duty. Reservists called on active duty would have the benefit of the SSCRA, for example with respect to home mortgage interest. In order to qualify, military service must have "materially affected" his or her ability to make payments. The law applies to any type of debt, including real estate debts, personal loans and credit card debts. Interest includes any service charges, fees and the like. The intent of the law was to provide relief from debt service, so relief from interest coupled with continued payments at the same level as before with the payments applied only to principal does not satisfy the law. Neither does accrual of the difference between the six percent ceiling amount and the actual rate of interest. The intent of the law was that the excess be forgiven by the lender. Under federal law, this provision does not apply to guaranteed student loans. 20 U.S.C.A. § 1078(d).

The SSCRA also protects against evictions. Court approval is required for eviction of a servicemember's spouse, children or other dependents during the period of active-duty service. Many of the provisions of the SSCRA, e.g., evictions, installment sales contracts, foreclosure, lease terminations, and life insurance policies, apply to dependents as well as to the servicemember.

Amendments to the SSCRA in 1991 protect servicemembers who utilize the law's protection from adverse actions respecting their credit ratings by lending institutions and credit reporting agencies. In addition, physicians and other health care providers acquired protections for their professional liability insurance coverage. One of the more important protections is a right to reinstatement of health care insurance coverage. Insurers may not require waiting periods or create exclusions for conditions that arose while the servicemember was on active duty.

E. COMPENSATING SERVICE-MEMBERS FOR INJURY AND DEATH

Injury and death afflict servicemembers and civilians alike. The law, however, provides far different routes for servicemembers and civilians to deal with these human conditions. Civilians seek compensation for injury and death largely through tort law and insurance mechanisms, supplemented by such public programs as Medicaid. Servicemembers are often precluded from tort remedies against the government which they serve. They are, however, provided with comprehensive medical treatment while in the military and thereafter are provided access to veterans' benefits, which are administered by the Department of Veterans' Affairs.

1. TORT CLAIMS OF SERVICE MEMBERS

In the absence of special legislation, all governmental entities enjoy sovereign immunity from liability for the acts of their agents and employees. The federal government has waived its immunity in some circumstances to provide remedies for service members and civilians through the Federal Tort Claims Act and several alternative less sweeping administrative claims procedures.

a. The Federal Tort Claims Act

The Federal Tort Claims Act (FTCA), 28 U.S.C.A. §§ 1346(b), 2671–2680, waives the United States' immunity for common law torts and is the exclusive remedy for torts committed by a federal official. As such, the FTCA creates absolute immunity for federal employees, and makes the United States the sole defendant. Plaintiffs who qualify for recovery under the FTCA are allowed 1) monetary recovery; 2) for damage to or loss of property, personal injury, and death; 3) caused by the negligent or wrongful act or omission; 4) of a

United States employee; 5) while acting within the scope of the person's office or employment; 6) under circumstances where the United States, if a private person, would be liable to the claimant; and 7) under the law of the place where the act or omission occurred.

There are several exceptions to liability listed in the Act, two of which bear on liability for damage or personal injury arising out of military actions. First, the FTCA bars claims arising out of combatant activities of the armed forces during time of war. 28 U.S.C.A. § 2680(j). This exception covers actions in both declared and undeclared wars. Koohi v. United States (9th. Cir.1992). Second, the FTCA bars "any claim arising in a foreign country." 28 U.S.C.A. § 2680(k). Claims arising on military facilities outside the United States are barred. The claim is considered foreign even if the base has been leased to the United States, or is located in a country that is being governed by the United States as a trustee for the United Nations. Cobb v. United States (9th Cir.1951) (Okinawa a "foreign country" where United States has de facto sovereignty over island); see also Smith v. United States (S.Ct.1993) (Antarctica is a "foreign country" although it lacks a recognized government). United States embassies in foreign countries also fall within this exception. See Meredith v. United States (9th Cir.1964).

The federal government can assert any defenses that would be available to a private person under the law of the state where the injury occurred. These defenses include contributory negligence, assumption of risk, comparative negligence, and release. In addition, the FTCA lists eleven specific exceptions to liability in addition to the combatant and foreign country exceptions. These include denial of claims for assault and battery, false imprisonment, false arrest, malicious prosecution, abuse of process, libel, slander, misrepresentation, deceit, and interference with contractual rights. 28 U.S.C.A. § 2680. A recent amendment to this section disallows claims based on "acts or omissions" of investigative or law enforcement officers.

The FTCA also excludes claims arising from "discretionary" acts or omissions of government employees, whether or not discretion was abused. 28 U.S.C.A. § 2680(a). In Westfall v. Erwin (S.Ct.1988), the Supreme Court ruled that a discretionary act is one which requires personal judgment, deliberation, and decision on the part of the employee. Discretionary acts usually occur at the planning rather than the operational stage of an activity; once discretion has been exercised and the decision made, the activity must be carried out with reasonable care. For example, the decision to admit a military dependent into a military hospital is discretionary, but the rendering of negligent treatment is not.   Similarly, a chief chemical officer's decision, made at the planning level, to use a particular strain of bacterium in a simulated biological warfare attack on San Francisco was a discretionary function. Nevin v. United States (9th Cir.1983). However, Congress superseded Westfall by the Federal Employees Liability Reform and Tort Compensation Act of 1988:

Upon certification by the Attorney General that the defendant employee was acting within the scope of his office or employment at the time of the incident out of which the claim arose, any civil action or proceeding commenced upon such claim in a United States district court shall be deemed an action against the United States under the provisions of this title and all references thereto, and the United States shall be substituted as the party defendant. 28 U.S.C.A. § 2679(d)(1).

b. Eligible Claimants: The Feres Doctrine

The eligibility of servicemembers to sue under the FTCA is governed by case law. For example, servicemen who were passengers in a car struck by a U.S. Army truck were allowed to recover under the FTCA because 1) the facts of the case did not meet any of the FTCA exceptions; and 2) the claims of the plaintiffs, who were off duty and off post when the incident occurred, had no significant relationship to military service. The fact that the claimants, because of their military status, received government benefits following the injuries did not bar the claim; the Court held such benefits were simply to be deducted from the final judgment. Brooks v. United States (S.Ct.1949).

Members of the armed services whose injuries are incident to their military service cannot recover under the FTCA. Feres v. United States (S.Ct.1950). The "Feres doctrine" or "incident to service rule" is based primarily on the "peculiar and special relationship of the soldier to his superiors" and "the [adverse] effects of the maintenance of such suits on discipline." The court believed that to allow suits against superior officers would disrupt military discipline. United States v. Brown (S.Ct.1954). Under the specific facts in Feres (one plaintiff was sleeping in barracks alleged to be a fire hazard, and two were victims of malpractice by military doctors) it is not clear why command and discipline would be disrupted. This apparent incongruity illustrates that while the underlying prohibition of FTCA suits by servicemembers is based upon discipline and command concerns, the Feres doctrine has been dramatically expanded to cover nearly any tort committed while an armed servicemember is on active duty, on a military base, or engaged in a military mission.

The scope of the Feres doctrine was further expanded in United States v. Shearer (S.Ct.1985), in which the Supreme Court modified the first element of a successful Brooks claim. No longer is the question to allow a military tort claim simply whether the claim itself was "incident to service"; rather, it is necessary to determine if the decision implicated a command decision. The Court ruled that "the situs of the murder is not nearly as important as whether the suit requires a civilian court to second-guess military decisions * * * ." While the Court distinguished Brooks, the line between Brooks and Feres was redrawn to preclude government liability even when a command decision led to a claim not "incident to service."

In 1987, the Supreme Court once again expanded the Feres doctrine, barring a claim by a deceased servicemember's dependent against civilian employees of the FAA. United States v. Johnson (S.Ct.1987). The lower court found that military discipline would not be implicated by such a tort action and allowed recovery. The Supreme Court reversed, holding that the claim, if incident to service, is precluded even if the effect on discipline is negligible.

For servicemembers or their surviving dependents to sue under the FTCA, the requirements of Brooks must be met and the components of Feres must be avoided. For a claim to succeed, the injury must have occurred (1) off-duty; (2) not on military property; (3) not during a military mission; and (4) not under military authority. The Feres doctrine may even bar claims of a servicemember which arise while he or she is on leave. See Lampitt v. United States (E.D.Mo.1984)(convalescent leave).

Although Bivens allowed civilians to sue the United States for constitutional torts, the Feres doctrine also bars non-FTCA claims against the federal government for constitutional torts, Bivens v. Six Unknown Named Federal Narcotics Agents (S.Ct.1971). In a case involving five black sailors who brought suit under Bivens against their commanding officers alleging racial discrimination, the Court ruled that allowing members of the armed services to challenge their supervisors in violation of Feres would undermine military discipline. Chappell v. Wallace (S.Ct.1983).

Numerous lower courts have held that the Feres doctrine protects state officials from suit by members of the National Guard. "It is beyond question that the Feres doctrine generally applies to claims brought by National Guard members." Bowen v. Oistead (9th Cir. 1997)(Feres doctrine bars suit against the Alaska National Guard, certain of its members, the United States, and certain commissioned officers of the United States Air Force); Stauber v. Cline (9th Cir. 1988)(Feres applied to a Guardsman's claims against individual members of the Alaska National Guard, the Alaska Adjutant General, the Alaska Department of Military and Veterans Affairs, and the State of Alaska itself); Uhl v. Swanstrom (8th Cir. 1996) (applying *Feres* bar to suit by National Guardsman against his commanding state officer, the Adjutant General of the Iowa Air National Guard, and the Iowa Air National Guard).

The Feres doctrine also extends to "suits between individual members of the military, recognizing an 'intramilitary immunity' from suits based on injuries sustained incident to service." Lutz v. Secretary of the Air Force (9th Cir. 1991). And it broadly applies "whenever a legal action 'would require a civilian court to examine decisions regarding management, discipline, supervision, and control of members of the armed forces of the United States.' " Hodge v. Dalton (9th Cir. 1997).

c. FTCA Claim Procedure

The FTCA provides for several administrative avenues of recovery which must be exhausted before resort to the courts is permitted. Any claim first (1) must be presented within two years of the date of accrual to the federal agency for whom the tortfeasor worked; (2) be filed in writing, preferably on a Standard Form 95, although other forms of written notice are permitted; (3) state specific damages for a sum certain; and (4) be signed and dated. If the claim is presented to the wrong agency, it will be forwarded promptly to the correct agency. The following chart summarizes the procedural requirements.

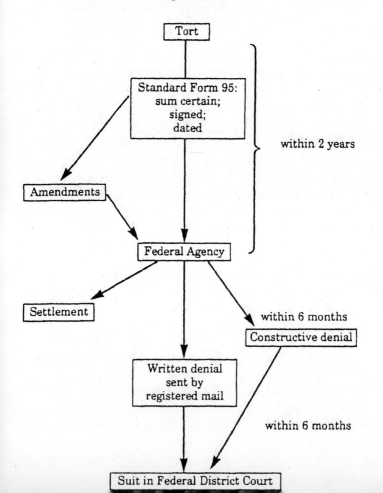

(1) Date of Accrual

The FTCA requires that the claim be received by the appropriate federal agency within two years of the date of accrual or it will be forever barred. This two year statute of limitations runs from the time of the tort injury for all plaintiffs who are not in active military service at the time of the incident. For those engaged in active military service at the time of the incident, the two-year statute of limitations begins to run at the conclusion of such military service. Soldiers' and Sailors Civil Relief Act, 50 U.S.C.A. App. § 525 (tolling provision). See also Lester v. United States (N.D.Tex.1980)(due to active military service, serviceman entitled to benefits of § 525); Wanner v. Glen Ellen Corp. (D.Vt.1974)(wife's claim barred by 2 year statute of limitations; husband in active military service could take advantage of § 525 and did not have claim barred). The Federal agency in question has 6 months in which to make a final disposition of the claim, either honoring it in whole or in part by settlement, or by denying any recovery. A final denial must be in writing and sent by registered mail. Failure of the agency to make a final disposition within 6 months may be deemed by the claimant to be a final denial.

Prior to 1979, "accrual" occurred when the tortious act was committed. However, in United States v. Kubrick (S.Ct.1979), the Supreme Court in a medical malpractice case held that claims accrue when the plaintiff learns of the existence and cause of his injury. This has become known as the "discovery rule." Thus, malpractice cases are an exception to the general FTCA rule that claims

accrue at the time of plaintiff's injury. Wilkinson
v. United States (4th Cir.1982); Snyder v. United
States (8th Cir.1983). The Eighth, Fourth, and the
Second Circuits have also refused to apply Kubrick
to continuing tort cases, where its application
would shorten the limitations period in cases of
continuous infliction of emotional distress and
cases where the plaintiff is under the doctor's
continuing care. Gross v. United States (8th
Cir.1982); Ulrich v. Veterans' Admin. Hosp. (2d
Cir.1988); Otto v. National Institute of Health (4th
Cir.1987).   Some Circuits have permitted an
exception to the "discovery rule" when the
plaintiff's injuries prevent awareness of the injury,
such as being comatose. Washington v. United
States (9th Cir.1985). Finally, Kubrick does not
apply where the plaintiff possesses insufficient
knowledge for the running of the statute of
limitations as, for example, where medical records
are unavailable or there is insufficient scientific
knowledge at the time of injury for the plaintiff to
bring a claim.   Harrison v. United States (5th
Cir.1983) (injury to spouse of retired airman when
a needle from a ventriculogram broke off in her
brain); Stoleson v. United States (7th Cir.1980)
(nitroglycerin exposure in a munitions plant).

(2) Sum Certain Requirement

Failure to specify a sum certain will result in
denial of the claim and will preclude a subsequent
FTCA action. The amount of damages stated in the
claim constitutes the upper limit of the award.
However, the claimant may amend the amount of
damages prior to final disposition of the claim if he
or she can show: (1) an increased amount based on

newly discovered evidence not reasonably discoverable at the time the claim was made, or (2) proof of intervening facts relating to the amount of the claim. Federal Courts generally hold that writings which specify dollar amounts, furnished to the agency prior to the end of the statute of limitations, are sufficient to satisfy the sum certain requirement. See FTCA Handbook I–B, e-f, USARCS Claims Manual. The head of the Federal agency concerned has authority to settle claims up to $25,000; any award in excess of that limit must have prior approval of the Attorney General or the Attorney General's designee. 28 C.F.R. § 14.10(a).

(3) Denial of a Claim

Upon the failure to settle, or a final agency denial of a claim, the claimant is permitted to bring suit in the United States District Court for the district in which the injury occurred. The action must commence within six months of the final denial by the Federal agency or it will be barred. 28 U.S.C.A. § 2401(b). The procedures for this action will be governed by the Federal Rules of Civil Procedure, while substantive issues of liability are governed by the law of the place where the claim arose. There is no right to a jury trial under the FTCA.

d. FTCA Cause of Action

Government liability under the FTCA is based on the doctrine of respondeat superior; that is, the actions of the employee are imputed to the employer. However, the government employee must have been acting within the scope of his office or employment when the injury occurred. The United States is then liable for this action only if a private employer would be held similarly liable under the agency laws of the state where the negligent or wrongful act occurred. Three basic points must be established to create liability on the part of the United States:

(1) Government Employee Causing Harm

Local law does not determine employment. Under 28 U.S.C.A. § 2671, "employees of the United States" include officers or employees of any Federal agency, members of the military or naval forces of the United States, and persons acting on behalf of a Federal agency in an official capacity, whether temporarily or permanently in the service of the United States, with or without compensation. For the purposes of the FTCA, all medical and dental personnel employed in government-maintained facilities are government employees. Local laws designating such professional personnel as independent contractors are not controlling.

(2) Employee Acting Within Scope of Employment

As applied to members of the military, the phrase "acting within the scope of employment" means "acting in the line of duty." 28 U.S.C.A. § 2671. Although the latter phrase seems to be broader than "scope of employment," it is not. Some courts have held that so long as the act was not intentional, and the servicemember did not incur the injury while engaging in an activity incident to service, relief is not barred. For example, in Elliott v. United States (11th Cir.1994), the court ruled that a servicemember injured on leave, though still on active duty, could bring suit for negligence by the military and was not barred by the Feres doctrine. In Taber v. Maine (2d Cir.1995) the drunk driving of a servicemember could render the government vicariously liable under state law and the claim would not be barred by the Feres doctrine. Drinking could fall within the scope of employment. See also Bates v. United States (8th Cir.1983) (military policeman's actions in stopping a vehicle and killing both occupants were not "incident to service"); Parker v. United States (5th Cir.1980)(four day furlough drive toward home off military base not "incident to service"); Mariano v. United States (4th Cir.1979)(plaintiff, on off-duty status when he was working, sustained injuries as a night manager of a recreational facility owned and operated by the United States; ruled "incident to service.")

Veterans may sue under the FTCA for injuries, death, and property damage caused by a government employee which occurred after the veteran was released from service. If the veteran is entitled to Federal disability payments, the amount of the judgment will be reduced accordingly. A veteran injured during the course of treatment at a VA hospital may sue under the FTCA for malpractice, even though the initial injury for which the treatment was being given was service-connected. United States v. Brown (S.Ct.1954).

(3) Claim Arising From Negligent or Wrongful Act or Omission

The question of negligence is determined in accordance with local law. Res ipsa loquitur, proximate cause, attractive nuisance, last clear chance, and other legal theories are available as permitted by local law. The Supreme Court has held, however, that claims based solely on strict liability are not authorized by the FTCA: there must be a showing of fault on the part of the government employee. Dalehite v. United States (S.Ct.1953); Laird v. Nelms (S.Ct.1972). The word "wrongful" was added to the FTCA in order to afford relief for acts or omissions which may be wrongful but not necessarily negligent. If the conduct of the government employee constitutes an actionable tort under state law, but is not clearly negligent or one of the expressly excluded claims, it may still be actionable under the FTCA. For example, "waste" has been held to be a "wrongful act". Palomo v. United States (D.Guam 1960). Similarly, the government was held liable for a tort in the nature of trespass when its agents wrongfully seized and destroyed the plaintiff's horses in an attempt to enforce a federal statute against unlawful grazing on a federal range. Hatahley v. United States (S.Ct.1956).

Subsequent to the end of the Second World War, the United States embarked on a series of experiments designed to study the effects on American soldiers of modern warfare techniques such as nuclear and biological weapons. This intentional use of military personnel as guinea pigs raised constitutional questions as well as issues about the scope of the Feres doctrine. Generally, in light of alternative remedies under the Veterans' Benefits Act and the effect of such suits on military effectiveness, courts generally have held that veterans exposed to such agents are ineligible for recovery. Jaffee v. United States (3d Cir.1981) (recovery denied for soldiers compelled to stand in a field without protection while nuclear device was exploded short distance away); Laswell v. Brown (8th Cir.1982)(recovery denied for soldier ordered to attend three atmospheric test explosions in the Eniwetok Atolls where he was exposed to low-level ionizing radiation); Gaspard v. United States (5th Cir.1983)(claims of serious disabilities incurred as a result of orders to participate in atmospheric atomic weapons tests precluded). See also United States v. Stanley (S.Ct.1987) (serviceman denied recovery for secret administration of LSD by the government in chemical warfare tests).

e. Personal Liability of the Employee

Recovery of a judgment under the FTCA completely bars further action against the employee responsible for the injury. However, where a suit against the United States is not available, the employee may be subject to personal liability. To counter this apparent imposition of liability on government agents when the government itself would not be liable, certain employees have been given separate statutory immunity. Two important areas in which such immunity has been granted relate to malpractice claims against military-affiliated doctors and claims against government contractors.

(1) Malpractice

Military medical personnel are immune from individual liability because the Military Malpractice Act of 1976, 10 U.S.C.A. § 1089, makes the FTCA the sole basis for malpractice suits. When plaintiffs turn to the FTCA, however, they generally find that Feres precludes malpractice claims where the injuries sustained are from service-related activities, or "incident to service." In Hayes v. United States (5th Cir.1995), for example, a servicemember suffered complications when he underwent an elective hernia operation for a non work-related injury. Despite the fact that the injury was not service-related, the court ruled that the tort—malpractice by a military doctor— was service related and barred by Feres. Likewise, in Borden v. Veterans Administration (1st Cir.1994), the Feres doctrine applied despite the fact that the knee injury suffered was caused during an off-duty basketball game, and the treatment the plaintiff received in military hospitals was partially at the hands of civilians. The "incident to service test" focus, the court held, is not on where the treatment was rendered or by whom, but rather on the service member's military status in relation to the treatment. See also Skees v. By and Through Dept. of Army (6th Cir. 1997) (FTCA claims denied in case of suicide of an off0duty soldier).

The Supreme Court in United States v. Smith (S.Ct.1991), considered the impact of the Military Malpractice Act on the FTCA foreign tort exception. The Court affirmed the FTCA exception despite the fact that this would leave some plaintiffs without redress; under the facts of the case the tortfeasor was immunized from liability, and suit was barred by the FTCA against the United States. This result would be more troubling from a policy perspective were it not for the fact that veterans and servicemembers are accorded extensive medical benefits which serve as part of a compensation system, making tort remedies less necessary than in a civilian context.

(2) Government Contractor Immunity

One of the most interesting expansions of immunity under the Feres doctrine occurred in Boyle v. United Technologies Corporation (S.Ct.1988). There, the father of a drowned serviceman claimed that the death could have been avoided if not for a defectively designed emergency escape system in a military helicopter. Lacking any legislation specifically immunizing government contractors, the plaintiff argued that there was no basis for judicial recognition of the government contractor defense. Writing for a majority, Justice Scalia recognized 1) that government contracting was an area involving "uniquely federal interests" so that 2) where a significant conflict exists between the application of state law and a federal policy or interest, the federal policy may override state law. The Court held that "Liability for design defects in military equipment cannot be imposed, pursuant to state law, when 1) the United States approved reasonably precise specifications; 2) the equipment conformed to those specifications; and 3) the supplier warned the United States about the dangers in the use of the equipment that were

known to the supplier but not to the United
States."

f. Damages

There is no limit on the amount of damages
available under the FTCA, but only monetary
damages are available under the Act; there is no
provision for equitable relief. In general, under
FTCA § 2674, the United States is liable only for
actual damages. However, in a 1992 decision, the
Supreme Court ruled that other measures of
damages which go beyond strict economic
compensation and are not intended to punish are
not prohibited by § 2674. Molzof v. United States
(S.Ct.1992). The claimant's attorney is restricted
to an attorney's fee payable out of the judgment
not to exceed 25% of a litigated claim and 20% of a
settlement of an administrative claim.

When a claimant receives injury-related
government benefits in addition to a FTCA
judgment or award, the FTCA award is reduced by
the amount of the benefit payments. The theory is
that both compensations come from the same
general revenues. But if the benefit payments are
paid from a special fund supplied in part by the
beneficiary, such as insurance, the FTCA award is
not reduced by that amount.

2. ADMINISTRATIVE CLAIM REMEDIES

a. Military Claims Act

The Military Claims Act, 10 U.S.C.A. § 2733,
provides an administrative remedy for damage to
or loss of property, personal injury, or death caused

by a civilian employee or member of the Army, Navy, Air Force, Marines, or Coast Guard. It is designed to provide relief for any persons, whether civilian or military, injured or killed as a result of noncombatant activities of the armed forces not covered by the FTCA. Specifically, recovery is permitted whether or not there is any indication of negligence or fault on the part of the military, or where the claim arises in a foreign country. Thus, if a claim is filed initially under FTCA and the claimant fails to demonstrate negligence on the part of a government employee, a claim under the Military Claims Act is possible. The reverse is also true: failure to settle a claim made under the Military Claims Act does not bar a subsequent suit under the FTCA. However, a filing under the Military Claims Act does not toll the two-year FTCA statute of limitations.

The Military Claims Act, like the FTCA, requires that the claim have arisen while the civilian employee or servicemember who caused the damage or injury was within the scope of his or her employment. The Act authorizes the Secretary of each service to settle claims up to $100,000. If the Secretary recommends the settlement of a claim in excess of this amount, it must be submitted to Congress for approval. Authority to settle claims for less than $25,000 may be delegated by the Secretary to any officer in the branch of the armed forces under the Secretary's control. Unlike the FTCA, there is no statutory limitation on the portion of the settled claim which may be paid as attorney's fees.

Payment of a settled claim under the Military Claims Acts is contingent upon its acceptance by the claimant as full satisfaction of the claim. The claim process is strictly administrative; there is no recourse to judicial review. The claimant, if dissatisfied with the initial disposition of the claim, has recourse only by appeal to the Secretary of the service involved, whose determination is final and binding.

Exceptions and defenses to liability under the Military Claims Act are similar to those under the FTCA. There is no recovery for personal injury to or death of a servicemember incident to service, but there can be recovery for property damage in this situation. In addition, local laws of contributory and comparative negligence apply and may reduce or bar potential recoveries. The statute of limitations under the Act is the same as that of the FTCA—two years from the date of accrual of the cause of action.

b. National Guard Tort Claims Act

The National Guard Tort Claims Act, 32 U.S.C.A. § 715, supplements the coverage of the Military Claims Act. It provides relief to any person, whether civilian or military, for property loss, personal injury or death caused by a member of the Army or Air National Guard. The provisions parallel those of the Military Claims Act.

As under the Military Claims Act, there is no recovery permitted to a guardsman for personal injuries or death incident to service. The statute of limitations is two years; meritorious claims in excess of $100,000 must be submitted to Congress for consideration. There is no limitation on attorney's fees. Claims are presented to the Army or Air Force, not to the National Guard offices or headquarters.

c. Foreign Claims Act

The United States has waived its sovereign immunity not only to permit its own citizens to recover for damage caused by government employees, but also to permit recovery by the nationals of foreign countries. The Foreign Claims Act, 10 U.S.C.A. §§ 2734–2735, authorizes the Secretaries of the various services to appoint officers to handle claims of damage to or loss of real or personal property of any foreign country or any inhabitant of that country. The claim must have arisen from the act or omission of a military or civilian government employee not acting incident to combat activities, with the limited exception that claims relating to aircraft traveling to or from combat zones are allowed. The Act covers incidents which occur either on or off military facilities located in foreign countries.

As under the Military and National Guard Claims Acts, the Secretary may settle and pay claims up to $100,000. Congressional approval is required for any award above this amount which the Secretary believes to be meritorious. Settlement of claims under the Act is final and conclusive. There is no limitation on the percentage of the award that can be paid by the claimant as attorney's fees. Consistent with the other statutes discussed above, all claims under the Act must be brought within two years of accrual.

Should a foreign national seek recovery in the courts of his or her country for damage or injury caused by a government employee, the United States will, where international agreements so provide, reimburse the foreign country any amount it may pay under its procedures. The United States will also pay the costs of arbitration or litigation.

Nationals of countries at war with the United States are given more limited rights of recovery. For such nationals to be entitled to any recovery, they must be determined to be "friendly" to the United States.

d. Military Personnel and Civilian Employees Claims Act

While the Military, National Guard, and Foreign Claims Acts create remedies against the United States for actions of government employees, the Military Personnel and Civilian Employees Claims Act, 31 U.S.C.A. § 3721, provides military personnel and civilian employees of the military an administrative remedy for damages inflicted on them by others. It covers damage to or loss of property, but not personal injury or death, which arises during activities incident to the service of the claimant. The claim may arise either in the United States or in a foreign country. There is no requirement of proof of negligence or wrongdoing. Rather, the claim must simply be "substantiated" and a determination made that possession of the property was "reasonable or useful under the circumstances." The government does not have to be responsible for the loss in any way. The Act excludes, however, any loss caused wholly or in part by the negligence of the claimant.

The claim is limited to $40,000 damages, and there is no provision for submission of greater amounts to Congress. Settlement of a claim is final and conclusive; there is no provision for appeal. Attorney's fees are limited to 10% of the award. The statute of limitations is two years from the date of accrual of the claim. If it accrues during time of war, or such conflict intervenes, the claim may be submitted two years after the activity ceases if good cause is shown. The claim must be submitted to the head of the organization to which the claimant is attached.

3. REEMPLOYMENT RIGHTS OF SERVICEMEMBERS

The Uniformed Services Employment and Reemployment Rights Act (USERRA) (38 U.S.C.A. § 4301 et seq.) protects the reemployment rights as well as rights respecting health insurance, pension benefits and fringe benefits following service in the armed forces. USERRA requires that all employers, regardless of size, reemploy former employees (both full- and part-time) returning from five years or less of military service. The reemployed servicemember is entitled to seniority credit both for pre-military service time as well as time spent serving in the military. Wrigglesworth v. Brumbaugh (W.D.Mich. F.Supp.2d 2001). Exceptions exist where (1) it would be impossible or unreasonable for the employer to do so, (2) reemployment would impose an undue hardship on the employer, or (3) the employee's job was for a brief, nonrecurrent period, with no reasonable expectation of continued employment. Once reemployed, a returning servicemember may be involuntarily terminated for "just cause."

Under USERRA, courts have the following remedies available: A court may (1) require the employer to comply with the provisions of USERRA, (2) require the employer to compensate the person for any loss of wages or benefits suffered by reason of such employer's failure to comply with USERRA, or (3) require the employer to pay liquidated damages, if the court determines that the employer's failure to comply with the law was willful. In addition, the law expressly provides that a court may use its full equity powers, including temporary or permanent injunctions, temporary restraining orders, and contempt orders, to vindicate fully the rights or benefits of servicemembers. Groom v. Department of Army (M.S.P.R. 1999) (holding that USERRA authorized remedies including reinstatement with like status and back pay).

States are made subject to the remedies under USERRA, including awards for prejudgment interest. The Supreme Court has restricted the ability of Congress to authorize damage awards against states in the interest of protecting federalism. Kimel v. Florida Board of Regents (S.Ct. 2000) and Board of Trustees of the Univ. of Alabama v. Garrett (S.Ct. 2001); but see Nevada Dept. of Human Resources v. Hibbs (S.Ct. 2003) (state employees may recover money damages in federal court in the event of the state's failure to comply with the family-care provision of the Family and Medical Leave Act).

Employee benefits constitute a specialized area of the law beyond the scope of this book. The extent of specific protections and their ascertainment requires the assistance of a legal professional.

CHAPTER 5

A BRIEF HISTORY OF
AMERICAN MILITARY LAW

Military law serves two broad purposes. One is to enhance command and control to make a band of fighters into a more effective force; the other is to reduce the exposure of civilian noncombatants to the harsh consequences of war. This chapter reviews the historical development of military law. The next two chapters, "The Military Criminal Justice System" and "The Law of Armed Conflict" examine, respectively, the current state of U.S. command and control law and international humanitarian law.

A. ANCIENT BEGINNINGS

The colloquy between Jesus and the centurion who appealed for the health of his servant reflects the idea that subjection to authority is basic to soldiering: "I also am a man under authority with soldiers under me; and I say to one, 'Go,' and he goes, and to another, 'Come,' and he comes * * *." (Mt. 8:9; NRSV, 1989 (NCC Christ USA).

Scripture also records many excesses of war. Captured kings and leaders were usually slain and the male populace either exterminated (I Kings 11:15), mutilated (Judges 1:6), or taken as slaves

(Deut. 20:11). Women and children were part of the spoils or war, and pregnant women were often disemboweled (II Kings 8:12; 15:15; Amos 1:13). Conquered cities were burned and destroyed, and anything of value became booty claimed by conquering forces. Even if a city paid tribute, it might nevertheless have to allow hostages to be taken (II Kings 18:14 - 16). Civilians remained at the mercy of the military; the Roman poet Juvenile, writing in the second century AD, described in his *Satires* the suffering of civilians (*togati* or noncombatants) at the hands of powerful soldiers who silenced opposition and bullied their way.

B. EARLY ENGLISH MILITARY CODES AND COMMENTARY

Early military codes and regulations promulgated to suppress killings and stealing within the ranks typically prescribed heavy punishments. For example, the Ordinance of Richard I (A.D. 1190), intended to guide Crusaders setting off for the Holy Land, provided: "[w]hoever shall slay a man on ship-board, he shall be bound to the dead man and thrown into the sea. If he shall slay him on land he shall be bound to the dead man and buried in the earth."

The Articles of War of Richard II (1385) encompassed additional concerns such as the protection of churches and church property, clergy and religious noncombatants and women. These provisions restricted rape, pillage, and rioting. They also enhanced command and control (e.g., "that no man go out on an expedition by night or by day, unless with the knowledge and by the permission of the chieftain of the battail"; "every man * * * of our party, shall bear a large sign of the arms of St. George").

The "English Military Discipline" of James II (1686) provided for the conduct of Councels of War or Courts-Martial. A senior officer was designated as the President or presiding officer, responsible for interrogating the accused regarding allegations against him and hearing his defense. The sixty-four "Articles of War" of James II (1688) for the governance of the English army echoed concerns expressed in earlier codes and expanded protections of civilian property. For example, Article XXI provided that "No person shall extort Free quarter, or shall commit any Waste, or spoil or deface Walks of Trees, Parks, Warrens, Fishponds, Houses, or Gardens, tread down, or otherwise destroy Standing Corn in the Ear, or shall put their Horses into Medows without Leave * * * ." Peculiarly military offenses such as failure to repair were codified ("[W]hoever shall fail at the Beating of a Drum, or sound of a Trumpet * * * to repair to his Coulours, with his Arms decently kept, and well fixed * * *."). See also Code of Articles of King Gustavus Adophus of Sweden (1621), Article No. 52 ("He that at the sound of Drumme or Trumpet repaires not to his Colours, shall be clapt in irons.").

The British Articles of War of 1765, the model for the 1775 American Articles of War, reflect a more mature administrative structure and include provisions similar to those in the Uniform Code of

Military Justice. For example, Section XIV (Of Duties in Quarters, in Garrison, or in the Field) included failure to repair (Art. IV), being drunk on duty (Art. V), sleeping on post (Art. VI), and misbehavior before the enemy (Art. XIII). Although the Articles of War were notably less protective of soldiers than modern rules, their eighteenth-century civilian counterparts also lacked many protections that both civilians and military personnel now take for granted. A major weakness that existed then and persists into modern American military law is the pervasive problem of command influence, treated in greater detail later in this treatise.

On the eve of the American Revolution, Sir William Blackstone's COMMENTARIES ON THE LAWS OF ENGLAND (1765-69) appeared, volumes generally judged to be among the most important legal treatises ever written in the English language. Blackstone's comments on the evolution and state of eighteenth-century British military law and national security law highlight issues that troubled the founding fathers such as a prejudice against standing armies and a preference for a citizen-based army. For example, Blackstone quoted Montesquieu's reservations about standing armies, a threat of oppression by the executive power and a sorry history of their abuses, concluding that "[i]n the land of liberty it is extremely dangerous to make a distinct order of the profession of arms." Vol. I, 395-401. Blackstone says that an army "should wholly be composed of natural subjects; * * * enlisted for a short and limited time; the soldiers also should live intermixed with the people; no separate camp, no barracks, no inland fortresses should be allowed. And perhaps it might be still better if, by dismissing a stated number and enlisting others at every renewal of their term, a circulation could be kept up between the army and the people, and the citizen and the soldier be more intimately connected together." Vol. I, 401-02.

Thus, English military law increasingly came to reflect democratic values by insuring that military commanders were ultimately accountable to civilian authority. Also, military discipline was progressively regularized and conformed to models of fairness and procedure imported from the sphere of civilian law. When America stood on the brink of revolution, it could adopt a well-developed system of military law from the British.

C. THE AMERICAN
REVOLUTIONARY ERA

In addition to being the father of his country, George Washington was also the father of American military justice. As the prospect of hostilities with the British became increasingly apparent, Washington was appointed by the Continental Congress to chair a committee that would draft a set of rules and regulations for the Continental Army. The drafting committee's work was approved and America's the first Articles of War were adopted on June 30, 1775.

British models served for the codes that governed both the American Army and Navy. The British Articles of War provided that "The

Judge Advocate General, or some person deputed by him, shall prosecute in His Majesty's name." One of General Washington's first acts upon taking command of the Continental Army was to ask that William Tudor be commissioned as an officer and the first Judge Advocate. The 1775 Articles of War authorized general and regimental court-martial and punishments "by order of the commanding officer." The commander-in-chief or general had the power to pardon as well as to mitigate sentences imposed by a general court, and regimental commanders had similar authority with regard to regimental courts. Punishments were not prescribed but rather left to the discretion of the court.

After a year's experience with the 1775 Articles, General Washington, acting through Judge Advocate Tudor, asked the Continental Congress to consider revising the Articles. The Congress appointed a committee comprised of John Adams, Thomas Jefferson, John Rutledge, James Wilson, and Robert R. Livingston to undertake the revision. The committee's handiwork closely followed the 1775 Articles modeled on the British Articles. Adams justified this approach and explained why the colonials followed in Britain's path: "There was extant one system of articles of war, which had carried two empires to the head of command, the Roman and the British, for the British Articles of War were only a literal translation of the Roman." Works of John Adams, 1850.

The 1776 revisions continued the practice of punishments within the court's discretion. The number of offenses for which the death penalty was authorized continued to expand although general court-martial sentences ordering executions were stayed until "after a report shall be made of the whole proceedings to Congress or to the General or Commander-in-Chief of the forces of the Untied States, and their or his direction be signified thereon." Appeals were permitted, but "if upon a second hearing, the appeal shall appear to be vexatious or groundless, the person so appealing shall be punished at the discretion of the * * * general court," a practice at odds with modern notions of appellate justice. Tudor's office was renamed and became the Judge Advocate General. He "or some person deputed by him [was to] prosecute in the name of the United States of America." The Judge Advocate General personally presided over many early courts-martial.

Strangely, little changed in military justice between the Revolutionary War and World War I; those who faced the Kaiser did so under a military justice system that had governed those who fought the Hessians. Military justice was immune to the improvements, both substantive and procedural, in the civilian justice system which could have served as models. During wartime, the country was too preoccupied to address deficiencies in military justice, and during peacetime there was no felt need.

D. JUDICIAL SEPARATION OF MILITARY AND CIVILIAN LAW

Two nineteenth century U.S. Supreme Court cases well illustrate the tension between treating military law as an aspect of command or subjecting the military justice system to the rule of law.

Shortly after the midpoint of the nineteenth century, in Dynes v. Hoover (S.Ct. 1857), Congress' eighteenth century system was subjected to scrutiny. Frank Dynes, a Navy seaman court-martialed for *desertion*, was found guilty of *attempting to desert* and sentenced to confinement for six months at hard labor. Dynes challenged his conviction on the ground that the offense for which he was convicted was not provided for in the Naval Articles and thus the court-martial lacked jurisdiction to try and punish him. The case defined several aspects of military law that would remain unchanged for decades to come. First, Justice Wayne's opinion for the Court acknowledged Congress' power to provide for the trial and punishment of military offenses, a power independent of and exercised apart from the judicial power conferred in Article III of the Constitution. As the Court said, "the two powers are entirely independent of each other." Second, Dynes' claim that he was convicted of a crime not defined in the law governing the Navy was disposed of by a Naval Article providing that "All crimes *** not specified in the foregoing articles, shall be punished according to the laws and customs in such cases at sea." The article's vagueness was dismissed: "Notwithstanding the apparent indeterminateness of such a provision, it is not liable to abuse; for what those crimes are, and how they are to be punished, is well known by practical men in the navy and army, and by those who have studied the law of courts martial, and the offenses of which the different courts martial have cognizance." Third, so long as a court-martial is convened regularly, has proceeded legally, and imposed punishment allowed by law, "no appeal or jurisdiction of any kind has been given to the civil magistrate or civil courts." Dynes limited civilian supervision of military justice for almost a century until the adoption of the Uniform Code of Military Justice in 1950.

Although Dynes provided the dominant paradigm, a Supreme Court case decided thirty years later placed military justice more squarely in the mainstream of constitutional and legal authority, deemphasizing its role as merely an aspect of a commander's disciplinary authority. Runkle v. United States (S.Ct. 1887) involved a claim for compensation filed by Major Benjamin P. Runkle, who had been court-martialed for allegedly embezzling money while serving as a disbursing officer with the Bureau of Refugees, Freedmen, and Abandoned Lands. Runkle was found guilty and sentenced to be cashiered, fined and imprisoned as the President of the United States might direct. The record of Runkle's court-martial was forwarded to the Secretary of War, who remitted the entire sentence except for the cashiering. In 1873, Runkle was ordered cashiered in General Order of the War Department No. 7. Runkle then petitioned President Grant to revoke and annul his conviction and sentence because they had not been approved by the President of the United States "as required by law" in the sixty-fifth Article of War. President Grant referred Runkle's petition to the Judge Advocate General of the Army. Though he expressed doubt as to whether Runkle could "justly be held liable," Grant apparently took no further action. When President Rutherford B. Hayes reviewed Runkle's case, he concluded that the "conviction is not sustained by the evidence in the case, and the same, together with the sentence of the court thereon, are hereby disapproved; and it is directed that said order No. 7, so far as it relates to said Runkle, be revoked." Order of August 4, 1877.

The Supreme Court found the duty of presidential review and approval nondelegable. In delineating the statutory duties of the President under the Articles of War, Justice Waite adopted the position taken by Attorney General Bates in an opinion provided to President Lincoln in 1864:

Undoubtedly the president, in passing upon the sentence of a court-martial, and giving to it the approval without which it cannot be executed, acts judicially. The whole proceeding, from its inception, is judicial. The trial, finding, and sentence are the solemn acts of a court organized and conducted under the authority of and according to the prescribed forms of law. It sits to pass upon the most sacred questions of human rights that are ever placed on trial in a court of justice—rights which, in the very nature of things, can neither be exposed to danger, nor subjected to the uncontrolled will of any man, but which must be adjudged *according to law*. And the act of the officer who reviews the proceedings of the court, whether he be the commander of the fleet or the president, and without whose approval the sentence cannot be executed, is as much a part of this judgment, according to law, as is the trial or the sentence. When the president, then, performs this duty of approving the sentence of a court-martial dismissing an officer, his act has all the solemnity and significance of the judgment of a court of law.

In place of the Dynes Court's emphasis on the separateness of the military justice system, Runkle affirms the subordination of the military command to the rule of law.

E. FRANCIS LIEBER'S CODE

Military law, particularly the international laws governing the conduct of warfare, has been heavily influenced by and is deeply indebted to the military code promulgated April 24, 1863, as General Order No. 100 "Instructions for the Government of Armies of the United States in the Field." These instructions, appropriately known as the "Lieber Code" because of Francis Lieber's role in their preparation, were unlike a traditional military order in that they were informational rather than directory in nature. The Lieber Code, appropriately called the "earliest official government codification of the laws of war," provided a documentary foundation for further development of the law of war and identified military necessity as a general legal principle to limit violence.

Lieber, a law professor, had a personal interest in the swift end to conflicts as well as a humanitarian concern for limiting war's devastation. He had been wounded in the war of 1815 against the French and, of his three sons who fought in the Civil War, one was killed at the Battle of Williamsburg on the Confederate side. Lieber began to promote the idea of a treatise on the law of war as early as 1861 in letters to friends as "something, which Congress might feel inclined to recommend to the army" and lectured at Columbia Law School in the winter of 1861 - 62 on "The Laws and Usages of War."

Lieber's lectures were noticed by General Henry Wager Halleck, who asked Lieber to prepare a short treatise on guerrillas. Lieber's work, valuable in distinguishing those who participated as part of the war effort and were entitled to treatment as prisoners of war when captured from bandits and criminals who were not, was approved by General Halleck and distributed for use by the Union Army. When Halleck, an authority on international law and the laws of war, was promoted to general in chief of the Union Army, Lieber was appointed as the only civilian on a special board created by the War Department "to propose amendments or changes in the Rules and Articles of War and a code of regulations for the government of Armies in the field as authorized by the laws and usages of War."

The drafting process proceeded rapidly in early 1863. Lieber drew on his recent lectures and other materials and by February had a manuscript ready which was promulgated as of April 24, 1863. Lieber's biographer made this assessment of the Code:

> Part propaganda and part expediency, but almost entirely sound international law at the core, the code was, like its chief author's personality, an admixture of military sternness with basic humanitarianism. * * * Perhaps one of the greatest merits of the order was its form, highly characteristic of Lieber's writing. It was less a rigid legal code than a persuasively written essay on the ethics of conducting war. This made it usable for tough-minded Union officers, unschooled in the laws of war, who must be convinced rather than ordered. It was realistic in its view that vigorous prosecution of war could most speedily bring peace, yet * * * humanitarian compared with treatises of earlier epochs * * * .

Freidel, FRANCIS LIEBER, p. 335.

The Lieber Code anticipates most of the subjects comprising the modern law of armed conflict. The document consists of 157 terse paragraphs treating such topics as martial law, military jurisdiction, military necessity, humanitarian protection for the persons and property of non-combatants, prisoners of war, pillage, partisans, spies, flags of truce, parole, armistice, assassination, insurrection, civil war, rebellion, and treason.

Three provisions provide a useful look into the workings of the Code. First, the provisions on slavery provided a legal foundation for freeing slaves liberated by the Union Army:

> [I]n a war between the United States and a belligerent which admits of slavery, if a person held in bondage by that belligerent be captured by or come as a fugitive under the protection of the military forces of the United States, such person is immediately entitled to the rights and privileges of a freeman. To return such person into slavery would amount to enslaving a free person, and neither the United States nor any officer under their authority can enslave any human being. Moreover, a person so made free by the law of war is under the shield of the law of nations, and the former owner or State can have, by the law of postliminy, no belligerent lien or claim of service.

U.S. War Department, General Order No. 100, Apr. 24, 1863, reprinted in Richard Shelly Hartigan, LIEBER'S CODE AND THE LAW OF WAR, p. 53.

Second, Articles 14 through 16 define military necessity as "those measures which are indispensable for securing the ends of war, and which are lawful according to the modern law and usages of war." This doctrine, which limits the scope and nature of warfare, was an important contribution to the law of warfare. Warfare was not unrestricted violence, but violence limited by an end. It could logically encompass the "direct destruction of life or limb of armed enemies, and of other persons whose destruction is incidentally unavoidable" as well as the "destruction of property" and of the "channels of traffic, travel, or communication," depriving the enemy of "whatever * * * [is] necessary for the subsistence and safety of the Army." Cruelty, defined as the "infliction of suffering for the sake of suffering or for revenge," is forbidden as are "maiming or wounding" unless done in the course of battle. Article 16 concludes that "military necessity does not include any act of hostility which makes the return to peace unnecessarily difficult."

Third, Article 19 requires "Commanders, whenever possible, inform the enemy of their intention to bombard a place, so that the non-combatants, and especially the women and children, may be removed before the bombardment commences. But it is no infraction of the common law of war to omit thus to inform the enemy. Surprise may be a necessity." The Code was informational rather than directory in nature, and history provides an apparent instance of a serious, albeit controversial, failure to abide by it. In August 1864, Atlanta was the scene of fierce and bloody combat designed to deprive the Confederacy of valuable rail communications and military stores. General Sherman bombarded Atlanta without warning. When General Hood protested that notification was "usual in war among civilized nations," Sherman denied that it was required. He later wrote: "I was not bound by the laws of war to give notice of the shelling of Atlanta, a fortified town, with magazines, arsenals, foundries [sic], and possible stores; you were bound to take notice. See the books." 2 Sherman, MEMOIRS 121, 128 (1904) quoted in James G. Garner, "General Order 100 Revisited," 27 MILITARY LAW REVIEW 1 (1965).

Bombardment of Atlanta–at the time full of noncombatants–cannot be reconciled with Article 19 of the Lieber Code.

The Lieber Code was cited by the Supreme Court in Ex parte Vallandigham (S.Ct. 1864), a case arising from "the most celebrated civil liberties case of the [Civil] war." James M. McPherson, BATTLE CRY OF FREEDOM: THE CIVIL WAR ERA (1988), p. 596. General Burnside, who commanded the military Department of the Ohio, issued a General Order No. 38 on April 13, 1863 declaring that anyone who committed acts benefiting the enemies of the Union, including declaring sympathies for the Confederacy, would be tried as spies or traitors. Clement L. Vallandigham, a candidate for governor in Ohio, at a rally on May 1, denounced the "wicked, cruel and unnecessary war" waged "for the purpose of crushing out liberty and erecting a despotism * * * a war for the freedom of the blacks and the enslavement of the whites." He was arrested and tried by a military commission, which convicted him "of having expressed sympathy" for the enemy and having uttered "disloyal sentiments and opinions, with the object and purpose of weakening the power of the Government [to suppress] an unlawful rebellion." Vallandigham avoided a death sentence when the commission recommended instead a sentence of imprisonment for the duration of the war which Burnside approved. Vallandigham's habeas corpus petition was denied by a federal judge on the ground that President Lincoln had suspended the writ.

Thereafter, Vallandigham sought review by the Supreme Court, which held that it lacked the power to review the proceedings of military commission by certiorari. Justice Wayne's opinion assessing the authority to conduct trials by military commission notes that Burnside acted "in conformity with the instructions for the government of the armies of the United States, approved by the President * * * [which] were prepared by Francis Leiber [sic]." For the military, Lieber's Code may have been informational rather than directory, but for the Court, it was law–binding and prescriptive. Time would secure within the military and the law of war the beachhead Lieber's Code gained early on in the Supreme Court. Even the unfortunate effect on judicial review of military commissions was temporary, for the Court soon allowed habeas review of a military commission conviction in Ex parte Milligan (S.Ct. 1866).

F. THE ANSELL-CROWDER CONTROVERSY

The Ansell-Crowder Controversy, a dispute between Major General Enoch H. Crowder, the Judge Advocate General of the Army from 1911-1923 and his senior assistant, Brigadier General Samuel T. Ansell, played a significant role in the reform of military justice. General Crowder assumed responsibility for administration of the Selective Service System in World War I but delegated the day-to-day operations of the office to General Ansell.

The two had diametrically opposed views on review of court martial proceedings. According to General Crowder:

> the court-martial simply [is] the right hand of the commanding officer to aid him in the maintenance of discipline. It is his agent. He controls it. It is answerable not to the law but to him * * * . The court-martial is not a court at all; it is by an agency of military command governed and controlled by the will of the commander ***.

Quoted in Brown, "The Crowder-Ansell Dispute: The Emergence of General Samuel T. Ansell," 35 MIL. L. REV. 1, 23 (1967). Conversely, General Ansell proposed a significant expansion of the powers of the Judge Advocate General to review the results of courts-martial. General Ansell believed that, under section 1199 of the Revised Statutes of 1878 ("Judge-Advocate-General shall receive, revise, and have recorded the proceedings of all courts-martial, courts of inquiry and military commissions"), the Judge Advocate General could modify or set aside the findings and sentence of a court-martial approved by a commander where jurisdiction was lacking or serious prejudicial error existed. The power to "revise," in Ansell's view, included the power "to reexamine for correction, to alter or amend."

Two extraordinary cases, both arising out of Texas in 1917, focused national attention on inadequacies of the system of military justice. The first involved a group of twelve or fifteen enlisted soldiers under arrest for a minor violation of the Articles of War of 1916 who refused to attend drill formation after being ordered to do so. The soldiers were correct as a matter of law; their refusal was based on an Army regulation that prohibited persons in arrest from attending drill. The soldiers were charged with mutiny, tried by general court-martial, convicted, given a dishonorable discharge, and sentenced to terms of imprisonment ranging from ten to twenty-five years. After the appointing authority reviewed and approved the cases and ordered the sentences executed, the cases were forwarded to the Office of the Judge Advocate General for disposition. Ansell and others in his office recognized the miscarriage of justice and directed that the findings be set aside. General Crowder objected, asserting that the Judge Advocate General lacked any authority to set aside findings after execution of sentence had been ordered by the appointing authority.

A second case further raised the profile of this dispute. After America's entry into World War I in 1917, the arrest of two African-American soldiers by local law enforcement officers in Houston, Texas for disorderly conduct was followed by a rumor that one of the soldiers arrested had been killed. A mob of armed black soldiers marched on the town and, before the riot stopped, fifteen whites were killed– civilians, police officers, and National Guard troops called upon to suppress the riot. Sixty-three soldiers were accused of murder, mutiny and riot and were tried by general court-martial. Thirteen were sentenced to death by hanging, forty-one to life imprisonment, four to short terms, and five were acquitted. The thirteen sentenced to death were hanged immediately after the trial. When news of the swift imposition of capital punishment reached Washington, the resulting furor led to stern action and swift reform measures. The commanding general was relieved, reduced in rank and retired. The War Department prohibited the execution of death sentences before review by the Judge Advocate General.

The commander's actions were authorized by military law; the commander of a territorial department could order the execution of a death sentence for murder, rape, mutiny, desertion or espionage in time of war. The crimes technically occurred during war, although obviously far from the European front and in the racially charged climate of the American south in the early twentieth century. The injustice of death sentences without appeal struck a nerve.

Late in 1917, Ansell defended his effort to review the convictions in the Texas Mutiny Cases in a memorandum submitted to the Secretary of War. His brief was answered by General Crowder shortly thereafter. From Ansell's perspective, the issue was whether review of courts-martial proceedings approved by the convening commander was provided for by statute under the authority to "revise" records. Crowder saw the issue as an absence of statutory authority and a question as to whether appellate review was desirable. Senior officers opposed a commander's order being overturned by a member of the Judge Advocate General's Department and expressed fears of disastrous effects on discipline. In addition, Crowder may have been reluctant to recognize substantial defects in the 1916 Articles of War, which he had revised and guided through Congress.

The controversy between Ansell and Crowder simmered in the War Department until the Armistice in Europe in November 1918, after which Senator Chamberlain of Oregon criticized the military justice system in a Senate speech for inequality, excessive sentences and command control of the justice process and called for the establishment of an appellate tribunal to address these problems. Eventually, Senator Chamberlain introduced a reform bill, drafted by Ansell, leading to extensive hearings on the reform of military justice. Though few were adopted at the time, Ansell's proposed reforms are worth noting because they set the agenda for military justice reform in the twentieth century.

The Ansell proposals included (1) increased specificity both as to crimes and punishments, (2) review of general court-martial charges by the Judge Advocate General's Department for legal sufficient and evidentiary support, (3) provision in a general court-martial of military counsel of the accused's choice if reasonably available, and, if circumstances warranted, civilian counsel provided at no expense to the accused, (4) having a fixed number of members of a court to prevent manipulation by the authorizing commander during the course of trial, (5) authorizing enlisted members to serve on a court, (6) appointing a Court Judge Advocate to select or augment the members of the court (to lessen the influence exercised by the appointing authority), rule on questions of law and challenges to the impartiality of the court members, summarize the evidence, insure the rights of the accused at trial, approve the court's finding of guilt or substitute a finding of guilty of a lesser included offense, announce the findings of the court, and suspend any sentence except death or dismissal, (7) allowing peremptory challenges to individual members of special and general courts-martial and challenges to an array from which members were selected, (8) requiring that, except as otherwise provided by Congress, the rules of evidence applicable to trials by courts-martial should be the same as those followed in U.S. district courts, (9) immediate announcement of acquittal in open court to prevent the appointing authority from returning the findings and sentence to the court-marital for reconsideration (the War Department prohibited the practice of returning acquittals to the court for reconsideration and the upward revision of sentences in the midst of the reform debate, thereby rectifying some of the worst abuses), and (10) providing appellate review by a Court of Military Appeals comprised of Article III judges.

Ansell's proposals, many far ahead of their time, were a product of a desire to treat military personnel charged with crimes fairly in accordance with the law. The Articles of War, in some respects unchanged from the eighteenth century, had by the end of World War I diverged considerably from civilian practice in the quality of treatment afforded an accused. Ansell play a catalytic role in prompting reform. But military justice would continue to be dispensed largely by amateurs of whatever rank, and those with legal training would have to wait their time. See generally Morgan, "The Existing Court-Martial System and the Ansell Army Articles," 29 YALE L. J. 52 (1919) and Morgan, "The Background of the Uniform Code of Military Justice," 6 VAND. L. REV. 169 (1953)).

G. THE UNIFORM CODE OF MILITARY JUSTICE

The size of the military shrank significantly in the period between the two world wars and little attention was paid to military justice, but World War II brought with it a significant expansion in manpower and strains on the military justice system. Jonathan Lurie in his careful history ARMING MILITARY JUSTICE: THE ORIGINS OF THE UNITED STATES COURT OF MILITARY APPEALS, 1775-1950 (Princeton, 1992), at p. 128, describes the scope of the problem as follows:

Ill prepared to cope with what was considered in 1917-1918 to be a major increase in American armed forces, the military justice system was in a much worse position to meet the dramatic needs engendered by the Second World War. The army expanded from 1,460,000 personnel to more than 8,000,000. By 1945, the navy's ranks had doubled in size to over 4,500,000. In all, at least 12,000,000 people were subject to military justice; and at the height of the war, approximately 600,000 courts-martial were convened per year. Over 1,700,000 trials were held, more than 100 executions were carried out, and at the end of the war in 1945, some 45,000 members of the armed forces were in prison.

The unfinished business of instrumental reform of military justice and the role of the commander in the process came back to haunt the military following World War II. Congress was flooded with complaints, and public pressure mounted for much-needed reforms in military justice. The complaints echoed those raised after World War I. A few examples well illustrate. First, although article 8 of the Articles of War provided that a law member from the Judge Advocate General's Department should be detailed to a general court-martial, an exception allowed an officer from another branch to be substituted. The exception often consumed the rule, and the task of assuring adherence to the law fell to clueless amateurs responsible for gross, and essentially unreviewable, miscarriages of justice. Second, command domination continued to be a problem. Commanders hectored hand-picked courts into sentencing defendants to the maximum allowable punishment and arrogated to themselves the task of setting punishment. Although allowed by the Articles, the practice contributed heavily to the perception that military justice was unduly harsh as well as unfair. Finally, indeterminate sentences continued the practice of "different spanks for different ranks." See Holtzoff, "Administration of Justice in the United States Army," 22 N.Y U. L. REV. 1 (1947).

Military justice reform for the Army came in two steps after World War II. The first step, the Elston Act of 1948, accommodated an on-going struggle between reformers and those who preferred the status quo by revising the Articles of War for the Army only (although the Air Force complied with it as well). The second step was the creation of one code of military justice to govern all branches of the service, a step realized with enactment of the Uniform Code of Military Justice in 1950.

The Elston Act modified the Articles of War to allow enlisted members to sit on general and special courts-martial if requested in writing by an enlisted accused. It also mandated increased use of professionally trained and qualified lawyers. The law member was required to be present throughout the trial and to rule on questions of law. In a general court-martial, if the trial judge advocate who represented the government was a lawyer, the defendant would be entitled to a lawyer. An accused who so requested would be entitled to counsel during a pretrial investigation.

The Elston Act had barely entered into force when Congress undertook the process of unifying military law and procedure by creating a uniform code to govern the Army, Navy, Marine Corps, Air Force, and Coast Guard. The current operation of this code is the subject of extended treatment in the next chapter, but a few of the highlights of the 1950 reform are worth mention here.

The Army's Articles of War served as the model, with modifications to accommodate the special needs or traditions of the Navy. Military crimes were continued in much the same way as previous codes, including peculiarly military offenses such as "conduct unbecoming an officer and a gentleman" and service discrediting conduct. The President was authorized to prescribe a table of maximum punishments for crimes as part of a revised Manual for Courts-Martial to go along with the new code. Before charges could be referred to a general court-marital, the UCMJ now required appointment of an investigating officer who would make "a thorough and impartial investigation" at which an accused would have an opportunity to present evidence and cross examine witnesses. As a partial check on commanders, a court-martial convening authority was required to refer the charge to his or her Staff Judge Advocate for "consideration and advice," although the commander was not bound by the recommendation. Some effort was made to prevent a commander from exercising undue influence over courts-martial (e.g., disqualifying a commander with "personal interest" in a case and prohibiting the convening authority from censuring, reprimanding or admonishing court members or counsel with respect to the findings or sentence). The UCMJ guaranteed the right of an accused in serious cases to be represented by a lawyer. Finally, in one of the most important changes, the UCMJ created the United States Court of Military Appeals, three civilian judges appointed by the President to 15-year terms.

CHAPTER 6

THE MILITARY CRIMINAL JUSTICE SYSTEM

The military criminal justice system has historically been one of the largest systems for processing crimes in the United States. During World War II, for example, approximately two million courts-martial were convened, of which 60,000 were general courts-martial. A dramatic reduction in the number of uniformed servicemembers and elimination of the draft have greatly reduced the size of the military criminal justice system. In FY 2001, the latest year for which figures are available, there were 7653 court-martial trials in the combined services: 4848 in the Navy, 1799 in the Army, 956 in the Air Force, and 50 in the Coast Guard. The number of Article 15 sanctions typically runs many times the volume of courts-martial; in FY 2001, there were 90,107 Art. 15s in the combined services.

In many respects, this system parallels state and federal civilian systems for dealing with crimes. Like state and federal law, military law is hierarchical, both substantively and procedurally. Substantively, the United States Constitution is at the apex of the military law system, followed by federal statutory law, regulations promulgated by the President, the secretaries of defense and of the various armed services, and rules of various commanders. Court decisions interpret these laws. Procedurally, the military court system is organized much like civilian courts: trials are conducted by courts-martial with review by two tiers of appellate courts, the first comprised of appellate military judges, the second comprised of civilian appellate judges. Judgments of the highest military court may, in turn, be reviewed by the United States Supreme Court.

In other particulars, military law and its processes diverge from civilian criminal law. As the Supreme Court of the United States noted in Parker v. Levy (S.Ct.1974): "Just as military society has been a society apart from civilian society, so military law is a jurisprudence which exists separate and apart from the law which governs in our federal judicial establishment."

There are two basic sources of this specialized jurisprudence: the Uniform Code of Military Justice (UCMJ) and the Manual for Courts-Martial (MCM). Congress originally enacted the UCMJ in 1950, extensively revised it in 1968, and has continued to update specific provisions over the years. The MCM, promulgated by executive order of the President, has been revised frequently, most recently in 2002. It includes specifications for UCMJ crimes, Rules for Courts-Martial (RCM), Military Rules of Evidence (MRE), and analyses of the code and rules. Additionally, military law incorporates regulations of the individual services. These primary sources of law are construed primarily by regulations of the various branches of the military and by two appellate courts: the

Court of Criminal Appeals (C.C.A.) of each service branch and the United States Court of Appeals for the Armed Forces (U.S.C.A.A.F.).*

A. ALTERNATIVE DISPOSITIONS

While reported civilian crimes are dealt with exclusively through judicial processes, military offenses may be dealt with through nonpunitive measures, nonjudicial punishment, and an array of judicial alternatives. This would appear strange if the conduct regulated by the UCMJ were equivalent to the conduct regulated by civilian criminal codes. However, as the Supreme Court noted in Parker v. Levy (S.Ct.1974), "[The UCMJ] regulates a far broader range of the conduct of military personnel than a typical state criminal code regulates of the conduct of civilians; but at the same time the enforcement of that code in the area of minor offenses is often by sanctions which are more akin to administrative or civil sanctions than to civilian criminal ones." In short, the broad range of offenses and the specialized nature of military society govern the alternatives used to treat offenders against the UCMJ.

---

* In 1995, the National Defense Authorization Act changed the nomenclature for the various military review courts. The "Court of Military Review" (C.M.R.) was changed to the "Court of Criminal Appeals" (C.C.A.), and the "United States Court for Military Appeals" (U.S.C.M.A.) was renamed the "United States Court of Appeals for the Armed Forces" (U.S.C.A.A.F.). Wherever appropriate, the latter designations will be used; when clarity requires it, the former will be utilized.

1. ADMINISTRATIVE CORRECTIVE MEASURES

To further the efficiency of his command or unit, a commanding officer or officer in charge is authorized to use nonpunitive disciplinary measures when faced with minor UCMJ violations or other deficiencies. Part V, ¶ 1(d), MCM. Such sanctions are appropriate vehicles for maintaining good order and discipline in the great majority of situations. Nonpunitive sanctions are appropriate for such deficiencies as neglect, laziness, inattention, and difficulty in adjusting to military life. Nonpunitive disciplinary measures are for correction, not for punishment. The sanction should be logically related to the offense charged and not excessive.

A commander can withhold privileges as a nonpunitive corrective measure. This could include pass privileges (the ability to leave the post), post exchange (px) or commissary privileges, on-post check cashing privileges, on-post driving privileges, or housing privileges. Appropriate regulations control the level of command appropriate to restrict or revoke privileges. The restriction should correspond to the privilege abused.

Other nonpunitive sanctions are admonitions (oral or written warnings); counseling; corrective training; reductions in rank, either for misconduct or inefficiency; revocation of a security clearance; bar to reenlistment; reclassification of one's military occupational specialty (MOS); and administrative elimination.

Some nonpunitive sanctions parallel punitive sanctions, but are not imposed for the purpose of punishment and are therefore not punitive. Armed servicemembers aggrieved by nonpunitive correction may seek redress through the complaint procedure of Article 138 (UCMJ, Article 138) or complaint to the appropriate Inspector General's office.

Administrative corrective measures are not always appropriate responses to UCMJ violations which come to a commanding officer's attention. In the first place, service regulations may prohibit or limit resort to these measures. Secondly, such measures are only appropriate for certain "minor offenses." Part V, ¶ 1(g)(1) MCM. It is clearly inappropriate, for example, to deal with rape, murder, mutiny, treason, or the like through administrative corrective measures. Nonpunitive sanctions may, however, be imposed for minor criminal conduct such as shoplifting, intoxication and fighting, bad checks, and driving under the influence.

2. NONJUDICIAL PUNISHMENT

a. Article 15

Art. 15 of the UCMJ grants authority to commanding officers and officers exercising command to impose "disciplinary punishments for minor offenses without the intervention of a court-martial." Such authority is frequently exercised. Art. 15 nonjudicial punishment (called "Captain's Mast" in the Navy and Coast Guard, "Office Hours" in the Marines, and simply "Art. 15's" in the Army and Air Force) is authorized on the ground that discipline and morale will be adversely affected if commanding officers are unable to impose punishment immediately for minor offenses. Moreover, requiring minor offenses to proceed through the court-martial system would be expensive and time-consuming.

Under the authority of the Manual for Courts Martial, MCM, Part V, ¶ 4 and regulations issued by the armed services, e.g., AR 27–10 Military Justice (8 September 1994) § 3, two types of Article 15 procedures are authorized—formal and summarized—as well as two levels of Article 15s—company grade and field grade—which refers to the rank of the commander imposing the Article 15. Based on the evidence against an accused service person, the commander chooses the appropriate level of Article 15, i.e., company grade or field grade, depending on the level of punishment appropriate, if it is concluded that the accused is guilty of the offense. A commander can refer an Article 15 up the chain of command to a commander more senior in rank in order to open the possibility of a more serious sanction if the imposing commander believes the accused is guilty of the offense charged.

Nonjudicial punishment is appropriate for minor offenses only when nonpunitive measures are inadequate. A "minor offense" is one in which the maximum punishment, if tried by court-martial, would be no more than a bad-conduct discharge or confinement for one year. Part V, ¶ 1(e), MCM. The theory of Art. 15 is that the punishment imposed is primarily for corrective, not retributive, purposes.

Jurisdiction to impose nonjudicial punishment pursuant to Art. 15 is dependent upon the existence of court-martial jurisdiction. The general rule for Art. 15 jurisdiction is that any member of a military command is subject to Art. 15 proceedings anywhere in the world, so long as the offender is attached or assigned to the command of the officer who imposes the punishment. Service regulations sometimes limit this broad jurisdictional rule, and the various services have by agreement prohibited the imposition of nonjudicial punishment upon members of other branches.

The infraction for which an Art. 15 is imposed must be a crime under the UCMJ. While no specific standard of proof applies to any phase of Art. 15 proceedings, a commander considering initiating such action must recognize that the servicemember is, in most cases, entitled to refuse the Art. 15 process and demand trial by court-martial. Since courts-martial employ the beyond a reasonable doubt standard of proof, as a policy matter, action under Article 15 is usually not warranted if the commander does not believe that that level of proof is available.

Table I summarizes the punishments allowed under the Manual for Courts–Martial, MCM, Part V, ¶ 5b for formal proceedings under Article 15.

Table 1
Formal Article 15 (U.S. Army)*
MAXIMUM NONJUDICIAL PUNISHMENTS UNDER ARTICLE 15 (Formal Proceedings)

Commanding Officer	Admonition or Reprimand	Restriction	Extra Duties	Correctional Custody	Forfeiture of Pay	Reduction in Rank
Company Grade:						
E-5 to E_9	Yes	14 days[1]	14 days[1]	No	7 days	No
E-1 to E-4	Yes	14 days[1]	14 days[1]	7 days[2][3]	7 days	To one grade lower
Field Grade:						
E-5 to E-9	Yes	60 days[1]	45 days[1]	No	1/2 pay per month for 2 months	To one grade lower if within promotion authority[4]
E-1 to E-4	Yes	60 days[1]	45 days[1]	30 days[2][3]	1/2 pay per month for 2 months	To one or more grades lower

---

* See Field Legal Guide for Officers (1995) edited by Col. Dennis R. Hunt.
[1] Restriction and extra duty may be combined, but the total may not exceed the maximum allowed for extra duty.
[2] Enlisted soldiers with a pay grade of E-4 or above may not be placed in correctional custody, but if their rank is reduced to pay grade of E-3, they may be placed in correctional custody as a part of the same punishment.
[3] Enlisted soldiers with pay grades of E-1 to E-3 may be confined for 3 days on bread and water when attached to or embarked on a vessel.
[4] The promotion authority for pay grades E-7, E-8, and E-9 rests with headquarters, Department of the Army; soldiers in these pay grades cannot be reduced by nonjudicial punishment.

The range of Art. 15 punishments against officers is more narrow than those against enlisted personnel, and the punishments commanding officers of lower grades may impose are more restricted than those which may be meted out by field grade, flag rank, or general officers. Part V, ¶ 5 (b), MCM. Any commander, officer in charge, or principal assistant may impose Art. 15 punishment if authorized by regulations of the Secretary concerned. Part V, ¶ 2, MCM.

While the procedure for Art. 15's may vary slightly from one branch of the service to another, the parameters are relatively uniform. A commander acting under Article 15 must notify the accused of the offense of which he or she has been accused, of the commander's intention to proceed under Article 15 with respect to the accusation, and the maximum punishment that could be imposed as a consequence of the Article 15. The notification must also apprise the servicemember of the following rights:

1. The right to remain silent. The servicemember need not say anything. Anything said may be used against him or her.

2. The right to consult with counsel and information about where to receive assistance from the JAG office. There is no right to representation by a military attorney.

3. The right to refuse the Article 15 and to demand trial by court-martial unless attached to or embarked on a vessel. The accused is not entitled to know what level court-martial the commander will recommend (i.e., summary, special or general) if the Article 15 is refused. If the accused believes the evidence against him or her is insubstantial, a demand for a court-martial may call the commander's hand, so to speak.

4. The right personally to present one's case in the commander's presence, unless the commander is unavailable or under extraordinary circumstances.

5. The right to call witnesses, if reasonably available.

6. The right to present evidence in defense, extenuation, and mitigation.

7. The right to request the presence of a spokesperson who may but need not be a civilian lawyer. Both the spokesperson and the accused may speak. Particularly if the accused is young or inexperienced, requesting a spokesperson is a good idea. Even innocent persons have trouble confronting accusations by themselves.

8. The right to an open hearing. Hearings are normally open, but the accused may request that his or hers be closed.

9. The right to examine available evidence.

10. The right to appeal.

Under regulations prescribed by the services (e.g., AR 27–10), forms for use in a formal Article 15 detail these rights. E.g., DA Form 2627, DA 27–10, Figure 3–2, pp. 21–22.

Use of a summarized Article 15 is permitted when the appropriate punishment imposed will not exceed 14 days extra duties, 14 days restriction and an oral reprimand or admonition. MCM, Part V, ¶ 4c.(1)(B) and (G); AR 27–10, ¶ 3–16. The rights of the accused in a summarized Article 15 are fewer in view of the limitations on the deprivations he or she can suffer upon a finding of guilt. The goal is an expeditious resolution of the matter with spare but adequate procedural safeguards. Because the type of Article 15— summarized or formal—is limited by the maximum punishment that can be imposed, a more senior commander would generally not elect to use a summarized procedure.

Under Army practice, a summarized Article 15 is handled utilizing DA Form 2627–1. A summarized Article 15 may be imposed by any commander, but only upon enlisted personnel. Because of the limitation on the punishment that can be imposed, the procedure is appropriate only for very minor offenses. The notice required is normally 24 hours and the commander may delegate the task of notification. There is no right to consult with a JAG officer. There is no open hearing and no entitlement to a spokesperson. The accused has a right to call witnesses and to be heard. There is a right to appeal to the next higher commander within 5 days. See DA 27–10, Form 2627–1, Figure 3–1, pp. 19–20.

One of the more important aspects of the Article 15 process is the disposition of the record of the Article 15. Adverse information such as an Article 15 can affect military career advancement possibilities. AR 27–10, ¶ 3–6. Under Army practice, for those in the rank of E–4 and below, records of a formal Article 15 are kept in the unit and destroyed upon transfer from the unit or after 2 years. For those in the rank of E–5 and above, at the commander's election, the original record of the Article 15 (DA Form 2627) can be kept in the unit records and destroyed upon transfer from the unit or after 2 years or it can be made a part of the soldier's Official Military Personnel File (OMPF). The OMPF has two portions, a restricted fiche which is not normally reviewed by career managers and selection boards which make assignment, school and promotion selections, and a performance fiche which is used for career decisions. Placement in the restricted fiché has less adverse impact on one found guilty in an Article 15. A non-commissioned officer (NCO) can have only one Article 15 in a restricted fiche. Any subsequent Article 15s would go into the performance fiche.

The accused who does not demand a court-martial receives merely an informal hearing before the commanding officer. His or her rights to a public hearing, to an advocate (in some branches, a lawyer), to present matters in defense or mitigation, to present and directly examine his witnesses, and to appeal any punishment to a superior commander are reiterated at this hearing. However, the option to consult counsel prior to accepting an Art. 15 punishment does not create a Sixth Amendment right to counsel and does not constitute the "appointment" of counsel. United States v. Kendig (C.M.A. 1993). Subsequent to reiteration of the rights of the accused, evidence is presented to the commander, who decides the question of guilt and, if necessary, imposes punishment.

Appeals of two sorts may follow imposition of Art. 15 punishment. First, the commander or a superior to the commander may suspend, set aside, remit or mitigate any punishment. Part V, ¶ 6, MCM. Second, one punished under Art. 15 who thinks the punishment is unjust or disproportionate to the offense may thereafter appeal within five days of imposition of punishment, absent good cause shown. This appeal, addressed to the commander's superior, must be in writing and must state the reasons for regarding the punishment as unjust or disproportionate. The appellate authority cannot increase the punishment imposed. Part V, ¶ 7, MCM. Before acting on such an appeal, the superior must refer the case to a Judge Advocate member or, with respect to the Coast Guard, to a lawyer of the Dept. of Transportation for review and advice. There is no further appeal beyond the commander's superior and no judicial review exists of Art.15 determinations.

Submission to Art. 15 punishment does not always bar subsequent court-martial for the same misconduct. In the usual case, where nonjudicial punishment is imposed for a minor offense and the court-martial concerns the same minor offense, the "former punishment" bars trial of the same offense. RCM 907 (b)(2)(D)(iv); United States v. Fretwell (C.M.A. 1960). However, if the original offense was "serious" rather than "minor," a court-martial could be initiated notwithstanding Art. 15 punishment because there was no prior judicial proceeding. Art. 15 (f), UCMJ; Part V, ¶ 1(e), MCM. The soldier would, of course, receive credit for any time served as a result of nonjudicial punishment.

The lack of procedural protections for the accused and the absence of judicial review over Art. 15 punishment have raised questions as to whether Art. 15 violates due process requirements of the Fifth Amendment to the United States Constitution. Some argue that most constitutional problems of Art. 15 procedure are overcome because the offender may demand trial by court-martial before punishment is imposed. Others disagree, arguing that the right to demand court-martial does not save Art. 15 from due process infirmities because, under the court-martial system, the accused runs the risk of incurring more severe punishment. In addition, the accused may suffer not only the Art. 15 punishment itself, but also serious administrative consequences resulting from that punishment. For example, in Bennett v. Tarquin (D. Haw. 1979), sailors found "guilty" of use and possession of marijuana were punished under Art. 15 with restrictions, reductions in rank, and fines. In addition, this punishment led to automatic removal under Navy regulations from nuclear submarine duty, which cost the sailors their monthly submarine pay and their eligibility for a reenlistment bonus.

There is as yet no definitive resolution to the due process question. However, Middendorf v. Henry (S.Ct.1976), provides some guidance. In Middendorf, the Court held that there was no constitutional right to counsel at a summary court-martial, in part because the accused could have demanded a special or general court-martial at which he would have been entitled to counsel. This reasoning was accepted by one court as validating Art. 15 procedures. Fairchild v. Lehman (Fed.Cir.1987). For further discussion of constitutional due process challenges to nonjudicial punishment and summary court-martial proceedings see infra at pp. 250-51.

b. Article 139

Under the seldom used Art. 139 of the UCMJ, a commanding officer may convene a board of one to three commissioned officers to investigate any complaint of willful injury to or wrongful taking of property by servicemembers. The board may summon witnesses, examine under oath, receive depositions and other evidence, and assess damages against the responsible parties. The damages assessed are subject to approval by the commanding officer; upon his approval, the amount assessed is charged against the offender's pay. When particular offenders cannot be ascertained, but their military unit is known, damages may be divided among those members present when the damage was done. Art. 139 is essentially an administrative restitutionary device. It does not supplant criminal sanctions for property-related offenses, such as Larceny (Art. 121, UCMJ), Robbery (Art. 122, UCMJ), and Burglary (Art. 129, UCMJ).

3. COURTS–MARTIAL

The Constitutional basis for a separate judicial system for military-related crimes is Art. I, § 8, which gives Congress the authority "to make Rules for the Government and Regulation of the land and naval Forces." The rationale for Congress' enactment of the UCMJ pursuant to this authorization is that the military has special needs for order, discipline, and efficiency which make resort to civilian courts for trial of military-related matters inappropriate. However, Congress was concerned that those accused of military crimes not be subjected to kangaroo courts. Therefore, it designed the court-martial system to avoid the phenomenon of "command influence," the improper interference by a superior in command with the independent judgment of persons responsible for judicial decision. As Chief Judge Everett said in United States v. Thomas (C.M.A.1986), "Command influence is the mortal enemy of military justice."

Unlawful command influence can be either actual or apparent. United States v. Osburn (A.F.C.M.R.1991). While the commanding officer within the ranks imposes Art. 15 punishment, Congress attempted to remove all courts-martial from such command influence by: (1) forbidding commanding officers from attempting to influence judicial proceedings (Art. 37, UCMJ); (2) authorizing disciplinary action against someone who obstructs court-martial proceedings (Art. 98, UCMJ); and (3) decreeing that defense counsel may not receive less favorable reports because of zealous advocacy on behalf of the accused (RCM 104(b)(2)). Additionally, Congress has established more extensive procedural safeguards for the benefit of the accused as the severity of punishments entrusted to the court-martial increases.

Military justice requires a role for commanders and some command influence is acceptable, such as orders requiring a company commander to refer specific types of cases, such as drug or alcohol cases, for disposition by a superior commander. However, a directive requiring all servicemembers with two previous incidents to be tried by court-martial would be unlawful command influence. United States v. Hawthorne (C.M.A. 1956); United States v. Hinton (A.C.M.R.1976) (per curiam).

Unlawful command influence is proscribed by Article 37. A partial solution to the problem of command influence is the DuBay hearing. In United States v. DuBay (CMA, 1967) the court discussed the hearing warranted when the defendant raises an issue of command influence as follows:

Whenever an issue of command influence is raised [on appeal,] the record will be remanded to a convening authority other than the one who appointed the court-martial concerned and one who is at a higher echelon of command. That convening authority will refer the record to a general court-martial for another trial. Upon convening the court, the law officer will order an out-of-court hearing, in which he will hear the respective contentions of the parties on the question, permit the presentation of witnesses and evidence in support thereof, and enter findings of fact and conclusions of law based thereon. If he determines the proceedings by which the accused was originally tried were infected with command control, he will set aside the findings or sentence, or both, as the case may require, and proceed with the necessary rehearing. If he determines that command control did not in fact exist, he will return the record to the convening authority, which will review the findings and take action thereon, in accordance with Articles 61 and 64 of the Uniform Code of Military Justice. The convening authority will forward the record, together with his action thereon, to the Judge Advocate General for review by a board of review, in accordance with Article 66 of the Code. From the board's decision, the accused may appeal to the Court of Military Appeals on petition, or the decision may be certified to the Court by the Judge Advocate General, under the provisions of Article 67 of the Code.

The threshold showing required to raise an issue of command influence is low. More than a mere allegation or speculation is required, but the quantum of evidence required to raise unlawful command influence is merely "some evidence." United States v. Stoneman (USCAAF, 2002). An appellant's burden is to "(1) show facts which, if true, constitute unlawful command influence; (2) show that the proceedings were unfair; and (3) show that the unlawful command influence was the cause of the unfairness." United States v. Stoneman (USCAAF, 2002). Some cases, as where a commander seeks to influence with the testimony of a witness at sentencing are clearer. United States v. Gore (MNCCA, 2003) (dismissal with prejudice is an improper remedy unless, as was not the cases here, the unlawful command influence rendered the entire trial process fundamentally unfair).

Policing improper command influence can, however, be an awkward and difficult task. See United States v. Dugan (USCAAF, 2003) in which the commander held a Commander's Call at which he discussed the problem of drugs in a way and at a time that may have influence the members of the court as they were considering what sentence to recommend. The Dugan court recalled a similar case, United States v. Brice (C.M.A., 1985) in which a new trial was ordered because "members of an ongoing court-martial attended a Commandant's meeting where drug problems in the military were discussed." The Court struggles to delineate a line between proper leadership by a commander and unlawful activity:

> We do not in any way wish to be viewed as condemning the contents of the Commandant's remarks since the drug problem in the military demands command attention; nor do we feel that such remarks necessarily constitute illegal command influence. Instead, we base our decision on the confluence of subject and timing, particularly as they affect the minds - however subtly or imperceptibly--of the triers of fact[.]

In many instances, this uncertain boundary may be an invitation to commanders to venture on their own to tiptoe through a minefield.

Pre-trial publicity in the form of public comments on the guilt of an accused which threaten the impartiality of court members down the chain of command are a special problem, albeit infrequent, with command influence. Such comments can come from an accused's military superiors or in some instances even from officials in the Department of Defense. The accused's well-grounded apprehension about the possibility of a fair trial may induce resignation or acceptance of an administrative discharge and deny the opportunity to clear one's name in a court-martial proceeding.

A case in point is that of Air Force Lieutenant Kelly Flinn whose experiences are recounted in her book, Proud to Be (1997). She writes:

> [D]espite his protestations that he could not comment on how to handle [her] case because to do so would constitute an exercise of unlawful command influence, General Fogelman weighed in. "In the end, this is not an issue of adultery," he told the congressional committee. "This is an issue about an officer entrusted to fly nuclear weapons who lied." He told the Congress and everyone in the entire nation who was listening that he expected the court-martial to find me guilty. [Air Force] Secretary Widnall sat next to him silently.

A service member in Lieutenant Flinn's position has no realistic opportunity to challenge what would appear to be unlawful command influence negating the possibility of a fair trial. Command domination in these circumstances should be subject to legal restraints.

The court-martial is not an Art. III court; rather, it is a creature of the executive branch, with limited powers and no life-tenured judiciary. We will turn first to examine the three varieties of court-martial procedures: the summary court-martial, the special court-martial, and the general court-martial.

a. Summary Court–Martial

The summary court-martial is the most limited of the three different courts-martial. Its jurisdiction is limited to enlisted personnel and it

may only impose sentence of confinement for not
more than one month, hard labor without
confinement for not more than 45 days, restriction
to specified limits for not more than two months, or
forfeiture of not more than two thirds of one
month's pay. Art. 20, UCMJ.

The summary court-martial is primarily
designed to try criminal cases promptly, although
it should "thoroughly and impartially inquire into
both sides of the matter." RCM 1301(b). A brief
overview of the composition of, and procedures for,
summary courts-martial reveals that these courts
follow the inquisitorial more than the adversarial
model of criminal justice. The accused in a
summary court-martial has a right to consult with
military counsel prior to trial, but does not have a
right to be represented by a military defense
counsel at the hearing. He or she may be
represented by a civilian attorney, so long as there
is no expense to the government.

A summary court-martial consists of one
impartial commissioned officer who is the judge.
The judge has an active, not a passive, role; the
role or even presence of adversarial counsel is
minimized; and the protections accorded the
accused in civilian trials or special and general
courts-martial are substantially diminished. As the
Supreme Court has noted, "the presiding officer
acts as judge, fact finder, prosecutor, and defense
counsel." Middendorf v. Henry (S.Ct.1976). Indeed,
the summary court-martial is so similar to an Art.
15 proceeding that expanded use of nonjudicial
punishment has greatly decreased the use of
summary courts-martial.

An accused member of an armed service can refuse trial by a summary court-martial. If the accused consents to summary court-martial, the charges are read and the accused is asked to plead to each charge. If the individual pleads guilty, the court must explain the meaning and effect of the plea. The court will not accept a guilty plea unless the accused understands the meaning and effect of the plea and it believes the accused is guilty. RCM 910 and RCM 1304(2)(D). If the court doubts that the accused's guilty pleas are made voluntarily and with understanding, or if at any time during trial any matter arises that is inconsistent with a guilty plea and that cannot be resolved, the court shall enter not guilty pleas regarding the specific charges affected. RCM 1304(b)(2)(D)(iii).

During the hearing on the merits, witnesses testify under oath, the accused may cross-examine witnesses, and the trial is public. As in civilian courts, the accused may testify or remain silent. When the evidence is in, the court makes its findings and announces them. Before a sentence is imposed, however, the accused may submit further evidence, make an unsworn statement, and correct the record as to previous convictions and personal data—all with an eye towards convincing the court of extenuating and mitigating factors. The court then imposes sentence, which cannot exceed the maximum punishments set forth above.

Because the summary court-martial departs substantially from the Anglo–American norm for criminal proceedings, much attention has focused on the constitutionally of these proceedings. One issue, whether counsel is required by the Sixth

Amendment in summary courts-martial, has been definitively resolved. In Middendorf v. Henry (S.Ct.1976), the Supreme Court held that "even were the Sixth Amendment to be held applicable to court-martial proceedings, the summary court-martial provided for in these cases was not a criminal prosecution within the meaning of that Amendment." The Court then examined whether denial of counsel violated the Fifth Amendment's prohibition against the deprivation of liberty without due process of law. It drew analogies to parole revocation proceedings and juvenile proceedings, then looked at special considerations of military efficiency and discipline in deciding there was no Fifth Amendment infirmity to summary courts-martial.

The Court of Military Appeals, while recognizing Middendorf's principles, has held that a decision to accept either Art. 15 or summary court-martial disciplinary action involves due process considerations. United States v. Booker (C.M.A. 1977). The individual must be told of his right to confer with independent counsel before he chooses the method of disposition of his case. Moreover, Booker further requires that any waiver of a statutory right to trial must be in writing and must constitute a voluntary, knowing, and intelligent decision to forego trial.

b. Special Courts–Martial

The special court-martial is the intermediate of the three kinds of courts-martial. The maximum punishments available to it include a bad conduct discharge, confinement for not more than one year, hard labor without confinement for not more than three months, and forfeiture of pay not exceeding two-thirds pay per month for no more than one year.   Unlike the summary court-martial, the special court-martial has the power to try any noncapital offense punishable under the UCMJ; that is, it may try "serious" crimes.   RCM 201(f)(2)(A). The jurisdiction of the special court-martial extends over all persons subject to the UCMJ; but it is seldom used for officers.   A member of the armed services cannot refuse trial by a special court-martial.

The special court-martial consists of not less than three members and in practice always involves a military judge. The accused, after learning the military judge's identity, may request in writing a trial by the judge alone. United States v. Amos (A.C.M.R.1988); RCM 501(a)(2). Members of a special court-martial may be from the convening authority's command or made available by their commander, even if they are members of an armed force different from that of the convening authority or the accused. RCM 503(a)(3).

Commissioned or warrant officers on active duty and enlisted personnel on active duty from units other than those of the accused may serve on special courts-martial. Art. 25, UCMJ; RCM 502(a)(1). Only commissioned officers may try another commissioned officer.   When an enlisted person is on trial, he may request orally on the record or in writing that at least one-third of the special court-martial members be enlisted personnel.   This request must be honored unless eligible enlisted personnel from other units cannot be obtained because of physical conditions or military exigencies. RCM 503(a)(2). Those excused for cause from service on the court-martial are: accusers, witnesses, investigating officers, counsel for any party, arrested or confined servicemembers, those who have acted or will act in conjunction with the convening authority or a reviewing authority, or those junior to the accused in grade or rank (unless this is unavoidable).

The convening authority generally should assign the "best qualified" people (by age, education, training, experience, length of service, and judicial temperament) available to serve on the court. Art. 25(d)(2); RCM 502(a)(1). In 1991, the USCMA affirmed this standard by reversing a sentence based on the finding that a subordinate to the convening authority had "stacked" the pool of potential court-martial members. United States v. Hilow (C.M.A. 1991). The court held that since the accused had pleaded guilty, and the plea was not affected by the stacking, the accused merely needed to be resentenced. However, the court noted that the right to trial by fair and impartial members is the cornerstone of the military justice system and any deviation from this standard creates the appearance of injustice.

Procedurally, a special court-martial operates more like a traditional Anglo–American trial court than an inquisitorial proceeding. The court usually is presided over by a military judge, the trial is generally recorded verbatim, and counsel must be appointed to ensure that the accused effectively exercises his right to call witnesses, to cross-examine adverse witnesses, and to remain silent.

RCM 501(b); 502(d)(5) & (6). A special court-martial may not adjudge punishment of a bad conduct discharge, confinement for more than six months, or pay forfeitures greater than 2/3 pay per month or for more than six months, unless all three of these conditions—military judge, verbatim recording, and defense counsel—have been satisfied. ¶ 15b. MCM. RCM 201(f)(2)(B)(ii); RCM 1103(c).

c. General Courts–Martial

The general courts-martial is the highest and most powerful trial court in the military criminal law system. It has the power to try any person subject to the UCMJ for any offense punishable by the UCMJ and may impose punishments which include the death penalty, dishonorable discharge, total forfeiture of all pay and allowances, confinement, and, of course, lesser punishments. RCM 201(f)(1). Additionally, when local civil authority is displaced by military occupation, general courts-martial may try persons subject to trial by military tribunal under the law of war. See Ex parte Quirin (S.Ct.1942).

General courts-martial consist of a military judge and not less than five members, unless the accused requests trial by military judge alone. RCM 501(a)(1)(A). In death penalty cases, however, a military judge may not sit alone. Procedures for general courts-martial parallel those for special courts-martial. The only notable differences are that in general courts-martial (1) appointed trial lawyers are always certified military lawyers and (2) military judges are always

detailed. RCM 1103(b)(2)(B). Procedures for both
special and general courts-martial are examined
later in more detail at pp. 289-99.

B. JURISDICTION
OF COURTS–MARTIAL

Broadly speaking, jurisdiction is the power to try
a case. In the military criminal law system,
jurisdiction of a court-martial exists when (1) the
court is properly convened; (2) the membership of
the court accords with the UCMJ requirements; (3)
the court has the power to try the person accused;
and (4) the offense charged is triable by the court
under the UCMJ. United States v. Choy
(A.C.M.R.1992). Courts-martial must be convened
and constituted in accordance with law in order to
have jurisdiction. The membership of courts-
martial has been described above, and only brief
preliminary attention need be paid to the
convening of a court-martial. More detailed
consideration of jurisdiction over the person and
jurisdiction over the offense is required. Finally,
brief mention will be made of the relationship
between Status of Forces agreements and court-
martial jurisdiction.

1. CONVENING A COURT–MARTIAL

After a preliminary inquiry (RCM 303, MCM)
and due consideration of administrative, nonpunitive and nonjudicial alternatives, a
commander may determine that a matter is
serious enough to warrant trial by court-martial.

The commander recommends trial up the chain of command to the Convening Authority. The Convening Authority is a person authorized by the UCMJ to create a court-martial by assigning members of the court and referring charges to it. The persons so authorized vary depending upon the type of court-martial convened. Thus, general courts-martial may only be convened by very senior officers such as territory, division, separate brigade, fleet, or air command commanders, or by the President of the United States, the Secretary of Defense, the Secretary of the armed force concerned, or an officer designated by the President or Secretary. Art. 22, UCMJ. Special courts-martial may be convened by any of the above as well as by commanding officers of districts, garrisons, forts, camps, stations, air fields, wings, groups, squadrons, vessels, bases, detached units, and the like. Art. 23, UCMJ. Summary courts-martial may be convened by any of the above plus commanding officers of detached companies. Art. 24, UCMJ.

General and special courts-martial may not be convened by any commanding officer who is the accuser of the person charged; the accusing officer must refer the charges to a superior commanding officer. Art. 22(b) & 23(b), UCMJ; RCM 504(c). For a summary court-martial, the accusing officer may either convene the court-martial or refer the charges to superior authority. Art. 24(b), UCMJ, RCM 1302(b).

The process of convening a court-martial is straightforward. A convening order which designates the kind of court, place and time it is to meet and members of the court, is issued by the convening authority. Appendix 6, MCM; RCM 504(d). When appropriate, the military judge and members of the prosecution and defense are also listed. In theory, a convened court-martial can exist indefinitely; however, the usual practice is for a small number of cases to be referred to the court and for the court then to adjourn permanently. United States v. Woods (C.M.A. 1988).

2. JURISDICTION OVER PERSONS

All U.S. citizens are normally entitled to criminal trial in Art. III federal courts or state courts with full Constitutional protections. Since courts-martial operate under legal and Constitutional limitations not identical to those binding these courts, specific Constitutional and statutory authorization must be found for subjecting citizens, whether civilians or servicemembers, to the authority of military tribunals.

a. Civilians

The general rule that court-martial jurisdiction does not extend over civilians was established long ago. In Ex parte Milligan (S.Ct.1866), a civilian was tried and convicted by a military commission for conspiracy, insurrection, and other crimes relating to an alleged plan to organize a secret military force in Indiana to aid the Confederacy during the Civil War. On petition for habeas corpus, the Supreme Court held that the military commission was without jurisdiction, stating: "This court has judicial knowledge that in Indiana the Federal authority was always unopposed, and its courts always open * * * and no usage of war could sanction a military trial there for any offense whatever of a citizen in civil life, in nowise connected with the military services." The important factors which led the Court to provide the full Constitutional safeguards of civilian courts were that Milligan: (1) was a citizen of a Union state not under military siege; (2) could have been tried, convicted, and punished in civilian court for these crimes; and (3) was not connected with the military services. These rationales are the core of four "exceptions" to the general rule that military court-martial jurisdiction does not extend to civilians.

Exception 1: Civilians of belligerent nations at war with the United States are subject to court-martial trial when the United States occupies that belligerent's territory. Upon the premise that the occupying nation has a duty to maintain the security of the inhabitants while the war continues, the Supreme Court upheld court-martial jurisdiction over civilians in territories seized from Mexico, Leitensdorfer v. Webb (S.Ct.1857), and sanctioned such authority over Confederate civilians in Louisiana during the Civil War. The Grapeshot (S.Ct.1869). In both these cases, non-citizen civilians were tried by court-martial; had the accused parties been U.S. citizens, the Court presumably would have required their trials in Art. III or state courts. See Reid v. Covert (S.Ct.1957)(plurality opinion).

Exception 2: "Unlawful belligerents" who commit hostile acts without identifying themselves as belligerents may be tried by court-martial. In Ex parte Quirin (S.Ct.1942), German nationals who attempted sabotage against the U.S. during World War II were permitted to be tried by military commission. The Court said:

> The spy who secretly and without uniform passes the military lines of a belligerent in time of war, seeking to gather military information and communicate it to the enemy, or any enemy combatant who without uniform comes secretly through the lines for the purposes of waging war by destruction of life or property, are familiar examples of belligerents who are generally deemed not be entitled to the status of prisoners or war, but to be offenders against the law of war subject to trial and punishment by military tribunals.

This rationale appears broad enough to encompass trial by courts-martial of even U.S. citizens who serve as "spies" or "enemy combatants" in this country during time of war.

Exception 3: Court–Martial jurisdiction was extended over "service-connected civilians" accompanying armed forces outside the U.S. by Art. 2(a)(11) of the UCMJ shortly after World War II. Congress' reason for expanding the reach of courts-martial was an absence of federal court jurisdiction to deal with certain military-related situations. Congress observed that: (1) federal district courts had extraterritorial jurisdiction over very few offenses; (2) host nation courts seldom entertained prosecutions of criminal offenses not involving their nationals; and (3) some offenses were subject to neither United States nor host country jurisdiction (e.g., violations of U.S. military regulations by civilians).

In a series of important cases, the Supreme Court cut back this Congressional expansion of military jurisdiction. In the first, an honorably discharged former airman was arrested at his home by military authorities on charges of murder and conspiracy while in Korea and was taken back to Korea to stand trial by court-martial. United States ex rel. Toth v. Quarles (S.Ct.1955). The Court held this application of UCMJ Art. 2(a)(11) unconstitutional; ex-servicemembers could not be subjected to court-martial trial for crimes committed during their tours of service.

After Toth, ex-servicemembers were removed from military jurisdiction while civilian dependents outside the United States were still subjected to UCMJ jurisdiction under Art. 2(a)(11). This anomaly was soon eliminated. In Reid v. Covert (S.Ct.1957), the Supreme Court held that Mrs. Covert, who killed her Air Force sergeant husband at an air base in England, could not be tried by military authorities, saying "we reject the idea that when the United States acts against citizens abroad it can do so free of the Bill of Rights." The Court emphasized that a similar crime on an air base in the United States would have been tried in an Art. III court. Significantly, the Court reached this conclusion despite the fact that no U.S. district court had extraterritorial jurisdiction over Mrs. Covert.

Subsequent Supreme Court cases have eliminated most of what arguably remained of Art.

2(a)(11) jurisdiction over civilians in peacetime. Kinsella v. United States ex rel. Singleton (S.Ct.1960) applied Reid to a case involving a dependent charged with a noncapital offense. Grisham v. Hagan (S.Ct.1960), and McElroy v. United States ex rel. Guagliardo (S.Ct.1960), held that military tribunals have no jurisdiction over civilian employees of the military, whether for capital or non-capital offenses. The Court therefore has narrowly confined court-martial jurisdiction to those who are within the "land or naval forces," i.e., no civilians whatsoever.

Exception 4: The sole extant branch of UCMJ jurisdiction over civilians appears to be based on the "war power" rather than the "land and naval forces power" of Art. I, § 8. The grant of this jurisdiction, Art. 2(a)(10), UCMJ, provides that "in time of war persons serving with or accompanying an armed force in the field" are subject to court-martial and military law.

"In time of war" has received little interpretation under Art. 2(a)(10). However, one court has held that, absent a Congressional declaration of war, the military lacks jurisdiction to try civilian employees of military contractors. United States v. Averette (C.M.A. 1970). "In the field" is not determined by the locality of the military force, but by the activity in which it is engaged. There must be military operations with a view toward actual wartime activity. For example, training operations preliminary to actual wartime combat are "in the field," Hines v. Mikell (4th Cir.1919), as are operations of a merchant ship transporting troops and supplies to a battle zone. McCune v. Kilpatrick (E.D.Va.1943).

One may be "accompanying" an armed force though not directly employed by the military. So long as the individual is moving with a military operation or has activities dependent upon and not merely incidental to the armed force's activities. For example, a person serving on a merchant ship carrying troops or supplies has been held to be accompanying the military. Perlstein v. United States (3d Cir.1945). "Accompanying" has been interpreted broader than "serving with": a civilian who no longer serves with the military but has continued to remain closely affiliated with a military community is subject to court-martial jurisdiction. Id.

b. Military Persons

Beginning with the first Article of War on June 30, 1775, the United States has always provided for a military justice system to discipline members of its armed forces. In Dynes v. Hoover (S.Ct.1857), the Supreme Court acknowledged Congress' power to provide for trial and punishment of military offenses. The source of this power is Art. I, § 8, authorizing Congress to make rules for the governing of the land and naval forces.

The jurisdiction of a court-martial depends upon the "military status" of the accused. In Solorio v. United States (S.Ct.1987), the Court held that "the proper exercise of court-martial jurisdiction over an offense [depends] on one factor: the military status of the accused." The Court rejected earlier decisions such as O'Callahan v. Parker (S.Ct. 1969) requiring that the crime also be "service connected" and held that a court-martial was proper even though the offenses, sexual abuses of two minors, were committed off-base in the accused's privately owned home.

The difficulty is in ascertaining an accused person's status: is the accused in the court-martial proceeding a person who can be regarded as falling within the term "land and naval forces?" Kinsella v. United States ex rel. Singleton (S.Ct.1960). Though there is no litmus test of military status, some indicia include accepting a position in writing, swearing to the oath of service, wearing a uniform, performing military duties, being paid according to rank, and being entitled to a pension. Ex parte Reed (S.Ct.1879); Art. 2(c), UCMJ.

Few categorization problems have arisen with respect to persons currently serving full-time active military duty. Moreover, while at their service academies cadets and midshipmen are subject to the jurisdiction of military tribunals. The problems of application focus on (1) entry into the military, (2) persons performing part-time military service, and (3) exit from the military.

(1) Entry into the Military

Most "time of entry" problems occur in connection with draftees and enlisted personnel. Draftees, unlike civilians, are technically subject to military jurisdiction. Arver v. United States (S.Ct.1918). However, because Congress imposes civil penalties on persons who are drafted and refuse induction, the UCMJ defers jurisdiction until the time of actual induction. Art. 2(a)(1),

UCMJ. Induction traditionally occurs when the oath is taken, but problems arise when draftees later claim not to have taken the oath. Today, the "step forward" made by the draftee after the oath communicates to witnesses his acceptance of military jurisdiction. Corrigan v. Secretary of Army (9th Cir.1954). Subsequent conduct consistent with the status of a soldier can remedy an earlier omission of the "step forward." Brown v. Resor (5th Cir.1969).

Jurisdiction over enlisted servicemembers attaches when a valid enlistment contract is signed. United States v. Williams (S.Ct.1937). However, several decisions rejecting military jurisdiction over persons who alleged enlistment under fraud or duress were overruled by Art. 2(b), UCMJ, which confers jurisdiction over "any person who has the capacity to understand the significance of enlisting."

(2) Part–Time Servicemembers

The status of persons performing part-time military service has been considered by courts in several contexts. For example, ROTC students have been held not subject to court-martial jurisdiction (because they are given a deferment from induction) even though service academy members may be tried by military tribunals. Allison v. United States (6th Cir.1970). Members of reserve components lawfully called to active duty for an initial training period or for delinquency in fulfilling inactive duty requirements may be subjected to court-martial. Art. 2(a)1, UCMJ.

Inactive reservists subject to proceedings under Art. 15 or 39 may be ordered to active duty involuntarily for investigation, court-martial, or nonjudicial Art. 15 punishment only if the offense was committed while the member was on active duty or inactive-duty for training (IDT). United States v. Ernest (C.M.A. 1991), Art. 2(d)(2). The general courts-martial convening authority or the Secretary of the particular armed force may order a reservist to active duty. Art. 2(d)(4), UCMJ. Additionally, reservists on IDT are subject to court-martial jurisdiction. Art. 2(a)(3), UCMJ.

Murphy v. Garrett (W.D.Pa.1990) noted Congress' expression of the importance of extending military jurisdiction over reservists. Thus, a reservist challenging military jurisdiction must first exhaust his military remedies before litigating in federal district court. On remand, the Court of Military Appeals held that there is jurisdiction to require a reservist to report for active duty to stand trial by court-martial. Murphy v. Garrett (C.M.A. 1990). In interpreting the term "active duty" in Art. 2(d)(2)(A), the court held: "[t]he fact that his regular service was terminated by the issuance of an Honorable Discharge and that his reserve service commences upon the simultaneous issuance of a new commission does not divest his armed force of jurisdiction."

Art. 3(d), UCMJ, now allows jurisdiction over a member of a reserve component, despite termination of a period of active duty or IDT, for an offense committed during that period of active duty or IDT. RCM 204 provides more specific guidance regarding jurisdiction over reservists. A reserve member must be on active duty before any arraignment at a general or special court-martial. A reservist so ordered to active duty may be kept in that status to serve any adjudged confinement or other restriction on liberty. However, that member may not be retained on active duty after service of the confinement or other restriction. All punishment remaining unserved when the member is released from active duty may be carried over to subsequent periods of IDT or active duty. RCM 204(b)(1). In contrast, a reservist may be tried by summary court-martial either while on active duty or IDT. But a summary court-martial conducted during IDT may be held only during normal periods of such training, and the accused may not be held beyond such training periods for trial or service of punishment. Moreover, a member of a reserve component at the time disciplinary action is initiated, who is alleged to have committed an offense while on active duty or IDT, is subject to court-martial jurisdiction regardless of any change between active and reserve service.

(3) Former Servicemembers

There is no jurisdiction over one whose military status has been completely terminated before commission of an offense. RCM 204(d). However, several exceptions exist to the general rule that court-martial jurisdiction over servicemembers ceases upon termination of military status.

First, jurisdiction extends to all offenses committed during the incarceration of a person who is in the custody of the military serving a sentence imposed by court-martial, even though the offense was committed after the prisoner's status as a servicemember ended. Kahn v. Anderson (S.Ct.1921).

Second, jurisdiction which attaches by apprehension, arrest, confinement or filing of charges continues in effect even after the servicemember's status later terminates. Messina v. Commanding Officer (S.D.Cal.1972).

Third, if military status terminates but there is "immediate" re-enlistment, the short gap between periods of military status does not sever military ties and jurisdiction remains over offenses committed on a previous tour of duty. United States v. Gallagher (C.M.A. 1957).

Fourth, retired members of regular armed forces components who are entitled to receive pay technically remain in the military service and may be tried by court-martial. United States v. Tyler (S.Ct.1881). However, this jurisdiction was limited to permit court-martial dismissal but not confinement of retired officers. Hooper v. United States (Ct.Cl.1964).

Finally, jurisdiction over a servicemember exists until the member's military status is terminated by formal discharge, regardless of any delay (even if unreasonable) by the government in discharging that person at the end of an enlistment. United States v. Poole (C.M.A. 1990).

3. JURISDICTION OVER OFFENSES

The law concerning the appropriate type of court-martial is simple at both ends but complex in the middle. Just as summary courts-martial may only try enlisted personnel, they are also limited to trial of relatively minor offenses. General courts-martial, at the other extreme, may try not only any person subject to the UCMJ, but any offense made punishable by the Code. The sole limitation on this broad jurisdiction is that a general court-martial composed of a military judge alone may not try capital cases.

Between these extremes is the special court-martial, which may try any non-capital offense punishable by the Code. What constitutes a "non-capital offense" is complicated because: (1) some offenses are capital only if committed "in time of war" (e.g., desertion, assaulting or willfully disobeying a superior commissioned officer, improperly using a countersign, spying, or misbehaving as a sentinel); (2) the President has the power, as yet unexercised, to limit punishments to less than death; (3) the convening authority may direct that the case be treated as non-capital; and (4) a sentence previously imposed, which is less than death, may not be increased to death upon retrial.

Of course, trial by court-martial is not required even if court-martial jurisdiction exists. Courts-martial have exclusive jurisdiction over purely military offenses. RCM 201(d)(1). See Florida v. Simanonok (11th Cir.1988). But, where an act violates both military and local criminal law, foreign or domestic, the accused may be tried by court-martial or by the appropriate civilian tribunal. RCM 201(d)(2). In that case, the determination of which tribunal will exercise jurisdiction rests with the nation, state, or agency concerned—it is not a right of the accused. RCM 201(d)(3). However, a court-martial proceeding will be dismissed if the accused has previously been tried by a federal civilian court for the same offense. RCM 907(b)(2)(C)(i). However, the accused may be tried by both a court-martial and a *state* civilian court for the same offense. This authority is rarely exercised and service regulations generally require approval of the service secretary to try an accused for an offense previously tried by a state court.

Under the UCMJ, military authorities, in their discretion, "may" deliver upon request a member of the armed forces accused of an offense against civilian authority to the civilian authorities for trial. Art. 14(a), UCMJ. But when such delivery interrupts the execution of the court-martial sentence, the offender shall be returned to military custody for the completion of his sentence upon request of the proper military authority. Art. 14(b), UCMJ. In practice, however, crimes committed in the civilian community by service personnel most likely will be investigated and prosecuted through a cooperative effort between military and civilian authorities.

4. STATUS OF FORCES AGREEMENTS AND COURT–MARTIAL JURISDICTION

Under international law, a state has jurisdiction over persons and events occurring within its borders. When members of an American armed service are in a foreign country in other than hostile circumstances, as for example when they are based or stationed abroad, they would be subject only to the domestic law of the foreign state unless treaties or other international agreements between the United States (the sending state or country in this example) and the foreign state (the host or receiving country) provide otherwise. Such an agreement is called a Status of Forces Agreement (SOFA). A SOFA is a pact between nations specifying which nation has jurisdiction in particular situations. For example, when a United States servicemember commits an offense within a foreign country, should the accused be tried in a court-martial or in a court of the host country? Because such questions have great potential for international dispute, it is not surprising that countries have tried to resolve them in advance of actual cases.

One typical and important SOFA is the one between all the parties to the North Atlantic Treaty. In the general provisions of this SOFA, Art. VII recites that the United States retains court-martial jurisdiction over all offenses committed by persons subject to such jurisdiction and that the host country has jurisdiction over all armed servicemembers, civilian components, and dependents with respect to offenses committed in the host country punishable by its laws. When one contracting nation does not have laws which punish a certain offense, the other gets exclusive jurisdiction over the accused. More important are the rules laid down for jurisdiction where the laws of both countries apply: (1) the United States gets primary jurisdiction when its personnel harm United States property or its personnel, or if the offense is duty-related; and (2) the host nation has primary jurisdiction in all other cases. Should the nation having primary jurisdiction decide not to prosecute, it is obligated to notify the other nation as soon as practicable.

SOFAs are not purely jurisdictional; they also provide some guarantees to accused persons. For example, when an accused has been tried by one nation, the other nation cannot retry him for the same offense. However, the United States military authorities may bring disciplinary charges against a servicemember even if he is tried by the other nation. Where trial is by the host nation, the accused is guaranteed a speedy trial, pretrial notice of the charges, the right to confront witnesses, compulsory process, legal representation, an interpreter, and the right to have a United States representative present at trial. There is no right to trial by jury.

C. THE CRIMINAL PROCESS

The military criminal justice system involves procedures for dealing with an accused which differ somewhat from civilian criminal law procedures. The criminal process, which extends from the time of initial restrictions upon the freedom of the accused through trial by court-martial, is the heart of the military criminal justice system.

1. RESTRICTIONS ON FREEDOM

An accused may be subjected to three types of pre-trial restrictions that are unique to military law. In increasing order of severity, they are called arrest (sometimes called restriction), apprehension, and confinement.

Arrest is a term of art in military law: it is simply an order, oral or written, issued by a competent authority which directs the accused to remain within certain specified limits. United States v. Harris (C.M.A. 1989); Art. 9(a), UCMJ; RCM 304(a)(3). Arrest is a moral and legal restriction, not a physical restraint; it may issue only upon probable cause and personal knowledge or inquiry of the arresting person. Art. 9(d), UCMJ; RCM 304(c). Enlisted members may be arrested by any commissioned officer or by delegates of commanding officers. Art. 9(b), UCMJ; RCM 304(b)(2) & (3). Officers may only be arrested by the commanding officer with authority over the accused. Art. 9(c), UCMJ; RCM 304(b)(1).

Apprehension is the military counterpart to civilian arrest, for it involves "the taking of a person into custody." United States v. Harris (C.M.A. 1989). Art. 7(a), UCMJ; RCM 302(a)(1). Apprehension involves restraint on the accused's personal freedom until he is handed over to the proper authorities, thus it goes beyond arrest by imposing physical restraint. Apprehension may be made by military police when in the exercise of their duties, provided there is probable cause to believe an offense has been committed by the accused. Art. 7(b), UCMJ; RCM 302(b) & (c). In addition, officers may apprehend persons to control quarrels and disorders. Art. 7(c), UCMJ; RCM 302(c). Though it is generally inappropriate for noncommissioned officers to apprehend warrant officers or commissioned officers, this may be done if so directed by a commissioned officer to prevent disgrace to the service or escape of a serious offender. RCM 302(b)(2).

Confinement is the most severe pre-trial restriction on the accused's freedom in that it involves incarceration or placement of a guard over the accused. Art. 9(a), UCMJ; RCM 305(a). The confining authority, whose power to confine is defined in the same manner as the power to arrest discussed above, gives written notice to the correction officer of the name and grade of the accused along with the offense allegedly committed. Within 24 hours, the correction officer transmits this information and the name of the person ordering confinement to the commanding officer of the accused. Art. 11(b), UCMJ; RCM 305(h)1. Following the standard that the accused arrested without a warrant must be given a prompt judicial determination (within 48 hours) of probable cause for his arrest, the U.S.C.A.A.F. has held that a non-judicial, neutral, commanding officer may constitutionally make a probable cause determination and choose to extend pretrial confinement. Gerstein v. Pugh (S.Ct.1975); United

States v. McLaughlin (A.C.M.R.1988). A servicemember in confinement may request a military counsel, which must be provided within 72 hours. RCM 305(f). Military magistrates may be appointed to review pretrial confinement. See AR 27–10, ch. 9.

2. INITIATING AND PROCESSING CHARGES

Charges are initiated when information is brought to the attention of military authorities concerning an offense suspected to have been committed by a person subject to the UCMJ. Charges are written and may be made only by one subject to the Code. Art. 30(a), UCMJ. Charges are usually made directly to the commanding officer authorized to impose Art. 15 punishment; if not, charges are soon brought to that person's attention.

The commander, after receiving a charge, has broad discretion concerning its disposition. First, the commander may order a preliminary inquiry. This is an informal investigation of the charges which involves little more than interviewing witnesses, collecting, marking, and securing physical evidence, and developing information sufficient to dispose of the charges intelligently. Second, the commander may dismiss trivial charges or charges unsupported by the evidence. Third, he or she may impose Art. 15 nonjudicial punishment unless his superiors have directed otherwise. Fourth, the commander may prefer charges by swearing to the truth of the charge.

Finally, the commander may forward charges too serious for Art. 15 disposition or administrative elimination to the officer exercising summary court-martial jurisdiction over the accused. When this is done, the accused must be informed of the charges and the summary court-martial officer should be provided with a summary of the evidence and the commander's recommendation for disposition. The summary court-martial commander may make any of the dispositions open to the Art. 15 commander; additionally, he or she may refer the charge for trial by summary court-martial, or forward the charge with a recommendation for special, or general court-martial, depending on the severity of the offense.

3. FORMAL INVESTIGATION

Before a charge may be referred to a general court-martial for trial, a formal Art. 32 investigation is required. This investigation has two purposes. First, it screens charges prior to trial by a general court-martial, impartially weighing the facts to determine whether the case should be brought to trial. United States v. Bramel (A.C.M.R.1990). In this respect, it parallels indictment by grand jury in the civilian trial process. However, this investigation need not follow grand jury procedures, since the Fifth Amendment exempts members of the Armed Services from the Constitutional requirement of indictment. Second, it provides the defense with some discovery and gives the defendant an opportunity for an early exoneration from charges.

In this sense, it bears some resemblance to a civilian preliminary examination.

The Art. 32 investigation commences when the commander appoints an investigating officer, who need not be an attorney. Because the Art. 32 investigation is required to be "thorough and impartial," an accuser may not serve as the investigating officer. United States v. Cunningham (C.M.A. 1961).

At the conclusion of the investigation, the investigating officer prepares a written report to the convening authority. This report includes a summary of testimony taken, other evidence, a statement concerning the likely mental state of the accused, a statement concerning availability of witnesses, and a recommendation of whether or not the accused should be tried.

While the Art. 32 investigation is not a trial, it is such a crucial pretrial procedure that a body of precedent has developed concerning the rights of one called before an investigating officer. The accused is entitled to representation by counsel; Art. 32(b), UCMJ. The investigating officer must forward any request for military counsel to the commander who directed the investigation. RCM 405(d)(2)(B). Alternatively upon request, the accused must be given a reasonable time to obtain civilian counsel. RCM 405(d)(2)(C). During the investigation, the accused may cross-examine witnesses and testimony must be under oath. However, because the investigation is advisory strict rules of evidence are not applied. Article 32 hearings are normally open to the press and public unless, on a case-by-case basis, "cause shown outweighs the value of openness." ABC, Inc. v. Powell (USCAAF 1997).

4. PREPARATION FOR TRIAL

The convening authority is the initial moving force in the pretrial stages of the court-martial. Appointment of the court-martial members, the military equivalent to jurors, is done by the convening authority.

Immediately after the convening authority's action, trial and defense counsel are detailed by their respective superiors. In both general and special courts-martial, counsel must be qualified attorneys. Additionally, counsel must be certified as competent to perform such duties in a general court-martial. For further discussion of the right to counsel in the military, see pages 223–28.

Following counsel's appointment, responsibility shifts from the convening authority to the attorneys. Defense counsel should consult with the accused, and should arrange for the attendance of witnesses at trial. Some questions have arisen, however, concerning a conflict between UCMJ Art. 46, giving both parties equal opportunity to obtain witnesses, and RCM 703(c)(2), requiring defense counsel to submit requests for witnesses to the prosecution for concurrence or resolution by the military judge. United States v. Carpenter (C.M.A. 1976). Service regulations may provide for a trial defense service to provide counsel independent of local commanders to represent service members before courts-martial, administrative boards, and other proceedings. See AR 27–10, ch. 6.

Generally, the rules applicable to subpoenaing witnesses in civilian trials also apply in courts-martial. However, the military defendant need not be indigent in order to have the costs of obtaining witnesses borne by the government, where the expected testimony would raise doubts concerning the defendant's guilt. In United States v. Sweeney (C.M.A. 1964), the court decided that character witnesses (two of defendant's former superior officers) should be subpoenaed at government expense. Since the character of an alleged co-conspirator testifying under immunity was impeached, the core of Sweeney's defense was his own good character and reputation. The court essentially balanced the equities, looking at the relevance of the testimony, the responsibilities of the witnesses sought, and the lack of readily available alternative sources of similar testimony.

Pretrial discovery is considerably more liberal in the military than in state and federal criminal proceedings. Generally, even evidence not required to be produced will be disclosed. It is also less formal than in civilian processes. Information is often obtained upon request, without resort to court processes. The basic sources for the rules of discovery in military proceedings are the MCM, the Jencks Act, and the Federal Rules of Criminal Procedure.

Under a 1991 modification of the MCM, a copy of the charge sheet, a list of prospective witnesses, and a list of any rebuttal witnesses to an "innocent ingestion" defense in a drug offense case is served upon the defense. Likewise, the defense is required to notify the prosecution of the name of all defense witnesses, provide sworn or written statements these witnesses may have made, and notify the prosecution if it intends to raise the defense of alibi, innocent ingestion, or lack of mental responsibility. RCM 701(a)(1) & (3) & (b)(1) & (2). The papers accompanying the charge sheet, including the report of the Art. 32 investigation, are also available to the defense.

Upon request, the defense may inspect evidentiary material in the hands of the military authorities relevant to the defense's preparation or which trial counsel intends to use as evidence. RCM 701(a)(2). Additionally, when a general court-martial is recommended, defense counsel is supplied with a copy of the substance of all testimony taken at the Art. 32 investigation. Evidence favorable to the accused may not be consciously suppressed by trial counsel. RCM 701(a)(6). This codifies and expands the civilian criminal procedure rule of Brady v. Maryland (S.Ct.1963), which is based upon the due process clause of the Fifth Amendment.

Trial counsel also is required to notify the defense of any records of prior convictions of the accused of which trial counsel is aware and plans to offer for any purpose. RCM 701(a)(4). Finally, upon request, the defense may inspect any information that trial counsel will present at presentencing proceedings as well as notify the defense of the witnesses to be called at those proceedings. RCM 701(a)(5).

The Jencks Act, 18 U.S.C.A. § 3500, requires production at trial of pre-trial statements of government witnesses. Such statements may substantially assist defense counsel on cross examination. In United States v. Albo (C.M.A. 1972), the Jencks Act was held applicable to courts-martial.

To the extent they are not displaced by the UCMJ or inconsistent with military justice, the Federal Rules of Criminal Procedure apply in courts-martial proceedings. For example, statements of the defendant in the government's possession or control may be inspected, copied, or photographed by defense counsel. Fed.R.Crim.P. 16(a)(1)(A). Defense counsel is also entitled to a copy of the defendant's prior criminal record and the results of physical or mental examinations which are material to the defense or intended for use by the government as evidence. Fed.R.Crim.P. 16(a)(1)(B), (C), and (D). RCM 701(a)(2)(B) & (4).

As in civilian criminal cases, there are some limitations on discovery in courts-martial proceedings. The most important limitations, contained in Military Rules of Evidence §§ 501–506, and 513, relate to privileged information. Military secrets, state secrets, and classified material are not discoverable. Neither are attorney work product or confidential communications between husband and wife, penitent and clergy, attorney and client, and, with some exceptions, psychotherapist and patient. All these limitations, of course, may be waived. Although confidential psychotherapist-patient communications are largely protected, there is no physician-patient privilege for military medical records.

5. SPEEDY TRIAL

The Sixth Amendment to the Constitution guarantees that "the accused shall enjoy the right to a speedy trial." In Federal courts, this right has been implemented by the Speedy Trial Act, 18 U.S.C.A. § 3161, which establishes time periods for indictment and trial, sets out delays excluded from the computation, and specifies sanctions for impermissible delay.

The Sixth Amendment guarantee to a speedy trial may not be expressly applicable to courts-martial, and the Speedy Trial Act does not apply to military tribunals. However, both the UCMJ and the MCM contain provisions which guarantee speedy disposition of criminal charges and the military appellate courts have further interpreted these provisions. The UCMJ contains three provisions concerning speedy trial. Art. 10 requires that immediate steps be taken to inform any person placed in arrest or confinement of the charges and that the charges be promptly tried or dismissed. Art. 33 states that when an accused faces a general court-martial, the charges and investigative documents generally should be forwarded to the convening authority within eight days of the accused's arrest or confinement. Art. 98, a seldom-used provision, makes causing "unnecessary delay" in disposition of a criminal case an offense against the UCMJ. An accused is entitled to trial within 120 days after notice to the accused of referral of charges, the imposition of restraint, or a reservist's entry into active duty to stand trial by court-martial, whichever occurs first. RCM 707(a), 905(c)(2)(B), and 907(b)(2)(A).

Before a 1991 change to the MCM, an accused held in pretrial confinement must have been tried within 90 days of confinement or violate the military court standards for speedy trial. United States v. Burton (C.M.A. 1971), United States v. Driver (C.M.A. 1974). The 1991 change eliminated the 90 day requirement and extended it to 120 days. The executive order warned, however, that unless the U.S.C.A.A.F. choose to reexamine the Burton decision, one might fully comply with the change to 707(d), yet fail to satisfy Burton. This concern was addressed in United States v. Kossman (C.M.A. 1993), in which the U.S.C.M.A. explicitly overturned Burton and replaced it with a system that vests military judges with broad powers of discretion to determine if the speedy trial requirement has been satisfied. The court saw nothing in Art. 10 that suggested a speedy trial motion could not succeed under either a 90 or 120-day limit if the government was seen to be dragging its feet. Likewise, the court recognized the peculiar difficulties experienced in the worldwide military justice system and that delays, not found in civilian practice, are possible and necessary. Thus, "If [the] decision today vests military judges with a degree of discretion, so be it. Judges who can decide difficult questions such as whether a confession was voluntary * * * can readily determine whether the government has been foot dragging on a particular case, under the circumstances then and there prevailing." It appears from the language of Kossman that while the 120-day limit is a good measuring device, it is not dispositive. Good faith motions may be made prior to that time, and requests for extensions may also be granted depending upon the particular circumstances.

Military court interpretations of Art. 10 have imposed more rigorous speedy trial requirements than the Sixth Amendment demands. United States v. Powell (C.M.A. 1975). These decisions have required more than the normal Sixth Amendment balancing of (1) length of delay, (2) reasons for delay, (3) timely assertion of speedy trial right, and (4) prejudice to the accused. Barker v. Wingo (S.Ct.1972). Moreover, military law protects the defendant against government delays in pressing charges, while the Sixth Amendment does not protect an accused against pre-indictment government delays. United States v. Marion (S.Ct.1971). In the military, government accountability for expediting the process begins with pretrial restraint or preferral of charges, whichever occurs first. RCM 707; United States v. Ward (C.M.A. 1975). However, civilian restraint of the accused for non-military offenses is not charged against the government.

Procedurally, the right to a speedy trial is implemented by the defendant and defense counsel. There is no automatic entitlement to expeditious process; the defendant must raise the issue. Normally, the issue is raised upon a motion to dismiss under RCM 907 (b)(2)(A). After a hearing on the motion, the judge makes a finding of fact and conclusions of law on the speedy trial issue.

The 2000 Edition of the Manual for Courts-Martial, RCM 707(c) reflects substantial changes and simplifications of the complex provisions concerning extensions of time for trial and excludable delays that have developed since the last edition of this book. Rather than setting forth extensive and incomplete rules on excludable delays, new 707(c) specifies automatic excludable delays only for appellate stays or when the accused is in the custody of the Attorney General for hospitalization due to incompetence or otherwise. Intentionally sweeping language then provides that "All other pretrial delays approved by a military judge or the convening authority shall be similarly excluded." In other words, requests for pretrial delay, with supporting reasons, must be brought to the military judge or convening authority for a decision, apparently in advance of the expiration of the 120-day period. See U.S. v. Thompson (U.S.C.A.A.F. 1997) (intent of rule is to eliminate after-the-fact determinations whether various delays are excludable).

Counsel for the accused, when moving for speedy trial relief, "should provide the court with a chronology detailing the processing of the case." RCM 707(c)(2). The remedy for the prosecution's failure to afford a speedy trial is dismissal of the charges. RCM 707(d). If there is a deprivation of the accused's constitutional right to a speedy trial, the dismissal will be with prejudice. If there has been a delay beyond that contemplated by Rule 707, but without a constitutional violation, the court may consider these factors in deciding whether to dismiss with or without prejudice: "the seriousness of the offense; the facts and circumstances of the case that lead to dismissal; the impact of a reprosecution on the administration of justice; and any prejudice to the accused resulting from the denial of a speedy trial."

6. PLEAS TO THE CHARGES AND PRETRIAL PLEA BARGAINING

The accused has three basic choices of pleas: guilty, not guilty, or guilty of a lesser offense. Pleas are first entered at arraignment but may be received up until the time of trial. Arraignment is a watershed because without consent of the accused no additional major alterations to the charges may be added following arraignment. RCM 601(e)(2); 603(d). Additionally, after arraignment, the accused can be tried even though absent from trial. RCM 804(b).

If the accused introduces a "not guilty" plea, all matters are placed in issue and the prosecution at trial must prove the accused's guilt beyond a reasonable doubt. A "guilty" plea admits every element of the crime specified, and if accepted is equivalent to a conviction. A "guilty of a lesser offense" plea generally occurs as a result of a pretrial agreement entered into between the convening authority and the accused.

If the accused makes an irregular plea or no plea at all, a plea of not guilty is entered and the court proceeds on that basis. Art. 45(a), UCMJ; RCM 910(b). Moreover, if the accused pleads guilty and later raises matters inconsistent with a guilty plea, or if it appears that the accused improvidently or through lack of understanding entered the guilty plea, the court will enter a plea of not guilty. Art. 45(a), UCMJ; RCM 910(h)(2). At any time up to announcement of the sentence, a guilty plea may be withdrawn by the accused. RCM 910(h)(1). Finally, military law does not permit any pleas of guilty to a charge for which the death penalty may be adjudged. Art. 45(b), UCMJ; RCM 910(a)(1).

Plea bargaining is "an essential component of the administration of justice," in military as well as civilian criminal cases. Santobello v. New York (S.Ct.1971). However, plea bargaining was approved of by military courts long before the Santobello decision. See United States v. Smith (John M.)(A.B.R. 1954). In the military, all pretrial plea bargaining agreements must be in writing and signed by the accused, defense counsel, and the convening authority. RCM 705(d)(2) and (3). Plea bargains are concluded with the convening authority, not the judge (as in civilian trials). Either side may initiate plea negotiations and propose terms. Before signing, defense counsel should be satisfied that the accused, if tried, would probably be found guilty. In addition, any pretrial agreement between the convening authority and the accused will be carefully scrutinized before being accepted by the military judge in lieu of a full-fledged trial of the facts. RCM 910(f). Further protection against abuse of the plea bargaining process in the military is the so-called "providency inquiry," set out in RCM 910(c)–(f) and most fully articulated in United States v. Care (C.M.A. 1969):

* * * the record of trial * * * must reflect not only
that the elements of each offense charged have
been explained to the accused but also that the
military trial judge or the president [of the court]
has questioned the accused about what he did or
did not do, and what he intended (where this is
pertinent), to make clear the basis for a
determination by military trial judge or
president whether the acts or the omissions of
the accused constitute the offense or offenses to
which he is pleading guilty * * * The record must
also demonstrate the military trial judge or
president personally addressed the accused,
advised him that his plea waives his right to a
trial of the facts by a court-martial, and his right
to be confronted by the witnesses against him * *
* .

This inquiry is conducted by the military judge
out of the presence of the court, and the judge may
immediately enter a finding of guilty after
accepting a plea of guilty. RCM 910(g). If the plea
is to a lesser offense, the judge should not enter a
finding until the evidence is received on the lesser
offense.

The common errors committed during providency
inquiries include: failure to inform the accused
that his constitutional rights are waived by a
guilty plea; misunderstanding by the accused
concerning the maximum sentence; failure to list
the elements of the offense to which the accused
pleads guilty; and failure to develop a factual basis
for the plea through responses of the accused to
questions by the judge. Moreover, the trial judge
dealing with such a plea should inquire carefully

into the terms and conditions of any pretrial agreement, "assuring on the record that an accused understands the meaning and effect of each condition as well as the sentence limitations imposed." United States v. Elmore (C.M.A. 1976). The judge is authorized to strike any conditions in the agreement which violate "appellate case law, public policy, or the trial judge's own notions of fundamental fairness." Id.

Problems arise when the judge too readily accepts or rejects the plea bargain. Acceptance of the sentencing terms of a pretrial agreement, for example, should not be done until the judge first announces sentence based on the rest of the plea following a providency inquiry. RCM 910(f)(3). On the other hand, if the judge refuses to accept the plea of guilty, the accused may seek to have the judge who has seen the plea recused from presiding over the trial. However, the courts which have considered such recusal motions have consistently rejected them.

7. TRIAL

There are relatively few important procedural differences between civilian and military trials, and some of the obvious ones are indicative of form rather than substance.   For example, courts-martial are conducted by attorneys who are uniformed officers of the armed services, and the court-martial members also are uniformed armed services members.

The Sixth Amendment right to a "public trial" applies to courts-martial, even in security-sensitive cases. United States v. Grunden (C.M.A. 1977). Military regulations provide that "courts-martial shall be open to the public." RCM 806(a). While exceptions are made for security requirements or "other good cause," this proviso has been narrowly construed to avoid constitutional problems. For example, the defendant in a case involving a charge of obscene language might successfully argue that members of the press could not be excluded from his trial.

a. The Military Jury System

There is no set number of members to a court-martial so long as the statutory minimum, discussed above in section A.3, is met. For whatever reason, it is also more common in military than civilian practice to try criminal cases before the military judge alone upon request of the accused than it is to have a judge-only civilian criminal trial.

In courts-martial, unanimous verdicts are not required except in death penalty cases, and no one may be sentenced to life imprisonment or confinement for more than ten years except by a three-fourths vote. A finding of guilty generally requires only a two-thirds vote, and if less than two-thirds of the jurors vote to convict, an acquittal will be entered. A tie vote on the accused's sanity is a determination against the accused. A tie vote on any other question is a determination in favor of the accused. Art. 52(b), UCMJ, RCM 1006(d)(4).

In military practice, the convening authority is authorized to select for the jury those members of the armed forces who are "best qualified for the duty by reason of age, education, training, experience, length of service, and judicial temperament." Art. 25(d)(2), UCMJ; RCM 502(a)(1). Though there has been some experimentation in the military with random jury selection techniques similar to civilian "jury wheels," court-martial members generally do not represent a "fair cross-section" of the military community. In addition, either trial or defense counsel's voir dire may challenge an unlimited number of court members for "cause," which includes prior contact with the case as accuser, witness, counsel, or investigating officer, as well as rigidity of opinions concerning guilt or penalty, and racial or other class prejudice. The basic test is that excusing the members would be appropriate "in the interest of having the trial and subsequent proceedings free from substantial doubt as to legality, fairness, and impartiality." RCM 912(f)(1)(N). A similar standard is applied in the recusal of a military judge.

b. Trial Procedures

The presiding officer sets the time and place for trial. After all court personnel have assembled but before the court is called to order, the presiding officer determines whether (1) the convening order is valid; (2) a quorum is present; (3) the accused is present; and (4) counsel are qualified. Unless arraigned at a previous Art. 39(a) session, the accused is informed of the charges and asked to plea. If a guilty plea is made, the court must ascertain whether the accused understands the ramifications of a guilty plea and the alternatives.

The members of the court are then seated
according to rank, the court is called to order, and
the court is sworn in. Witnesses can be excluded
from the courtroom at the request of the
prosecution or defense, or the military judge may
order exclusion sua sponte. MRE 615. The charge
is read, and members of the court are challenged, if
at all, by trial counsel and then defense counsel.
Each of the challenges must be race neutral and
adhere to the untainted analysis approach. United
States v. Greene (C.M.A. 1993). There are an
unlimited number of challenges for cause, and one
peremptory challenge for each party. Art. 41,
UCMJ; RCM 912(f)-(g). If a military judge is
present, he determines challenges for cause; if not,
then a simple majority vote of the members of the
court decides challenges for cause. RCM 912(f)(3),
(h). In United States v. White (CMA 1993) the
U.S.C.M.A. ruled that judges should grant
challenges for cause liberally, and appellate courts
should not overrule lower court challenge
determinations.

The court members are provided a copy of the
charges and are informed of the plea made to each
charge. If the plea is "not guilty," counsel may
make an opening statement. Following the opening
statement, if any, the evidence is presented.
Ordinarily, the prosecution's witnesses are
examined first, followed by the defense witnesses,
then by each side's rebuttal witnesses. RCM 913.

At the conclusion of the presentation of evidence,
the prosecution and then the defense counsel may
present their arguments. RCM 919. Occasionally,
these arguments raise issues, for example, whether

prosecutorial arguments exceeded the bounds of earnest and forceful presentation, United States v. Doctor (C.M.A. 1956).

At the close of argument, the presiding officer instructs the members of the court on the applicable law. Art. 51(c), UCMJ. The members then meet alone to determine the guilt or innocence of the accused. A substantial body of law has given necessary detail to the bare requirement of Art. 51(c) that the presiding officer instruct court members concerning their general responsibilities and the elements of the offense. For example, the military judge should define any terms with special meanings, tailor all instructions to the facts, and give such other explanations, descriptions or directions as may be necessary and which are requested by a party or which the military judge decides should be given. RCM 920(e). The military judge may summarize and comment on the evidence as long as it is an accurate, fair, and dispassionate statement of what the evidence shows.

c. Sentencing Procedures

If there is a finding of guilty, the sentence is imposed at a second stage of the court-martial proceeding. Like the findings stage, the second stage is adversarial: first prosecution and then defense counsel present evidence relevant to sentencing and make arguments to the court. RCM 1001(a). At one time, any evidence that the prosecution could introduce was generally limited to data from the accused's official records and rebuttal of defense evidence, RCM 1001(b), a limitation which generally favored the defense. Recent amendments, however, largely removed the limitations, bringing the Rules for Court Martial more in line with Federal civilian standards. (RCM 1001 Analysis). Evidence admissible by prosecution at sentencing now includes prior civilian convictions, including pleas of nolo contendere, evidence of "hate crime" motivation, and character evidence of the accused. (RCM 1001(b)(3)-(5)). The military judge must advise the accused of the right to present matters in extenuation and mitigation. RCM 1001(a)(3). The accused may testify under oath on his or her own behalf, but may be cross-examined or impeached. The accused also has the option of making an unsworn statement, oral, written, or both, which is not subject to cross-examination. RCM 1001(c). The accused may also choose simply to have counsel argue on his behalf.

After receiving instructions from the court concerning the sentence, such as the maximum sentence possible, the trier of fact determines a sentence. RCM 1005 & 1006(a). All evidence admitted during the trial and reasonable inferences therefrom may be considered in determining the appropriate sentence. RCM 1001(f)(2); United States v. Stevens (A.C.M.R.1985). When a decision has been reached, the court is opened, and the accused is informed of the sentence. The judge then reviews the sentence for proper form and adjourns the court after sentence is adjudged. If there is no agreement on a sentence by the required number of jurors, the military judge may declare a mistrial; the case is returned to the convening authority who may direct a rehearing on the sentence. RCM 1006(d)(6).

Defense counsel may then prepare a recommendation for clemency to be submitted to the convening authority. Any members of the court who desire to do so may sign the recommendation and state their reasons for signing. The recommendation properly may include matters not admissible at trial and should not merely cumulate evidence considered at trial.

Military sentences are not executed when adjudged. However the accused will normally begin serving any adjudged confinement immediately and forfeitures will normally take effect 14 days later. Art. 57, UCMJ. Except when a sentence of death is adjudged, the convening authority has the discretion to suspend or remit a sentence. RCM 1108(b). Unless the sentence includes a dishonorable or bad-conduct discharge, dismissal of a commissioned officer or cadet, or a punishment of death, the sentence is executed when approved by the convening authority. RCM 1113(a)-(c). Otherwise, the sentence is not executed until approved by a Military Court of Criminal Appeals, which exercises all the traditional authority of appellate courts as well as "[a]wesome, plenary, de novo power of review * * * ." United States v. Cole (C.M.A. 1990). Subsequent to review by the C.C.A., the U.S.C.A.A.F. may, upon petition, review the case as well. The U.S.C.A.A.F. may decline review altogether; moreover, so long as there is some competent evidence, it will not reevaluate the facts of a particular case.

d. Evidence in Courts–Martial

UCMJ Art. 36(a) states in part that in military trials, procedures: "may be prescribed by the President by regulations which shall, so far as he considers practicable, apply the principles of law and the rules of evidence generally recognized in the trial of criminal cases in the United States district courts * * * "

These regulations, which specify many evidentiary rules in detail, also expressly state that courts-martial shall apply "the rules of evidence generally recognized in the trial of criminal cases in the United States district courts and * * *, when not inconsistent with * * *, the rules of evidence at common law." MRE 101(b). The President has set out the rules of evidence applicable to courts-martial in the Military Rules of Evidence (MRE). They are based on the Federal Rules of Evidence and amendments to the Federal Rules are automatically incorporated into the Military Rules 18 months after their Federal Rule effective date, unless the President takes affirmative action to prevent their incorporation. MRE 1102.

When evidence regulations conflict with the UCMJ, the regulations must give way. United States v. Eggers (C.M.A. 1953). Further, when either conflicts with a constitutional principle, the constitutional right governs. For example, in United States v. Jacoby (C.M.A. 1960), an accused successfully argued that her Sixth Amendment right to confront the witnesses against her was violated by former UCMJ Art. 49, which allowed admission into evidence of depositions taken upon written interrogatories.

While a detailed discussion of all issues of evidence in courts-martial is beyond the scope of this chapter, a discussion of some major points is in order.

First, neither the prosecution nor the defense need present at trial all available evidence or present evidence in any particular order. However, failure to present evidence known to and within the sole control of one party may lead to adverse inferences being drawn against that party. Moreover, while the court generally must refrain from becoming an advocate in a court-martial proceeding, it may play an active role in obtaining further evidence from the parties.   RCM 801(c); MRE 614.

Second, court-martial counsel generally present evidence in the sequence in which the relevant events occurred. The prosecution presents its case first, attempting to establish every essential element of the offense.   Thereafter, the defense often moves for a finding of not guilty which, if denied, is followed by defense evidence concerning justification, denial, or affirmative defense. The prosecution is afforded an opportunity to rebut the defense's case-in-chief, and the defense may present evidence in surrebuttal.   Finally, additional rebuttal evidence is allowed in the discretion of the military judge, as is evidence requested by the military judge or members. RCM 913(c).

Third, either prosecution or defense counsel may make an offer of evidence to which the opposing party may object. Failure to object at trial to admission of evidence is generally deemed, upon appeal, to waive objections relating to admission, especially where a party consciously chooses not to object, asserts a position inconsistent with reliance on an objection, or appears to invite error by failing to object. MRE 103(a); RCM 905(e).

The primary objections to admissibility are irrelevancy, hearsay, and illegality. Relevancy, of course, depends on the charges brought and the circumstances sought to be presented. MRE 401–403. Likewise, the hearsay rule is difficult to circumscribe: in court-martial proceedings, as in civilian criminal trials, exceptions to the hearsay rule swallow the rule itself. MRE 801's definitions of hearsay is taken verbatim from the Federal Rules of Evidence. MRE 803 thereafter sets forth extensive categories of exceptions which parallel exceptions to the Federal Rule with the necessary modifications for adaptation to military practice. Analysis of MRE 803, Appendix 22, MCM. Illegality of evidence is separately considered in section F.1, infra.

Finally, once evidence has been admitted in a court-martial, it is the role of the trier of fact to draw conclusions from the evidence. Simply stated, some evidence will appear more indicative of particular conclusions than other evidence. Several so-called presumptions, which demand certain conclusions absent contrary evidence, deserve separate treatment. The "presumption of innocence" reiterates the fundamental proposition that to obtain a conviction in a criminal trial, the prosecution must demonstrate the defendant's guilt beyond a reasonable doubt. See RCM 920(e)(5)(A). The "presumption of sanity" simply absolves the government from proving the defendant's sanity until such time as the defendant presents credible evidence questioning his or her sanity. See RCM 916(k)(3)(A). Finally, the "presumption of competency of witnesses" merely indicates that witnesses' testimony usually will be believed unless context, demeanor, internal contradictions and so forth indicate that it should be disbelieved. MRE 601.

D. REVIEW OF COURTS–MARTIAL

Both civilian and military appellate review processes are designed to correct errors in individual cases and establish a body of law for application to subsequent cases. However, the military review system is more protective of the rights of convicted persons than state or federal review systems because several military reviews are automatic. Moreover, some military reviews correct factual errors and exercise clemency as well as reviewing questions of law and "clearly erroneous" factual findings. Appointment of new counsel at government expense to handle appeals also encourages a thorough and detached review of the court-martial trial process. Finally, defense counsel is mandatory when requested by the accused, when the United States is represented by counsel, or when the Judge Advocate General (TJAG) has sent the case to the U.S.C.A.A.F. The court's obligation to appoint defense counsel in these circumstances is broad but not absolute. United States v. Smith (C.M.A. 1992).

The military appellate process involves mandatory review by the convening authority, often with the advice of a staff judge advocate (SJA). Additionally, further reviews may be appropriate by superiors of the convening authority, TJAG, the Court of Criminal Appeals , and the United States Court of Appeals for the Armed Services. In rare cases, subsequent review by civilian federal courts is also appropriate.

1. CONVENING AUTHORITY

Until the commander who convened the court-martial affirms the court's actions, the findings and sentence, with the exception of any confinement or forfeitures, do not take effect. Art. 57(c), UCMJ; RCM 1113(a). Following the trial, therefore, the record of the proceedings is submitted automatically to the convening authority. Art. 60(a), UCMJ; RCM 1101(a). The commander may not disturb any finding of not guilty, RCM 1107(b)(4), but has the discretion to disapprove all or any portion of a finding of guilty and to reduce, mitigate, or disapprove any sentence or portion of a sentence. Art. 60(c)(2), UCMJ; RCM 1107(c)-(d). While the commander may reduce, mitigate, or disapprove a sentence, neither the commander nor the court-martial can "correct" upwards a previously announced sentence. United States v. Baker (C.M.A. 1991); Art. 60(e)(2)(c), UCMJ ("In no case * * * may the record be returned for increasing the severity of the sentence unless the sentence prescribed for the offense is mandatory"). The commander must evaluate all aspects of the trial, calling upon the SJA in appropriate cases (see section D.2, infra). RCM 1107(b)(3). In this process, the commander should weigh the evidence, pass on the credibility of witnesses, ensuring that the accused is guilty beyond a reasonable doubt, and ensure that each aspect of the sentence accords with his or her notions of justice. This review, a hybrid between trial and appellate process, is heavily weighted in favor of the defendant. Reductions of sentences by convening authorities are common.

The convening authority who is biased or has become so involved in the prosecution as to give the appearance of impropriety is obligated to pass the record on to a superior field commander for review. For example, when the convening authority grants immunity to one involved in a crime with the accused, that action raises some doubt as to his or her ability to be impartial. In that case, someone else should review the record to avoid even the appearance of bias. However, the mere granting of immunity is not equivalent to actual bias, and each case must be examined to determine if such bias exists. United States v. Lilly (N.C.M.R. 1979).

2. STAFF JUDGE ADVOCATE

Before acting on the record of trial by a general court-martial or a special court-martial which adjudged a sentence of bad conduct discharge or one-year confinement, a convening authority must refer the case to the SJA for a written opinion. Art. 60(d), UCMJ; RCM 1106(a). The purposes of this evaluation are to advise the convening authority concerning the legal posture of the case and to apprise appellate agencies, in condensed form, of the trial proceedings and results.

Cases involving acquittals are given very limited SJA review. The SJA merely provides an opinion concerning the existence of court-martial jurisdiction and determines the propriety of the court's appointment. However, no such review is required. RCM 1112(b).

Cases involving convictions are given much more thorough SJA review. This review must be in writing and must contain concise information regarding: (1) the findings and sentence adjudged by the court-martial; (2) a summary of the accused's service record, including length and character of service, awards received, and any records of nonjudicial punishment and previous convictions; (3) a statement of the nature and duration of any pretrial restraint; (4) a statement of any action the convening authority is obligated to take under a pretrial agreement, if any, or the reason why there is no such obligation; and (5) a specific recommendation concerning what action the convening authority should take. If an allegation of legal error is raised, the SJA should state whether corrective action on the findings or sentence should be taken. Additionally, the SJA may include any other matters deemed appropriate. RCM 1106(d).

The SJA review must be supplied to defense counsel for examination and rebuttal. RCM 1106(f); following receipt of the SJA review, the convening authority is required to state his reasons if he takes action different from that recommended by the SJA. These reasons, if any, are then transmitted along with the record to the Judge Advocate General. United States v. Keller (C.M.A. 1975).

3. THE JUDGE ADVOCATE GENERAL

Regardless of whether there has been an SJA review, the convening authority is required to forward the entire record, complete with disposition and the SJA's opinion, to the Judge Advocate General of the appropriate branch of the service. Art. 64(b), 65(a), and 69(a), UCMJ; RCM 1111 and 1112. TJAG's review is administrative rather than judicial; the record may be examined to determine if the findings and sentence are supported in law. RCM 1112. If any questions arise concerning the legality of any aspect of the court-martial or the convening authority's action, TJAG may modify or set aside the findings and/or sentence and then must forward the record to the Court of Criminal Appeals. Art. 66(b) and 69(a), UCMJ; RCM 1201 (a), (b)(1).

4. COURT OF CRIMINAL APPEALS

Each service branch TJAG appoints the members of that branch's Court of Criminal Appeals. Art. 66(a), UCMJ. The C.C.A. is composed of not less than three members, usually selected from among senior active or retired JAG officers who have previously been appointed as military judges. C.C.A. jurisdiction is mandatory and automatic for all courts-martial where (1) there is a sentence of death, dismissal of an officer, cadet, or midshipman, dishonorable or bad-conduct discharge of any servicemember, or imprisonment of a servicemember for one year or more and (2) the right to appellate review has not been waived or an appeal has not been withdrawn. Art. 66(b), 67(a), 71(c), and 72(c), UCMJ. Additionally, C.C.A. has jurisdiction to review cases referred to it by TJAG. Art. 69(d).

The scope of review exercised by C.C.A. is unusually broad. The court is permitted to "weigh the evidence, judge the credibility of witnesses, and determine controverted questions of fact." Art. 66(c), UCMJ; United States v. Turner (C.M.A. 1987). It also may decide any questions of law raised by the record. C.C.A. may affirm a court-martial decision, set aside its findings, order a rehearing, or dismiss charges against the accused. Art. 66(c), (d). When the C.C.A. finds an error of law in the court-martial, it will hold the findings or sentence incorrect only if the error "materially prejudices the substantial rights of the accused." Art. 59(a), UCMJ.

The C.C.A. judges have neither tenure nor fixed terms of appointment but serve, as do court-martial judges, at the pleasure of TJAG. This method of "detailing" judges has been attacked for failure to satisfy requirements of the United States Constitution. In Graf v. United States (1994), the accused argued that the lack of a fixed term of office violated the necessary independence for the judiciary under the Fifth Amendment. However, the Supreme Court held that while a fixed term of office was one part of judicial independence, it was not the only factor in such independence and that, in a military context, fixed judicial terms were not mandatory. In Weiss v. United States (S.Ct.1994), the defendants contended that, because military judges are not confirmed by the Senate, their appointments violated the Appointments Clause of the Constitution. The U.S. Supreme Court held that duties of military judges were not significantly different than those of other servicemembers: initial appointment as a commissioned officer of one later detailed to serve as a judge was sufficient to satisfy the Appointments Clause.

One year later, the Supreme Court decided another Appointments Clause issue which casts much doubt on the legitimacy of many decisions of the former Coast Guard Court of Military Appeals. United States v. Ryder (S.Ct.1995), was premised on the underlying illegality of civilians having no proper appointment serving on this court. The Secretary of Transportation exercised his constitutional authority to appoint these judges, but Ryder involved convictions upheld by the CMA prior to proper appointment. The Supreme Court unanimously held that the conviction was unlawful, refusing to find that decisions of improperly appointed judges were "de facto valid." The Court said that its decision would directly affect no more than ten cases raising this issue on direct appeals.

5. UNITED STATES COURT OF APPEALS FOR THE ARMED FORCES

The U.S.C.A.A.F. (formally the C.M.A.) is the highest civilian court specializing in appeals from military tribunals. It consists of five civilian judges appointed by the President and confirmed by the Senate for staggered 15–year terms. These judges may be removed by the President only for neglect of duty, malfeasance in office, or for mental or physical disability.

U.S.C.A.A.F. jurisdiction extends to (1) all cases in which the death sentence is imposed; (2) all cases sent by TJAG for review after C.C.A. review; and (3) those cases reviewed by C.C.A. which, upon petition of the accused and on good cause shown, the U.S.C.A.A.F. agrees to review.   Art. 67(a), UCMJ; RCM 1204(a).

The review functions of this court are very similar to those of other civilian appeals courts. First, review extends only to questions of law. Art. 67(c). Second, the court's authority includes the power to supervise the administration of the military criminal justice system. The court has taken the position that any accused person deprived of a fundamental right under the UCMJ "need not go outside the military justice system to find relief in the civilian courts of the Federal judiciary." United   States   v.   Bevilacqua (C.M.A.1968). Thus, acting pursuant to the All Writs Act, 28 U.S.C.A. § 1651 (a), the court has issued writs of habeas corpus, prohibition, and coram nobis.

6. PETITION FOR A NEW TRIAL

Any time within two years following approval of sentence by the convening authority, the accused or defense counsel may petition TJAG in writing for a new trial. Such a petition may be grounded upon either newly discovered evidence or fraud upon the initial court-martial. Art. 73, UCMJ; RCM 1210(a). Military regulations require further that the petitioner establish that a new trial "would probably produce a substantially more favorable result for the accused." RCM 1210(f)(2)(C).

When the petition is based on newly discovered evidence, the petitioner is limited to post-trial evidence which could not have been discovered with due diligence before trial. When fraud is the basis for the petition, the fraud must have had a "substantial contributing effect" upon the determination of guilt or the sentence. RCM 1210(f). For example, perjury by witnesses, forgery of documents, and willful prosecutorial concealment of evidence will be construed as fraud upon the court if the outcome probably would have been different absent those actions. RCM 1210.

If an appeal is pending before a military appellate court, TJAG refers the petition to the appropriate court for action. RCM 1210(e). When no such appeal is pending, TJAG is empowered to "vacate or modify, in whole or in part," the court-martial findings, sentence, or both. RCM 1201(b)(2).

When a new trial is ordered by a military appellate court or TJAG, the latter designates a new convening authority. RCM 1210(h)(1). The new convening authority sets the time, place, and personnel for the retrial. RCM 1210(h)(3). The military judge may be the same judge who presided over the original trial, but all members of the court must be different from those who first heard the case. RCM 810(b)(1). Upon retrial, the accused may not be tried for any offense of which he or she was acquitted or not tried at the earlier court-martial. RCM 1210(h)(2). Furthermore, the sentence imposed at retrial may not be more severe than the first sentence. RCM 810(d)(1).

7. CIVILIAN REVIEW OF COURTS–MARTIAL

The UCMJ provides that military review of court-martial convictions is "final and conclusive" and "binding upon all * * * courts * * * of the United States" (Art. 76) except that decisions may be reviewed by the Supreme Court by writ of certiorari. Art. 67a; 28 U.S.C.A. § 1259. Despite this language, indicating that no collateral review by civilian courts is appropriate, some limited review of courts-martial in the federal courts has always been permitted. The real difficulty has been in determining when civilian review is allowed.

Burns v. Wilson (S.Ct.1953), is both the seminal case on civilian review and the source of most of the confusion in this field. In Burns, a plurality of the Court found it appropriate to review whether the military courts had "dealt fully and fairly with an allegation raised" in the habeas corpus petition. It was inappropriate, said the plurality, for civilian courts to reexamine and weigh the evidence in a court-martial. In dictum, the Court noted that "in military habeas corpus the inquiry * * * has always been more narrow than in civil cases" and that "this court has played no role in [military law's] development; we have exerted no supervisory power over the courts which enforce it." In Burns, various concurring or dissenting members of the Court argued (1) that the federal courts have only the more limited function of seeing whether the military court had jurisdiction, (2) that the case should be reargued; and (3) that federal courts should review the decisions of courts-martial for constitutional errors like the decisions of federal agencies.

Several problems are raised by Burns. First, may the federal courts collaterally review military court decisions only in habeas corpus cases? Various other avenues of review accepted in courts of appeals after Burns are (1) Court of Claims suits for back pay, (2) mandamus to compel performance of duties, (3) declaratory judgments under 28 U.S.C.A. § 2201, and (4) injunctive relief under Fed.R.Crim.P. 65. In Schlesinger v. Councilman (S.Ct.1975), where an injunction was sought, the Supreme Court held that habeas corpus was not the sole vehicle for attacking military court decisions. However, the Court did not address the appropriateness of each of the avenues listed above; moreover, it held that civilian review was inappropriate in Schlesinger itself.

Second, what is the scope of civilian court review over military court decisions? As one court noted: "The Supreme Court has never clarified the [Burns] standard of full and fair consideration, and it has meant many things to many courts." Kauffman v. Secretary of Air Force (D.C.Cir.1969). Some civilian courts have been satisfied to review only whether the military courts considered the petitioner's allegations, while others have stressed the "fullness" and "fairness" of the military court deliberations over the allegations. To date, this divergence of opinion has not been resolved by the Supreme Court.

Third, what prerequisites to and bars from review limit the availability of civilian court review of military court decisions? The most important prerequisite to civilian review is that the accused first exhaust his military appeals. Parisi v. Davidson (S.Ct.1972). If the attack is upon conviction, the general rule is that all forms of direct military appellate review, automatic and discretionary, must be exhausted. If the attack is upon confinement (e.g., habeas corpus), the accused should (1) petition the U.S.C.A.A.F. for extraordinary relief or (2) request administrative relief from his commanding officer under Art. 138.

Finally, considerations of comity will preclude civilian courts from granting injunctive relief for an accused while a court-martial or the military appellate processes are in progress. The comity doctrine of Younger v. Harris (S.Ct.1971), premised upon federal non-intervention in ongoing state criminal proceedings, was applied in Schlesinger even though the Court stated that "the peculiar demands of federalism are not implicated." The Schlesinger Court noted that this deficiency was supplied by equally compelling factors: the separateness of military and civilian societies and the mission of the military to fight or be ready to fight wars. Congress, noted the Court, attempted to balance military necessities and demands for fairness by placing a court comprised of civilian judges with lengthy tenure at the apex of the military court hierarchy.

Confusion over the application of Burns has resulted in an array of approaches taken by the federal courts. Several of the early decisions avoided reaching the issue of the scope of review under Burns entirely. Others refused to review any claims unless the military court "manifestly refused" to consider the accused's constitutional claims. Most courts are conducting de novo reviews of constitutional claims in collateral proceedings, disregarding the military court's determination. Thus, courts either ignore Burns or expressly refuse to follow it. Rosen, Civilian Courts and the Military Justice System: Collateral Review of Courts–Martial, 108 Military L. Rev. 5, 56–61 (Spring 1985); Annotation, Review by Federal Civil Courts of Court–Martial Convictions—Modern Status, 95 A.L.R. Fed. 472 (1989).

E. MILITARY LAW CRIMES, DEFENSES, AND PUNISHMENTS

UCMJ Arts. 77–134, known as the Punitive Articles, contain the substantive offenses for which one subject to the UCMJ may be held accountable.

These crimes may be classified in many ways. For convenience, this chapter divides crimes into "Specified Offenses" and "Unspecified Offenses." The former category encompasses both common law crimes and offenses peculiar to the military. Common law crimes will be treated only briefly, for they do not differ significantly from the civilian crimes treated in numerous criminal law texts. The peculiarly military crimes discussed are "Absence Offenses," "Duties and Orders Offenses," "Superior–Inferior Relationship Offenses," and "Combat–Related Offenses." The "Unspecified Offenses" discussed are violations of the "General Articles." Finally, selected defenses will be surveyed and a brief overview of military law punishments will be presented.

1. SPECIFIED OFFENSES

Simply stated, the specified military law offenses are those in which each element of the offense is specified in one or another of UCMJ Arts. 77 through 132. If the prosecution fails to prove any element of the specified offenses with which the accused is charged, the accused must be found not guilty of that charge. As in civilian law, the prosecution must demonstrate each element of the offense "beyond a reasonable doubt." While there is some inevitable tedium to the process, the only way to study the specified offenses is by examining the statutory wording and case interpretation of each offense separately.

Principals and accessories alike are liable for crimes. Art. 77 and 78, UCMJ. Also, the accused may be found guilty of a lesser offense "necessarily included" in the crime charged. Art. 79, UCMJ. Previously, military courts followed the practice established in United States v. Baker (C.M.A. 1983), excluding lesser offenses if pleadings and proof demonstrated that the offenses fairly embraced each other. United States v. Teters (C.M.A. 1993), however, overruled Baker and held that if the statutory elements of the crime, as enumerated by Congress, were met, then the offenses did not merge. In Teters, the court held that the defendant could therefore be convicted of both theft and forgery, even though the latter was solely designed to accomplish the former. Thus, unless to do so would be contrary to the intent of Congress a court may impose multiple convictions and punishments under different statutes for the same act.

a. Common Law Crimes

The so-called "common law crimes" in the military are in fact codified in great detail. Within its jurisdictional limitations, the military not surprisingly proscribes conduct which would be felonious or misdemeanant if committed in civilian life.   However, the military does not draw the felony/misdemeanor line often drawn under state law. Rather, punishments are established for each crime by various UCMJ Articles and MCM regulations.

While little purpose would be served by a detailed enumeration of all the elements of the common law crimes recognized by the military, a few general comments about homicidal offenses, sex offenses, property offenses, and alcohol and drug related offenses may be helpful.

(1) Homicidal Offenses

In the military, unlawful killings (homicides) are classified along modified Model Penal Code lines. No distinction is made between first and second degree murder. There is, however, a distinction drawn between murder and manslaughter. Murder involves unlawful killings which are premeditated, intentional, inherently and wantonly dangerous to human life, or committed in perpetration or attempted perpetration of burglary, sodomy, rape, robbery, or aggravated arson. Art. 118(1)-(4), UCMJ; Part IV, ¶ 43, MCM. Premeditated murders and felony murders are punishable by death or mandatory life imprisonment with or without eligibility for parole; intentional but unpremeditated murders and reckless murders are punishable by life imprisonment or less. Premeditation requires both a specific intent to kill and consideration of the act intended to bring about death. Part IV, ¶ 43c(2)(a), MCM.

Death may be not be adjudged unless all of the members find, beyond a reasonable doubt, at least one of the aggravating factors set out in RCM 1004(c). The members must also concur that any extenuating or mitigating circumstances are substantially outweighed by the aggravating circumstances.

Manslaughter is classified as voluntary or involuntary under Art. 119(a) or (b) of the UCMJ.

Voluntary manslaughter has the same elements as unpremeditated murder (intent to kill or do great bodily harm but no consideration of the act intended to bring about death) but it occurs in the "heat of sudden passion caused by adequate provocation." In other words, a reasonable person in the accused's place would have been provoked, and the accused must actually have been provoked. Involuntary manslaughter involves any unlawful, unintentional killing of a human being by "culpable negligence" or during perpetration of an offense other than those offenses listed in Art. 118(4), discussed above. Negligent homicide is an unspecified offense under Art. 134. United States v. Kick (C.M.A. 1979).

(2) Sex Offenses

Military law makes rape or carnal knowledge unlawful (Art. 120) and also proscribes sodomy (Art. 125). Rape is defined as forcible, nonconsensual sexual intercourse involving penetration. Art. 120(a), UCMJ. Rape is a general intent crime, and even slight penetration will suffice to convict if the other elements of rape are present. Art. 120 (c), UCMJ. Carnal knowledge is defined as sexual intercourse involving penetration with a person, other than the accused's spouse, who has not attained the age of sixteen years. Art. 120(b), UCMJ. Neither force nor lack of consent is an element of a carnal knowledge offense. As long as the person whom the accused had sexual intercourse was at least 12 years of age, it is an affirmative defense, which the accused must prove by a preponderance of the evidence, that he or she reasonably believed that the other person was at least 16 years of age. Part IV, ¶ 45C(2), MCM. Both rape and carnal knowledge are defined in gender-neutral terms. Art. 20(d)(1)(B).

Sodomy is defined as "unnatural carnal copulation" with another person of either sex or with an animal. Art. 125(a), UCMJ. Penetration, however slight, is required. However, neither consent nor lack of force is a defense. Unlike rape and carnal knowledge, sodomy is criminalized between persons of the same sex and persons of the opposite sex under the UCMJ. See United States v. Fagg (C.M.A. 1992).

Indecent assault, bigamy, adultery, indecent exposure, pandering, indecent acts, and the like have been brought within the ambit of the unspecified offenses.

(3) Theft Offenses

Art. 121, Larceny and Wrongful Appropriation, combines various common law crimes involving taking, obtaining, and withholding tangible personal property or other articles of value. One who "steals" services may not be convicted under this provision, but may be convicted for a violation of Art. 134. United States v. Herndon (C.M.A.1965); United States v. Cornell (N.M.C.M.R.1983). The "theft" must be wrongful, and the defendant must have specific intent to deprive another of property, either permanently or temporarily. Art. 121 does not cover misappropriation of U.S. Government property, for such offenses are separately treated in Art. 108 (military property), Art. 109 (other government property), and Art. 132 (frauds against the United States).

Robbery, dealt with in Art. 122, may be proved under either of two theories. The first, a taking by "force or violence," requires proof of the amount of force used, but no proof that the victim was placed in fear by the force. Part IV, ¶ 47c(2), MCM. The second, a taking "by fear of immediate or future injury to his person or property" or to the person or property of a relative, family member, or someone in his presence, requires proof of the victim's reasonably held fear but not proof of actual force or violence by the accused. Part IV, ¶ 47, c(3), MCM. Under both theories, robbery only occurs when the victim is in the presence of the accused.

Extortion (Art. 127) involves threats to the victim to obtain things of value, but does not involve force and need not be accomplished in the victim's presence.

Burglary (Art. 129) is cast in a traditional common law mold. There must be (1) a breaking and (2) entering (3) at night (4) into the dwelling house (5) of another (6) with the intent to a commit a serious crime (those listed in Arts. 118–128). Civilian law relaxations of such elements as the time of day and the place burgled have not made their way into military law.

(4) Alcohol and Drug Related Offenses

Any servicemember who operates a vehicle while drunk or under the influence of any illegal substance or in a reckless or wanton manner may be punished. Art. 111, UCMJ. Similarly, any member who uses, possesses, manufactures, distributes, or imports a proscribed substance is subject to military punishment. Art. 112a(a), UCMJ. Such substances include opium, heroin, cocaine, amphetamines, and marijuana as well as any other drug considered a "controlled substance" under U.S. law. Art. 112a(b)(1)-(3), UCMJ. Running contrary to civilian court precedent, the Air Force Court of Military Review rejected the argument that the accused must possess a "usable quantity "of a controlled substance to be convicted. United States v. Birbeck (A.F.C.M.R.1992).

The impact of alcohol and illegal drug use on military society is substantial. From 1984–1987, 34% to 41% of general courts-martial annually having the power to issue bad-conduct discharges involved alcohol or drug offenses.

b. Peculiarly Military Offenses

Many offenses specified in the UCMJ are strictly military in nature. Other offenses, denounced by military law rather severely because of the nature of military duty and martial responsibilities, would be minor offenses under civilian law. These offenses can be organized into the following four categories:

(1) Absences Offenses: Missing Movement (Art. 87); Absence Without Leave (Art. 86); Desertion (Art. 85);

(2) Duties and Orders Offenses: Failure to Obey Order or Regulation (Art. 92); Willfully Disobeying Officers (Art. 90(2) and Art. 91(2); Dereliction of Duty (Art. 92(3)); Drunk on Duty

(Art. 112); Misbehavior of Sentinel (Art. 113); Malingering (Art. 115);

(3)   Superior–Subordinate   Relationship Offenses: Mutiny (Art. 94); Failure to Suppress or Report Mutiny (Art. 94(a)(3)); Contempt Toward Officials (Art. 88); Assault of a Superior Commissioned Officer (Art. 90(1)); Insubordinate Conduct Toward Other Officers (Art. 91(1), (3)); and

(4) Combat–Related Offenses: Aiding the Enemy (Art. 104); Spying (Art. 106); Espionage (Art. 106a); Misbehavior Before the Enemy (Art. 99); Subordinate Compelling Surrender (Art. 100); Improper Use of Countersign (Art. 101); Forcing a Safeguard (Art. 102); Captured or Abandoned Property (Art. 103); Misconduct as Prisoner (Art. 105).

Each of these types of uniquely military offenses deserves separate, though necessarily abbreviated, treatment.

(1) Absence Offenses

Absence offenses are the most prevalent military offenses. Of all military offenses actually tried, 70–80% fall under Art. 86, which includes Absence Without Leave (AWOL) and Failure to Repair. To convict a servicemember of AWOL, the prosecution must prove that (1) the accused was required to be a certain place at a certain time; (2) the place or time had been lawfully prescribed; (3) the accused knew of the time or place; (4) the accused either failed to show up, left after showing up, or failed to return at the proper time; and (5) the failure to show, departure, absence, or failure to return was without authority. Part IV, ¶ 10b, MCM. AWOL is a residual offense when Desertion and Missing Movement (discussed below) are inappropriate. AWOL, a general intent crime, may be established merely by proof of the unauthorized absence and proof that the accused actually knew of the appointed time and place of duty. Part IV, ¶ 10(c), MCM.   Such proof often takes the form of documentary evidence called SIDPERS (Standard Installation Division Personnel System), a system of personnel accounting which has replaced the military Morning Report. Factors such as time of war, type of duty, and duration of absence will aggravate the punishment imposed for AWOL. Part IV, ¶ 10c(4), MCM. Impossibility due to physical disability, transportation misfortune, or civilian confinement, mistake of fact negating intent, and duress are commonly argued defenses in AWOL prosecutions.

Desertion, the most serious absence offense, has been said to rank with mutiny as "one of the two greatest crimes a soldier can commit." Ayde, Essay on Punishments and Rewards: A Treatise on Court–Martial 236 (4th Ed. 1797). It requires that the accused (1) absent himself from his unit, organization, or place of duty with intent to remain away permanently; (2) absent himself with intent to avoid hazardous duty or important service; (3) enter into a new armed force or a foreign force without disclosing a lack of regular separation from the first force; or (4) if a commissioned officer, before acceptance of his resignation, quits his post or duties without leave and with intent not to return. Art. 85(a) & (b), UCMJ. Desertion is very similar to AWOL except the prosecution must demonstrate specific intent such as by circumstantial evidence the length and particulars of the absence.

In United States v. Thun (C.M.A. 1993), a serviceman was ordered to prepare to deploy for duty in the Persian Gulf. Upon inspection it was determined that the while his gear was present, the servicemember was not. While the servicemember was only absent for just over three hours, it was sufficient to sustain a conviction of desertion in light of the fact that his unit was to leave for important duty that day. Thus, duration of absence is considered in the context of the circumstances surrounding the absence. Other examples of aggravating circumstances in desertion cases include apprehension rather than voluntary surrender and desertion in time of war.

Occasionally, small pleading irregularities have invalidated prosecutions of desertion cases. For example, in United States v. Smith (C.M.A. 1968), the prosecution specified that the accused deserted with intent to avoid "hazardous duty." Service in Vietnam was determined as a "important service", but the court found that "hazardous duty" was a term of art limited by regulation to parachuting, demolition, and experimental guinea-pig duty, not necessarily duty in a combat zone. The conviction was overturned, though it appears the prosecution may have erred in not pursuing an Art. 85 case of desertion with intent to shirk important service.

The MCM further provides that hazardous duty or important service may include combat duty, embarkation for foreign or sea duty, strike or riot duty, or training for duty on the border or coast in time of war or threatened invasion. Services such as drill, target practice, maneuvers, and practice marches usually do not qualify as "hazardous" or "important." In any event, "[w]hether a duty is hazardous or a service is important depends upon the circumstances of the particular case, and is a question of fact for the court-martial to decide." Part IV, ¶ 9c(2)(a), MCM.

Missing Movement (Art. 87) is a little-used provision developed in World War II when servicemembers failed to show up when their units or ships moved out. It fills the gap between the generally minor offense of AWOL and the serious offense of Desertion. Missing Movement has two forms: absence through design and absence through neglect.

(2) Duties and Orders Offenses

Like absence offenses, duties and orders offenses are very common and have no criminal law counterparts in the civilian sector. Duties and orders offenses generally may be seen as those involving (1) violations of general orders or other lawful orders, (2) willful disobedience of orders, and (3) slovenliness or drunkenness in the performance of military duties.

It is unlawful to violate or fail to obey a lawful general order which the accused had a duty to obey and knowledge of general orders is presumed by all persons subject to the UCMJ. Art. 92, UCMJ; Part

IV, ¶ 16c(1)(d), MCM. General Orders may be issued by the President, Secretary of a service branch, a commander of flag or general rank or a general court-martial convening authority. In each instance, they must apply generally to the force commanded.   Part IV, ¶ 16c(1)(a), MCM. A regulation issued by a general officer for an entire military post is an example of a general order. United States v. Snyder (C.M.A. 1952). Orders, including general ones, are deemed lawful unless "contrary to the Constitution, the laws of the United States, or lawful superior orders" or "beyond the authority of the official issuing it." Part IV, ¶ 16c(1)(C), MCM.   General policy directives requiring implementing directives, directives of an informational nature only, and regulations not clearly punitive on their face do not give rise to a duty of obedience punishable if violated under 92(1). Like other penal statutes, this one has been strictly construed for the benefit of the accused.

Failure to obey orders other than General Orders is punishable under Art. 92(2) if (1) the order was lawful; (2) the accused knew of the order; (3) was duty bound to obey it; and (4) failed to obey it. As with General Orders, other orders are inferred to be lawful unless violative of Part IV, ¶ 16c(1)(c), MCM.

Many colorful cases illustrate unlawful orders. For example, an order establishing a six-month waiting period before an application for permission to marry by a member of the command would even be considered, was held to interfere unreasonably and unlawfully with servicemembers' personal

affairs.   United States v. Nation (C.M.A. 1958).
Orders unrelated to military duty, such as
performance of personal services for the person
issuing the order and performance of military
duties while on leave, are unlawful.   Part IV, ¶
14c(2)(a), MCM.   A proposed amendment to the
MCM would make the lawfulness of an order a
question of law to be determined by the military
judge.

Willful disobedience of lawful orders of superiors
is made unlawful under Arts. 90(2) and 91(2).   The
elements of these offenses include (1) a lawful
order given to the accused; (2) by a superior
commissioned, warrant, or noncommissioned
officer of the accused; (3) which order the accused
knew to be from that superior; and (4) which the
accused willfully disobeyed.   Part IV, ¶¶ 14b(2) &
15b(2), MCM.   Whether an ordering party is
superior to the accused is specified in Art. 89.
When an off-duty captain dressed in civilian
clothes sought to quell disorderly conduct of an
airman and was struck by the airman, the court
found the captain to be performing a duty required
by Art. 7(c) of quelling a fray between persons
subject to the UCMJ.   United States v. Nelson
(C.M.A. 1968).   However, when a marine major
called a private a "coward with a yellow streak
down your back," the private replied he would like
to "see the Marine Corps flat on its back with its
heels in the air," and the major said, "Let's see you
put me on my back," the officer was found to have
abandoned his superior position.   United States v.
Struckman (C.M.A. 1971).

Though the superior need not say, "This is a direct order, Private Jones," the order must be directed specifically to the subordinate. Part IV, ¶ 14c(2)(b), MCM. A subordinate who disobeys an order to comply with a pre-existing duty such as a higher directive, a statute or regulation, or a previous order cannot be convicted of willful disobedience of a command since disobedience of the prior directive provides an adequate basis for punishing the accused. Finally, because willfulness is a difficult mental state for the prosecution to establish, many "willful disobedience" cases ultimately are resolved with conviction of the lesser included offense of "failure to obey"(Art. 92(2)), "disrespect" (Art. 89) or "insubordination" (Art. 91(3)). There is no obligation to obey an unlawful order.

Punishment for dereliction or drunkenness while on duty is dealt with under UCMJ Arts. 92(3), 112, 113, and 115. The general dereliction provision, Art. 92(3), involves cases of willful or negligent failure to perform duties or performance in a culpably inefficient manner. Part IV, ¶ 16c(3c), MCM. In United States v. Lawson (C.M.A. 1993), the court clarified the standard of nonperformance as simple negligence. The duties must be specifically prescribed, and "mere ineptitude" is said not to be punishable. Part IV, ¶ 16c(3)(d), MCM. Though the reach of this provision is potentially quite broad, it has in fact been applied to a narrow range of cases not specified within other Articles. For instance, soldiers found drunk on duty, unless involuntarily intoxicated, are charged under Art. 112; sentinels found sleeping, drunk, or absent from their posts are charged under Art. 113; soldiers who avoid performance of duty by feigning illness, disablement, or the like are charged under Art. 115 as malingerers. In none of these cases would Art. 92(3) be involved.

(3) Superior–Subordinate Offenses

Obedience to authority has always been a primary characteristic of military society. Such obedience often has been viewed, even in our democratic society, as a necessary aspect of an organization whose primary function is fighting or being prepared to fight wars. It is not surprising, therefore, that rebellion against higher authority is made a criminal offense by the UCMJ. Such offenses include mutiny (Art. 94), contempt for officials (Art. 88), disrespect toward or assaulting superior commissioned officers (Arts. 89 and 90(1)), and insubordinate conduct toward various officers (Art. 91(1) and (3)).

Both mutiny and failure to prevent, suppress, or report a mutiny are capital offenses. Art. 94(b), UCMJ. The elements of mutiny are (1) creation of any violence or disturbance or acting in concert with others to refuse to obey orders (2) with the intent to usurp or override lawful military authority. One fails to prevent, suppress, or report mutiny when he does not take all reasonable means to overcome or report mutiny. Concert of action is not required for mutiny when the accused creates violence or disturbance. Part IV, ¶ 18b & c, MCM.

Contempt toward officials (Art. 88) involves use by a commissioned officer of contemptuous words directed at the President or various other civilian political officials. To date, the only case decided under Art. 88 is United States v. Howe (C.M.A. 1967). Second Lieutenant Howe was convicted of using contemptuous language against President Johnson while off-duty and in civilian clothes. At the time of his offense, Howe was participating in an anti-war demonstration in Texas and carrying a sign calling the President a fascist aggressor in Vietnam. The CMA held that Art. 88 does not violate the First or Fifth Amendments, that "contemptuous" is used in its ordinary sense in Art. 88, that intent for the words used to be disrespectful is not an element of the offense, and that Howe's language was contemptuous per se. See generally Lt. Col. Davidson, "Contemptuous Speech Against the President," July 1999, The Army Lawyer.

Disrespect and insubordination towards superiors (Arts. 89 and 91(3)) require that the disrespected person be a superior officer of the accused, that the accused know that the victim is his superior, and that the accused did or omitted to do certain acts or used certain language disrespectful of the victim. One form of disrespect, Assault Upon a Superior Commissioned Officer, is specially treated in Art. 90(1).

It is sufficient that the victim, if in the same military service, either be superior in rank or superior in command for these offenses to occur. Part IV, ¶ 13c(1)(a), MCM. Though knowledge of superiority is clearly an element of these offenses, there is a split of authority as to whether, for pleading purposes, the prosecution must allege knowledge as part of the charges. Examples of disrespectful behavior include use of denunciatory language, contemptuously walking away from a superior who is addressing him, and intentional failure to salute. See Part IV, ¶ 13c(3), MCM for other examples. Though disrespect offenses may occur in off-duty situations, more familiarity with a superior may be permitted during the course of social circumstances. United States v. Montgomery (A.C.M.R.1953). While the disrespect must be directed at a particular officer, there is a distinction made in military law between Disrespect Towards Commissioned Officers (Art. 89) and Disrespect Toward a Superior Warrant Officer or Noncommissioned Officer (Art. 91(3)). The former offense need not be committed in the officer's presence, but the latter must occur within the sight or hearing of the warrant or noncommissioned officer. Part IV, ¶ 13c(4) & 15c(5), MCM. In neither case does truth of the disrespectful language appear to be a defense. Part IV, ¶ 13c(3), MCM.

(4) Combat–Related Offenses

Several UCMJ offenses relate exclusively to combat situations. They are tailored to punishment of individuals who assist the enemy or engage in activities which might assist the enemy. These offenses, due to their ramifications on the military mission, are often punishable by death.

Aiding the Enemy (Art. 104) occurs when the accused provides arms, money, ammunition, supplies or other things to a known enemy, knowingly harbors or protects an enemy, or knowingly communicates with the enemy. Part IV, ¶ 28c, MCM. The offense is capital. For purposes of Art. 104, "enemy" includes civilians as well as armed forces members. Part IV, ¶ 23(c)(1)(b), MCM. Though the MCM says this Article "denounces offenses by all persons whether or not otherwise subject to military law" (Part IV, ¶ 28c(1), MCM), this appears overly broad in light of the Supreme Court's limitations on court-martial jurisdiction over civilians.

Spying (Art. 106) involves clandestine activity or actions under false pretenses. The accused must be obtaining or endeavoring to obtain information during wartime with the intent to communicate this information to the enemy. Part IV, ¶ 30b, MCM. The UCMJ requires a mandatory punishment of death upon conviction of the offense. The rationale, of course, is the preservation of national security during wartime.

Three other capital offenses are (1) Subordinate Compelling Surrender (Art. 100; Part IV, ¶ 24, MCM), which differs from mutiny in requiring surrender by acts rather than words; (2) Improper Use of Countersign (Art. 101; Part IV, ¶ 25, MCM), which involves wartime disclosure of a secret signal to unauthorized personnel or wartime disclosure of an erroneous secret signal to one entitled to receive and use the correct signal; and (3) Forcing a Safeguard (Art. 102; Part IV, ¶ 26, MCM), involving the violation of protective measures during wartime.

Misbehavior Before the Enemy (Art. 99; Part IV, ¶ 23, MCM) is a multifaceted crime which involves running away to avoid combat, abandoning or surrendering rather than defending against enemy actions, casting away arms or ammunition, committing acts of cowardice, etc. In all instances, the accused must be before or in the presence of the enemy for a conviction to ensue. A similar offense related to misdealings with enemy property such as pillaging and profiting from seized, abandoned, or captured property is outlined in Art. 103 and Part IV, ¶ 27 MCM.

Finally, it is criminal to engage in misconduct as a prisoner, either by acting to the detriment of others to gain favorable treatment by enemy captors (Art. 105(1)) or by maltreating prisoners while in a position of authority (Art. 105(2)). Art. 105(1) is intended to apply to all unauthorized conduct by a POW, except escaping, which tends to ameliorate his condition to the detriment of other prisoners. Part IV, ¶ 29c(3)(b), MCM. The obligations of a POW under the Code of Conduct are considered infra. Chapter 5.

2. UNSPECIFIED OFFENSES— THE GENERAL ARTICLES

In addition to the specified common law and peculiarly military law offenses surveyed above, the UCMJ contains two articles which encompass a wide range of unspecified conduct. These articles, which overlap considerably, deserve quotation in full:

Art. 133: Conduct Unbecoming an Officer and Gentleman

Any commissioned officer, cadet, or midshipman who is convicted of conduct unbecoming an officer and a gentleman shall be punished as a court-martial may direct.

Art. 134: General Article

Though not specifically mentioned in this chapter, all disorders and neglects to the prejudice of good order and discipline in the armed forces, all conduct of a nature to bring discredit upon the armed forces, and crimes and offenses not capital, of which persons subject to this chapter may be guilty, shall be taken cognizance of by a general, special, or summary court-martial, according to the nature and degree of the offense, and shall be punished at the discretion of that court.

In some respects, these two general articles diverge. First, the coverage as to persons differs between them; the former applies only to commissioned officers, cadets, and midshipmen, while the latter applies equally to officers and enlisted personnel. Second, the articles differ in their coverage of offenses specifically enumerated elsewhere in the UCMJ. Art. 133 includes acts made punishable by any other article. Thus, a commissioned officer who steals property violates both Art. 121 and Art. 133. Part IV, ¶ 59c(2), MCM. Conversely, Art. 134 on its face applies only to disorders and neglects "not specifically mentioned in this chapter." Third, the language of the two articles is similar but not equivalent. Art.

133 criminalizes "conduct unbecoming an officer and a gentleman," while Art. 134 criminalizes conduct prejudicial to "good order and discipline in the armed forces" or of a nature bringing "discredit upon the armed forces".

The MCM gives examples under the two articles which are not identical. Examples given of "conduct unbecoming" include: knowingly making a false official statement; using insulting or defamatory language to or about another officer; being drunk and disorderly in a public place; and failing without good cause to support one's family. Part IV, ¶ 59c(3), MCM. In a recent case, United States v. Frazier (C.M.A. 1992), the court upheld a verdict of Conduct Unbecoming based upon an officer maintaining an intimate relationship with another soldier's wife. The court found that such actions brought discredit to the military. Among the more than 60 purportedly distinct offenses to Art. 134 are assaults with intent to commit murder, rape, robbery, etc.; dishonorable failure to pay debts; bigamy; and child molestation. Part IV, ¶¶ 64, 95, 71, 65, and 87, MCM. Art. 134 can subsume state crimes through the Federal Assimilative Crimes Act, if they meet the "prejudice" and "discredit" requirements of the article. Part IV, ¶ 60c(2)(a)-(3), MCM.

The similarity between Art. 133 and 134 should also be apparent. Both serve as residual categories of prohibited activities which are not listed and subdivided element-by-element. In this respect, they resemble common law crimes such as "conspiracy to corrupt the public morality." Shaw v. Director of Public Prosecutions [1962] A.C. 220

(H.L.). While many states have expressly disapproved convictions for any activities not fairly within the ambit of narrowly-drawn criminal statutes, the UCMJ expressly endorses the concept of unspecified crimes.

Not surprisingly, this divergence between civilian law and the general articles has spawned constitutional challenges to their validity. Until 1974, most commentators argued that the general articles were constitutionally defective because of vagueness, overbreadth, potential for abuse of prosecutorial discretion, and lack of delineation of punishment. Those who disagreed, including various military courts, relied primarily on court decisions construing the articles, statutory language limiting the possibilities for abuse, a long military custom and history behind the articles, special constitutional standards applicable to military law, and restraint by the military in use of the articles.

In Parker v. Levy (S.Ct.1974), this debate was terminated when the Supreme Court upheld the general articles against a wide range of constitutional challenges raised by Captain Howard Levy, an army physician on active duty at the Fort Jackson Army Hospital. As part of his duties, Levy was to conduct a clinic for Special Forces troops. Upon discovering that these duties were being neglected, his commander called Levy to his office and handed him a written order to conduct the training. Levy read the order and stated that he would not obey it because of medical ethics. About the same time, Levy made several public statements to enlisted personnel at the post which urged black soldiers to refuse to go to Vietnam because "they are discriminated against and denied their freedom in the United States." He also referred to Special Forces troops as "liars and thieves and killers of peasants and murderers of women and children." Levy was charged and convicted by general court-martial of violating Arts. 133 and 134. The conviction was sustained by the military courts of appeal, and habeas corpus relief was denied in federal district court. Reversing a Third Circuit decision holding Art. 133 and 134 void for vagueness, the Supreme Court found the articles to be neither vague nor overbroad.

Much of the majority opinion rested on differences between military and civilian law and the need for immediate obedience and discipline in the military: "Just as military society has been a society apart from civilian society, so military law is a jurisprudence which exists separate and apart from the law which governs in our federal judicial establishment." Additionally, the opinion cited several factors narrowing the broad language of the general articles. Furthermore, the court concluded that numerous examples in the MCM have imparted "accepted meaning to the seemingly imprecise standards of Arts. 133 and 134" and that: [e]ach of these articles has been construed by the United States Court of Military Appeals or by other military authorities in such a manner as to at least partially narrow its otherwise broad scope * * * .

The effect of these constructions of Arts. 133 and 134 by the Court of Military Appeals and by other military authorities has been twofold: It has narrowed the very broad reach of the literal articles, and at the same time has supplied considerable specificity by way of examples of the conduct which they cover.

Finally, the Court conceded that some areas of vagueness remain even after such construction, but that these areas of uncertainty are narrowed further by less formalized custom and usage. Levy's conduct, said the Court, clearly fell within the prohibited range of the article's proscriptions in light of an example in the MCM that squarely covered his statements.

In dissent, Justice Stewart said, "I find it hard to imagine criminal statutes more patently unconstitutional than these vague and uncertain general articles * * * ." Moreover, he found little comfort in the narrowing effects of history, regulations, and court decisions:

If there be any doubt as to the absence of truly limiting constructions of the general articles, it is swiftly dispelled by even the most cursory review of convictions under them in the military courts. Art. 133 has been recently employed to punish such widely disparate conduct as dishonorable failure to repay debts, selling whiskey at an unconscionable price to an enlisted man, cheating at cards, and having an extramarital affair. Art. 134 has been given an even wider sweep, having been applied to sexual acts with a chicken, window peeping in a trailer park, and cheating while calling bingo numbers.

3. DEFENSES TO CRIMINAL LIABILITY

As in the civilian sector, the military criminal law system contains many potential defenses which may be raised by motion or introduced at trial. Motions which may result in dismissal of the charges without reaching the guilt or innocence of the defendant include motions to dismiss for lack of jurisdiction or expiration of the statute of limitations period and motions based on former jeopardy, pardon, former punishment, and denial of speedy trial. RCM 907. Special or "affirmative" defenses, which deny criminal responsibility wholly or partially while admitting the objective acts charged, include justification or excuse, self-defense, obedience to lawful orders, entrapment, ignorance or mistake of fact and insanity. RCM 916. Other defenses, such as mistaken identity, alibi, and good character, deny that the accused committed the acts charged. RCM 916(a).

There is little substantive difference between civilian and military affirmative defenses. Justification is a defense to death, injury, or other acts done in proper performance of a legal duty. Thus, military police engaged in lawful apprehension may use force, if reasonably necessary. When an accident (not negligence) results in death or injury during the performance of a lawful act in a lawful manner, the result is excusable. RCM 916(f).

Obedience to apparently lawful orders is also a defense. However, this defense is inapplicable where "the accused knew the orders to be unlawful or a person of ordinary sense and understanding would have known the orders to be unlawful." RCM 916(d). For example, in United States v. Calley (A.C.M.R.1973), the superior orders defense was rejected in connection with murder charges relating to the killing of unarmed civilians, including women and children. The court noted that, under the circumstances, the order to kill was so far removed from combat necessities as to be patently illegal.

Entrapment is a defense when "the criminal design or suggestion to commit the offense originated in the Government and the accused had no predisposition to commit the offense." RCM 916(g). The principal aspect of the defense is the accused's lack of predisposition to commit the offense alleged, not the deterrence of government involvement in criminal activity: "The fact that persons acting for the Government merely afford opportunities or facilities for the commission of the offense does not constitute entrapment." RCM 916(g).

Ignorance or mistake of fact is a defense when knowledge of that fact is an element of the offense, or when the mistake negates the mental state required for the offense. RCM 916(j). Thus, in general intent offenses, mistaken belief must be reasonable and must have existed in the accused's mind to serve as a defense, while in specific intent crimes, the mistake need only have existed in the mind of the accused. Even an honest and reasonable mistake of law is generally no defense unless the mistake negates the mental state required for the crime. RCM 916(l)(1). The generalization that "ignorance of the law is no defense" refers to the usual offense which requires no actual knowledge by the accused of the law or the legal effects of his actions.

Voluntary drunkenness does not excuse offenses committed while intoxicated, nor can it be used to lower a charge of premeditated murder or unpremeditated murder to manslaughter. However, intoxication may negate actual knowledge, specific intent, or premeditation such that a charge of premeditation may be reduced to unpremeditated. RCM 916(l)(2); United States v. Morgan (C.M.A. 1993).

In military law, one is insane who "lacked mental responsibility" at the time of the offense or who lacks the requisite mental capacity at the time of trial. Art. 50a, UCMJ; RCM 916(k), 909(a). The test applied for the former type of insanity is based in part on the American Law Institute's Model Penal Code test and United States v. Frederick (C.M.A. 1977). Under the test, one is not criminally responsible if, (1) at the time of the acts (2) as a result of a severe mental disease or defect, (3) he or she was unable to appreciate the nature and quality or the wrongfulness of the acts. Art. 50a(a), UCMJ; RCM 916(k). Obviously, application of this test involves considerable exercise of discretion by the trier of fact.

A finding that the defendant lacks mental capacity at the time of trial does not necessarily exonerate the accused of the offense, but merely suspends the proceedings. The case may be continued or charges withdrawn or dismissed depending upon the nature and potential duration of the accused's incapacity. RCM 909(f).

4. PUNISHMENT

Most of the Punitive Articles merely recite that violations will be punished "as a court-martial may direct." While military punishment goals include those of civilian punishment such as deterrence and rehabilitation, military punishment is also imposed to further discipline and maintain order in fulfilling the military's mission. The limitations on the severity of punishments which may be imposed by summary, special, and general courts-martial are discussed supra at Section A.3. Moreover, this limitation is further circumscribed by the maximum punishments set forth in RCM 1003.   The heart of this regulation limiting punishment is the Maximum Punishment Chart found in Appendix 12, MCM.

Rather than restate the information available in the Maximum Punishments Chart, only a few general comments on the sweep of military punishments will be made here. First, cruel or unusual punishment, such as flogging, branding or tattooing, is prohibited. Art. 55, UCMJ. Congress "intended to grant protection covering even wider limits" than those encompassed by the Eighth Amendment. United States v. Matthews (C.M.A. 1983).   Second, military punishments may take more varied forms than straight imprisonment (called "confinement at hard labor" in the military). Serious offenses may be punished by dishonorable or bad conduct discharges, and most offenses will lead to varying lengths of imprisonment. Differing amounts of pay forfeitures also may be adjudged. Third, as in civilian law, prior convictions may provide grounds for increasing punishment beyond the limits established for first offenders. Finally, RCM 1004 lists specific procedures that must be followed before the death penalty may be imposed.

Inequities in the treatment of offenders based on their rank continue to challenge the asserted fairness of military justice and prompt calls for reform. See Pound, "Unequal Justice," 133 U.S. News & World Report 18-30 (Dec. 16, 2002). For example, the notorious case of Army General David Hale, now retired, illustrates how these problems infect the perception, both by those within the military as well as the public at large, of the fairness and impartiality of the military.

General Hale was court-martialed on charges that he carried on affairs with the wives of four subordinate officers and lied to Pentagon investigators about his adultery. He could have been sentenced to 11 years in prison, forfeiture of all retirement pay, and dismissal from the service. Instead, he got a plea bargain, amounting to little more than a slap on the wrist; in return for pleading guilty to eight of the charges, he was reprimanded, fined $10,000, and ordered to forfeit $1,000 monthly pay for a year. He was subsequently demoted from a major general to brigadier general, but nevertheless retired as a general officer. Although it is difficult to conceive of activity more corrosive to morale, good order and discipline than Hale's (cf. 2 Sam. ch. 11, David and

Bathsheba), his punishment was mild. A survey of reported appellate cases of adultery prosecutions presenting similar facts shows that enlisted service members and company grade officers receive far harsher punishment.

F. CONSTITUTIONAL SAFEGUARDS IN THE MILITARY CRIMINAL JUSTICE SYSTEM

The only explicit textual difference between civilian and military criminal defendants' rights under the Bill of Rights is the Fifth Amendment's exception of the requirement for grand jury indictment in the military during "time of War or public danger." While there has been no definitive ruling on the general issue whether the Bill of Rights has full applicability to the military, "the burden of showing that military conditions require a different rule than that prevailing in the civilian community is upon the party arguing for a different rule." Courtney v. Williams (C.M.A. 1976). The crossover between military constitutional rights and civilian rights was affirmed in the case of United States v. Davis (S.Ct.1994). In Davis, the petitioner made an ambiguous request for counsel which was immediately clarified by naval investigators as a comment about counsel and not a request. The Supreme Court ruled that investigators need not honor an ambiguous request for counsel, nor must they even clarify the intent of the suspect. This case has far broader implications for the civilian community than the military community.

Three aspects of the Bill of Rights which deserve careful study in connection with the military criminal law system are search and seizure, self-incrimination, and the right to counsel.

1. SEARCH AND SEIZURE

The Fourth Amendment's prohibition against "unreasonable searches and seizures" applies to searches of military personnel. United States v. Jacoby (C.M.A. 1960). Probable cause also is required to conduct most searches, within certain exceptions paralleling those in civilian law. MRE 314, 315; United States v. Stuckey (C.M.A. 1981).

The "exclusionary rule" (evidence illegally obtained may not be used to convict) of Mapp v. Ohio (S.Ct.1961), applies in court-martial proceedings. MRE 311(a) states that evidence is "inadmissible" where obtained (1) as a result of (2) an unlawful (3) search or seizure (4) made by one acting in a governmental capacity (5) if the defendant makes a timely motion to suppress or an objection to evidence and (6) the defendant had a reasonable expectation of privacy in the person, place, or property searched, a legitimate interest in the evidence seized, or grounds to object to the search or seizure under the Constitution as applied to members of the military. However, such illegally obtained evidence may be used to impeach by contradiction the in-court testimony of the accused or when the evidence would have been obtained even without the unlawful search. MRE 311(b).

Evidence is admissible if the search resulted from a search authorization where the issuer had a substantial basis for determining the existence of probable cause and the officials executing the authorization or warrant reasonably and with good faith relied on its issuance. MRE 311(b)(3). In United States v. Lopez (C.M.A. 1992), the Court of Military Appeals affirmed the "good faith" exception for search and seizure. The test for determining "good faith" is "whether a reasonably well-trained law enforcement officer would have known the search or seizure was illegal despite the authorization", and that the commander be neutral, detached, and impartial.

The MCM does not define whether every action productive of incriminating information is a "search or seizure" in the Fourth Amendment sense. However, both the MCM and the CMA acknowledge that military authorities may engage in administrative inspections or inventories to a greater extent than may civilian law enforcement officials without engaging in prohibited "searches or seizures." MRE 313; United States v. Middleton (C.M.A. 1981). MRE 314 sets forth a list of "reasonable searches not requiring probable cause." For searches requiring probable cause, MRE 315 delineates the procedures for obtaining a search authorization or warrant, but then lists certain "exigencies" for which an authorization or warrant is unnecessary. The following, based upon these rules and case law developments, is a helpful but nondefinitive list of lawful searches.

a. Lawful Warrant or Authorization

The warrant must be issued by a neutral and detached official acting in a judicial or quasijudicial capacity. See United States v. Sloan (A.F.C.M.R.1990). It must be based upon probable cause and be limited at least as to the place to be searched and the things to be seized. However, military officials generally do not obtain civilian search warrants because military law also recognizes as reasonable a search conducted pursuant to a military commander's properly granted authority.

MRE 315(d) allows the issuance of an "authorization to search" by an impartial commander or other officer in a position of command or by a military judge or magistrate. United States v. Sloan (A.F.C.M.R.1990). The search authorization, which must be based upon probable cause, grants permission to search a person or area for specified property or evidence or for a specific person. MRE 315(b), (f). A search authorization may be issued for a search of persons subject to military law, military property, persons and property within military control, and non-military property in a foreign country. MRE 315(c).

This variety of lawful search is peculiar to the military. It theoretically involves authorization by one in the position of a neutral and detached civilian magistrate who issues a search warrant. One might question how close this analogy is, for the commander is responsible for the efficient operation of the military unit and therefore has a stake in troop performance that the magistrate does not have in civilian society. A more straightforward explanation of this broad exception to civilian "lawful search" principles is that military missions and expectations of military personnel may make otherwise unjustified searches reasonable. This explanation is buttressed by the limitation of these searches to military property and persons. "An otherwise impartial authorizing official does not lose that character" merely because that official is present at a search or available to those seeking the issuance of an authorization or because the official previously authorized investigative activities. MRE 315(d)(2).

b. Lawful Apprehension

An apprehension is lawful if made by an authorized person or upon the reasonable belief that an offense was committed by the person apprehended. Searches incident to lawful apprehensions are lawful if made to discover and seize weapons or destructible evidence, but not if made as a pretext to further connect the apprehended person with a crime. These searches are limited to the person of the accused and an area within his or her "immediate control"—the area within which the individual searching could reasonably believe that the person apprehended could reach within a sudden movement to obtain weapons or reach destructible evidence. MRE 314(g)(2). Such searches must be made at the time of apprehension or during efforts thereafter to continue custody of the accused.

In addition, a search also may be made of the passenger compartment of an automobile and containers within that compartment as a contemporaneous incident of apprehending the automobile's occupant, regardless of whether he or she has been removed from the vehicle. MRE 314(g)(2). Furthermore, when the apprehension occurs at a place where others reasonably may be present who might interfere with or pose a danger to the apprehension efforts, a reasonable examination may be made of the general area where these persons may be located. MRE 314(g)(3)(A).

c. Lawful Hot Pursuit

Based upon Warden, Maryland Penitentiary v. Hayden (S.Ct.1967), this doctrine is responsive to an emergency: stopping pursuit to obtain a warrant would assist escape of the accused and removal or destruction of evidence. Such pursuit must be "lawful" (probable cause to suspect the one pursued committed a crime) and "hot" (little lag time between suspect's flight and apprehender's chase). Once the fleeing suspect is caught, law enforcement officers have broader rights to search the premises in which the accused is apprehended than under the "lawful apprehension" doctrine.

d. Open Fields or Woodlands

There is no reasonable expectation of privacy in open fields or woodlands, and therefore unrestricted searches of such areas are lawful. Katz v. United States (S.Ct.1967). MRE 314(j) similarly declares that such searches are not unlawful. The main issue here is whether a particular place is truly an "open field" or a semi-private abutment to a dwelling. The case law is split as to whether items seen from outside such an area may lawfully be seized when located within an abutment.

e. Removal or Disposal of Contraband

Usually, such searches are permitted when officials learn of contraband in a vehicle. There must be reasonable grounds for believing they are in the place searched, and that the emergency justified the action to prevent removal or disposal. If the vehicle allegedly containing contraband already has been seized or otherwise immobilized, consent of the owner of the vehicle or a search pursuant to a warrant is required. Similarly, MRE 315(g)(3) allows a search of an operable vehicle, except where a search warrant or authorization is required by the Constitution, the MCM, or the MRE.

f. Consent

Consent may be given by the accused or by one who exercises control over the property searched. Consent must be given voluntarily in order to be valid. If there is physical or psychological duress or coercion applied by government officials, consent is deemed involuntary. Whether consent is voluntary is an oft litigated question, and one "to be determined from all the circumstances". Important factors have been whether the defendant was in custody and whether pressure to answer questions was applied by one superior in rank to the defendant. Knowledge of the right to refuse consent is another factor to be considered. But the prosecution is not required to show such knowledge to establish voluntariness. The burden of proving that consent was voluntary is on the prosecution and must be shown by "clear and convincing evidence."

g. Administrative Inspection or Inventory

Military law distinguishes between "inspections" and "searches". Under MRE 313, inspections are lawful only if (1) they are not conducted primarily to obtain evidence to use in a court-martial or disciplinary proceeding and (2) they are ordered and conducted primarily to ensure the security, fitness, or good order and discipline of the military unit. In United States v. Roberts (C.M.A. 1976), the court said that the "traditional military inspection which looks at the overall fitness of a unit to perform its military mission is a permissible deviation from what may be tolerated in civilian society generally." The court held that "shakedown inspections" instituted "in search specifically of criminal goods or evidences is not such a permissible intrusion into a person's reasonable expectation of privacy, even in the military setting." Thus, the commander who tailors a barracks or field area inspection to legitimate military reasons can have an entire group searched without probable cause. But, if the commander expressly searches for criminal evidence or contraband among the same group, one of whose members is suspect, the search is illegal. Indeed, MRE 313(b) allows inspections to locate and confiscate weapons or contraband. However, if 1) the inspection was ordered immediately after a reported offense and was not previously scheduled; 2) specific persons are selected for examination or 3) those examined are subjected to substantially different intrusions during the same inspection, then the prosecution must prove by clear and convincing evidence that the examination was an "inspection" under the rule and not a subterfuge.

h. E-mail

A recent line of cases has addressed the issue of searches and seizures of messages in e-mail accounts. A person who has an e-mail account through a private company has a reasonable expectation of privacy regarding any messages stored in a computer to which he alone can gain access through the use of a password. A person also has an expectation of privacy for any messages to other subscribers of an e-mail service who have passwords. Probable cause to search an e-mail account does not attach to other user names held by the same individual. There must be probable cause to search each user name. U.S. v. Maxwell (USCAAF 1997). However, an accused does not have a recognizable expectation of privacy for e-mail stored in a government computer, which serves as the base's electronic mail host, when all personal mailboxes are issued for official business only, and all users of the system receive notice that the system is subject to monitoring whenever they log on. U.S. v. Monroe (USCAAF 1997).

i. Other Searches

There are a number of other types of searches considered reasonable that do not require probable cause. First, more liberty to search lawfully is given with respect to "border searches," military or civilian, because of "national self-protection reasonably requiring one entering the country to identify himself as entitled to come in, and his belongings as effects which may lawfully come in."

Carroll v. United States (S.Ct.1925); MRE 314(b). This liberty has been construed so broadly that a warrantless gate search at Camp Casey Korea was determined to be functionally equivalent to a border inspection for purposes of the Fourth Amendment and the court admitted evidence found during such a search over objection. United States v. Stringer (C.M.A. 1993). Second, searches are routinely permitted of persons reporting to confinement within, or returning from, military or civilian confinement or restriction because such persons have no reasonable expectation of privacy. MRE 314(h). Third, "stop and frisk" searches, approved by the Supreme Court upon "reasonable suspicion" (which is less than "probable cause") in Terry v. Ohio (S.Ct.1968), are justified by the immediacy of the law enforcement need and the limited scope of the search. MRE 314(f). Fourth, security concerns may justify random searches of vehicles upon entry to or exit from military installations, United States v. Poundstone (C.M.A. 1973); MRE 314(c). Fifth, no probable cause is required for the taking of urine samples, if part of a nontargeted administrative inspection. Finally, searches of a type not otherwise included in MRE 314 and not requiring probable cause may be conducted if allowed under the Constitution as applied to members of the military. MRE 314(k).

2. SELF–INCRIMINATION

The Fifth Amendment prohibits compelling any person to incriminate himself in a criminal case. Art. 31 of the UCMJ, which generally conforms to this prohibition, has been construed to grant broader protection in some respects than does the Constitution. There are four parts to Art. 31:

(A) No person subject to the UCMJ may compel any person to incriminate himself or to answer any question, the answer to which might tend to incriminate him.

(B) No person subject to the UCMJ may interrogate an accused or a suspect without first informing him of (a) the nature of the accusation; (b) that he does not have to make a statement; and (c) that any statement made may be used against him.

(C) No person subject to the UCMJ may compel any person to make a statement or produce evidence before any military tribunal which is not material and which may degrade him.

(D) Any statement received in violation of Art. 31 is inadmissible at trial by court-martial.

MRE 301(a) states that a servicemember has the protections of both the Fifth Amendment and Art. 31 and can assert the privilege most beneficial to him or her. In United States v. Tempia (C.M.A. 1967), the Court of Military Appeals held that Art. 31 custodial interrogations of suspects did not fully comply with Miranda v. Arizona (S.Ct.1966). Prospectively, it required that warnings also include telling the accused that he is entitled to the presence of an attorney, either retained or appointed. After Tempia, the MCM was revised to require full Miranda warnings when evidence of a testimonial or communicative nature with the meaning of the Fifth Amendment is sought. MRE

305(d). Moreover, unlike civilian Miranda warnings, Art. 31 warnings are required even when the accused is not in custody. However, no indication was given as to whether these regulations were intended merely to reaffirm then-existing law or were supposed to set forth an independent standard for military practice. This became important when the Supreme Court, in Harris v. New York (S.Ct.1971), withdrew from its reasoning in Miranda somewhat and permitted use of statements obtained after a defective warning to impeach the accused's credibility. MRE 304(b)(1) adopts Harris, permitting impeachment when "the accused first introduces into evidence such [privileged] statement or derivative evidence."

Military law permits taking handwriting exemplars, urine samples, blood samples, and statements for voice identifications. Because such body evidence and exemplars are not protected by the privilege against self-incrimination, their production may be compelled. See MRE 301.

3. RIGHT TO COUNSEL

Whether the Sixth Amendment right to counsel applies fully in courts-martial is a question over which commentators disagree and which the courts have never squarely faced. UCMJ provisions, MCM regulations, and case law developments have diminished the issue to little practical significance. However, the Sixth Amendment backdrop has substantially influenced statutory, regulatory, and judicial approaches to the right to counsel in the military.

a. Types of Court–Martial

Military law gives the accused the right to counsel before a general or special court-martial or at an Art. 32 investigation. Art. 38(b), UCMJ. Military regulations do not extend this right to summary courts-martial, RCM 1301(e), and in Middendorf v. Henry (S.Ct.1976), the Supreme Court held that there was no constitutional right to counsel in summary courts-martial. The Court avoided the issue of the Sixth Amendment's general applicability to the military by deciding that summary courts-martial are not "criminal proceedings" because of the limits on penalties imposable, the procedural distinctions present between summary and other courts-martial, and the historical differences between the military and civilian communities. At the same time that it found no Sixth Amendment right to counsel in summary courts-martial, the Court declined to find any deprivation of due process under the Fifth Amendment. Thus, summary courts-martial may be held without any involvement of counsel. However, when the accused is convicted in such a counsel-free disciplinary proceeding, the "conviction" may not be used later (1) to increase punishment under the "escalator clause" of Section B of RCM 1003(d), (2) to upgrade an offense under RCM 1001 or (3) to impeach a witness under MRE 609(a) absent a valid personal waiver by the accused of counsel prior to the earlier disciplinary hearing. United States v. Booker (C.M.A. 1977).

Generally in special courts-martial, the accused has the right to 1) civilian counsel of his own choosing, 2) military counsel of his own selection at government expense if such counsel is reasonably available, or 3) appointed military counsel at government expense. Art. 38(b), UCMJ. In multiple defendant cases, separate counsel normally should be appointed for each defendant to avoid any problem of conflict of interest. United States v. Blakey (C.M.A. 1976). The accused who chooses counsel is still entitled to appointed military associate counsel. Art. 38(b)(4). Moreover, the accused may refuse counsel altogether and proceed pro se if he effectively waives his right to counsel and satisfies the court of his mental competence.

For all general courts-martial, at a minimum, counsel must be admitted to a federal bar or the highest court of a state and military counsel must be certified as competent to perform such duties by the Judge Advocate General of the applicable armed force. Art. 27(b), UCMJ; RCM 502(d). In special courts-martial, similar requirements apply "unless counsel having such qualifications cannot be obtained on account of physical conditions or military exigencies." Art. 27(c)(1), UCMJ. Only if it is impossible or impracticable to obtain such qualified counsel will someone with lesser qualifications be acceptable in special courts-martial. RCM 502(d)(2). Persons chosen as counsel by the accused must meet the same general standards that are applied for assigned counsel. RCM 502(d)(3). However, if the military counsel selected by the accused is not "reasonably available," the defendant must select another counsel. Art. 38(b)(3)(B), UCMJ. The decision concerning availability is made by counsel's commanding officer but is subject to the convening authority's review. Two cases upholding decisions of unavailability involved the only officer of a unit ordered to immediate post-war Germany and an officer who was facing charges of his own and undergoing psychiatric examination.

Once an attorney-client relationship has attached, the "reasonably available" standard ceases to apply; once appointed, counsel may be severed from the case only if the accused so demands or "good cause" is shown for severance based on extraordinary problems. United States v. Taylor (N.C.M.R. 1977). Routine transfers, financial, logistical, or administrative burdens are not sufficient "good cause." The test is met, however, when original counsel leaves the service or becomes ill.

b. Stages of the Proceedings

The right to counsel attaches not only at trial, but also at pretrial investigations, Art. 32 investigations, pretrial lineups (more broadly than in civilian practice), depositions, and upon appeal. The warning requirement of Tempia, supra, insures that counsel often will be brought into criminal matters quickly and the Art. 70 practice of appointing new counsel upon appeal helps insure a fresh look at trial errors and competency of trial defense counsel.

There are, however, problems which may arise in the transition from trial counsel to appellate counsel. For example, in United States v. Palenius, (C.M.A. 1977), trial counsel persuaded the accused not to request appellate counsel for his automatic appeal to the Court of Military Review on the erroneous theory that waiver of counsel would speed reversal on appeal of the court-martial conviction. When such relief was denied, the accused raised the issue of inadequate post-conviction representation of counsel. The court agreed with the accused, citing the right to appellate defense counsel. Furthermore, it outlined the responsibilities of trial defense counsel after conviction so that effective representation will not fall in the cracks during the transition from trial to appeal. The court said that, to avoid "fragmented, noncontinuous representation," trial defense counsel should (1) advise his client concerning the appeal process, taking action as necessary during such intermediate stages as the SJA review and presentation of pleas to the convening authority for modification or reduction of sentence; (2) familiarize himself with any issues that should be argued on appeal and discuss these with both the accused and appellate defense counsel; (3) remain attentive to his client's needs for advice on such matters as the possibility of an Art. 57(b) deferment of sentence; and (4) maintain the attorney-client relationship until substitute defense counsel or appellate counsel have been properly designated and have commenced the performance of their duties.

c. Competency and Integrity

The general test of competency of counsel, whether appointed or selected, was explored in depth by the Court of Military Appeals in United States v. Rivas (C.M.A. 1977). The Rivas court rejected the low standard that incompetency will be found only when the "attorney's efforts [were] so poor as to have rendered the trial a farce or mockery." Rather, a two-pronged standard of average competency was adopted: (1) counsel must be of average competency in recognizing legal issues and defenses in the military criminal law field and (2) counsel must exercise that competence "without omission throughout the trial." While it is inappropriate for appellate courts to "second-guess the strategic or tactical decisions made at trial by defense counsel," inaction where there is no "realistic strategic or tactical decision" behind counsel's silence constitutes incompetency.

Finally, defense counsel must be careful to avoid command pressures which might weaken the professional and moral obligation to provide the best possible defense of the client. For example, a conviction was reversed when defense counsel, after repeated requests for a witness he felt was essential to his client's case, caved in and withdrew his request following the military judge's stern and intimidating lecture. United States v. Giermek (C.G.C.M.R. 1977). In another instance, the appeals court noted that defense counsel was obligated to present at the court-martial level any evidence of command pressure or improper SJA remarks to court members which might taint the fairness of the trial. United States v. Borner (C.M.A. 1953).

CHAPTER 7

THE LAW OF ARMED CONFLICT

A. SCOPE AND APPLICATION

Various terms used interchangeably by international law scholars apply to the branch of international law that deals most directly with warfare. Variously called the "law of war," the "international law of armed conflict" and "international humanitarian law," the field is defined by the United States Department of Defense (DoD) as:

> That part of international law that regulates the conduct of armed hostilities. It is often called the law of armed conflict. The law of war encompasses all international law for the conduct of hostilities binding on the United States or its individual citizens, including treaties and international agreements to which the United States is a party, and applicable customary international law.

DoD Dir. 5100.77, DoD Law of War Program, para. 3.1 (9 Dec. 1998).

Historically, the application of international humanitarian law turned on whether the armed conflict was classified as a belligerency or insurgency. A belligerency is an armed conflict between sovereign States (unless there was recognition of belligerency in a civil war); an insurgency is a civil commotion caused by armed violence within the territory of a sovereign State that is subject to internal domestic laws. Consistent with this traditional view, the Department of the Army Field Manual, THE LAW OF LAND WARFARE (July 1956) defines war as "a legal condition of armed hostility between States * * * usually accompanied by the commission of acts of violence * * *." (FM 27-10, App. A-3, para. 8).

It is now clear that the law of armed conflict reaches more hostilities than "war" and includes internal armed conflicts. Expansion in the scope of international humanitarian law was brought about by Prosecutor v. Tadic (a/k/a Dule), No. IT-94-1-AR72 (Oct. 2, 1995) a decision of the Appeals Chamber of the International Criminal Tribunal for the Former Yugoslavia (ICTY). The issue in Tadic was whether the Trial Chamber had jurisdiction over violations occurring in internal conflicts as opposed to international conflicts that had risen to the level of a belligerency. After an extensive review of the of the emergence of customary rules to govern internal armed strife and the authority conferred on the ICTY by the United Nations Security Council in the ICTY Statute, the appellate court concluded that:

[C]ustomary rules have developed to govern internal strife. These rules ***cover such areas as protection of civilians from *** indiscriminate attacks, protection of civilian objects, in particular cultural property, protection of all those who do not (or no longer) take active part in hostilities, as well as prohibition of means of warfare proscribed in international armed conflicts and ban of certain methods of conducting hostilities. Para. 127.

Until Tadic, internal armed conflicts were governed almost exclusively by Common Article 3 of the Geneva Conventions of 1949 and Additional Protocol II to the Geneva Conventions. (See discussion below.) After Tadic, however, internal armed conflict has been viewed as governed by rules of customary international law. The practical impact of these rules for American combat forces is likely to be limited in view of the requirement of the DoD Law of War Program that all members of the U.S. armed forces "comply with the law of war during all armed conflicts, however such conflicts are characterized, and with the principles and spirit of the law of war during all other operations." DoD Dir. 5100.77, DoD Law of War Program, para. 5.3.1 (9 Dec. 1998).

1. LAWFUL WAR AND UNLAWFUL WAR

War results when one nation seeks to impose its will on another by force. War's hostile contention need not embrace armed resistance as, for example, with the German invasion of Denmark in World War II. The nineteenth-century military theorist Carl von Clausewitz described war as the continuation of foreign policy by other means, i.e., violent means.

Efforts to impose moral restraints on war date back at least to the writings of Saint Augustine and Saint Thomas Aquinas. Modern approaches to restraining the conduct of war begin with the writings of Hugo Grotius in the 17th century. Such efforts were later furthered by the evolution of total war, of which the American Civil War is an example, with its devastating effects on civilians. More efforts were made in the nineteenth century through the work of the Swiss humanitarian Henri Dunant whose efforts led to the founding of the International Red Cross. In the twentieth century, the Kellogg–Briand Pact (1928) sought to outlaw war as an instrument of national policy, but lacked effective enforcement mechanisms. Even the United Nations Charter, while outlawing aggressive war, preserves to nations the right of individual and collective self-defense of member states in Article 51. Compare U.N. Charter Article 2(4) with Article 51. The lawfulness of war under international law thus turns on its conformity to the international norms that regulate it.

A formal declaration of war is not required for the application of the law of war (FM 27-10, App. A-4, para. 9). The applicability of international humanitarian law will turn on the nature and extent of hostilities including the number of troops involved, the duration of the conflict and its disruptive impact and the methods of combat.

Every nation has a right to maintain its political and territorial integrity. Thus, regulation of civil war is left to the discretion of the sovereign entity in which the conflict occurs until it reaches the status of a belligerency.   (FM 27-10, App. A-4, para. 11.)

Although simple on its face, this international/civil war distinction has proven difficult to apply. No precise test exists to separate purely internal hostilities from international war. Entities which are not yet recognized by the world community as constituting separate nations may, during a struggle for independence, either claim the protection of international law, or have its requirements imposed upon them. In general, humanitarian laws of warfare such as the Geneva Conventions (discussed below), which reflect the general rules in this area, would apply to the conflict if this entity qualifies either 1) as a "power" or "state" capable of becoming a party to the conventions, or 2) as a "belligerent" involved in a conflict of international dimensions.

A group of people can claim to be a "state" or "nation" when they 1) have an indigenous population, 2) reside in a defined territory, 3) have effective governmental control over that territory, and 4) can enter into relations with other nations.

Customary international laws of war apply to more than just recognized or recognizable "nations" on the theory that at some point fighting becomes significant enough to require international attention, even though no international boundaries may have been crossed and the conditions for statehood have not yet been met. Thus, for example, the Geneva Conventions protect and bind entities termed "belligerents" which fill the conceptual gap between recognized nations and isolated bands of rebels within a nation. To qualify as a belligerent, scholars have argued that five prerequisites must be met: 1) recognition by other parties to the struggle that the entity is a belligerent; 2) observation by the entity of the law of war; 3) possession by the entity of an armed force with a responsible command structure; 4) existence within the entity of some semblance of a government; and 5) control by that government over a significant amount of territory.

Even if a conflict is categorized as a civil insurrection as opposed to belligerency, some portions of international humanitarian law will apply. For example, the case of Prosecutor v. Tadic (ICTY 1995) established that international humanitarian law applies to all parties in internal conflicts that fall short of belligerency.

Intricacies of international law beyond the scope of this treatise can affect the status even of the rulings of international tribunals such as the International Court of Justice (ICJ). Consider for example, the case of Military and Paramilitary Activities in and Against Nicaragua (Nicar. v. U.S.), 1986 I.C.J 14, in which Nicaragua challenged the support extended by the United States to the Contras, a paramilitary force seeking to overthrow the government of Nicaragua. The United States withdrew from proceedings before the ICJ after concerns arose about the objectivity of the court. The tangled course of the proceedings and their effect on the authoritativeness of that opinion are well-captured in the following synopsis of the ICJ's proceedings in conformity with the Statute governing it:

Although the Court was [placed] in an awkward position [by the withdrawal of the United States], it by no means "had to believe" Nicaragua's evidence and witnesses. Pursuant to Article 53 of the Statute, in the absence of a party, the Court must, before deciding in favor of the claim of the present party, "satisfy itself ... that the claim is well founded in fact and law." *** [The] United States withdrew from the proceedings *** convinced, as it publicly stated, that the Court was not proceeding objectively. That charge was true, as demonstrated by several departures from due process, the most serious of which was refusing intervention by El Salvador. *** Subsequently, the Court's whitewash of Nicaragua's actions became all too clear. It had chosen to endorse Nicaragua's claim that it was lending no material support to rebellion in El Salvador. But in 1993, an explosion in Managua of an arms cache of the Salvadoran rebels led to condemnation by the UN Secretary-General and the Security Council and to an admission and apology by the rebels.

Richard B. Bilder and Stephen M. Schwebel, "Book Review and Note on The Settlement of Disputes in International Law: Institutions and Procedures," 95 Am. J. Int. Law 464 (2001) (internal citations omitted). After withdrawing from the proceedings in the Nicaragua case, the United States in 1985 withdrew from the compulsory jurisdiction of the ICJ.

Even the President as commander in chief of the nation's military is required to "take care" to follow the requirements of customary international law "where there is no treaty, and no controlling executive or legislative act or judicial decision." The Paquette Habana (S.Ct. 1900). That obligation extends as well to the President's inferiors down the chain of command. Even official written guidance from military authorities can quickly become stale or outdated by changes in customary international humanitarian law, so it is imperative that field commanders during hostilities follow advice from attorney advisors competent on the requirements of international humanitarian law.

2. INITIATION AND TERMINATION OF AN INTERNATIONAL ARMED CONFLICT

a. Initiation

An international armed conflict may begin in any one of three ways: (1) by declaration of war; (2) by the announcement of one state that it considers itself to be at war with another state; or (3) through the commission of hostile acts employing military forces by one state against another. Traditionally, where war is commenced by the outbreak of hostilities followed by a declaration of war, the legal beginning of the war is the time of the declaration. Savage v. Sun Life Assurance Co. of Canada (W.D.La.1944) (insured killed in Japanese sneak attack on Pearl Harbor). The more modern view, particularly where insurance policies are involved, is that the word "war" should be given its ordinary meaning rather than a strict legal interpretation. New York Life Ins. Co. v. Bennion (10th Cir.1946).

The Third Hague Convention of 1907 attempted to formalize the commencement of war. It required a prior and explicit warning before hostilities could commence. The ensuing declaration of war was required to state the motives behind the war. Furthermore, all neutral states had to be notified without delay that a state of war existed. The Convention, ratified by only 28 states, soon became obsolete. Today, the outbreak of hostilities without a formal declaration or ultimatum would be regarded as war in a legal sense unless both parties clearly denied the existence of a state of war.

b. Anticipatory Self-Defense

The Bush Administration takes the view that anticipatory self-defense, also known as preventive self-defense or preemptive self-defense, is a necessary aspect of the policy of United States in the War on Terrorism. See Authorization of Force Against Terrorism, Pub.L. No. 107-40, 115 Stat. 224 (2001). The right of nations to individual and collective self-defense is preserved in Article 51 of the U.N. Charter.

Historically, the right of anticipatory self-defense has been limited to circumstances involving "a necessity of self-defense, instant, overwhelming, leaving no choice of means, no moment for deliberation." These limitations emerged from an exchange of correspondence in 1841 between United States Secretary of State Daniel Webster and Henry Fox, the British minister in Washington, regarding an 1837 incident when the American steamer Caroline, while preparing an attack on Canada, was attacked in U.S. territory by Canadians.

The overriding issue today is whether Webster's limits on recourse to anticipatory self-defense are obsolete. The demands of modern high-technology warfare may have rendered the Caroline limitations obsolete. Alternatively, the limitations may be inapplicable in the case of terrorist attacks by non-state actors or state surrogates. Modern instances of acts of anticipatory self-defense include Israel's air strike on an Arab airfield in the 1967 War, the 1981 Israeli air raid on an Iraqi nuclear reactor, and the 2003 war against Iraq.

c. Termination

An armed conflict may be terminated by 1) a treaty of peace; 2) a cessation of hostilities and establishment of peaceful relations without a treaty; 3) unconditional surrender; or 4) subjugation.

The actual signing of the peace treaty leads only to a cessation of hostilities. The state of war is not ended until the treaty becomes effective through ratification. At that point all normal peacetime rights and duties between the parties to the agreement go back into effect. Furthermore, Art. 118 of the 1949 Geneva Convention Relative to the Treatment of Prisoners of War requires immediate release and repatriation of all prisoners.

The cessation of hostilities alone cannot terminate the state of war. Rather, both parties must deny the continued existence of the state of war and must reestablish peaceful relations.

Uncertainty as to the date of termination is generally avoided by issuing a suitable declaration of peace. An armistice, which is a contractual agreement between belligerents to bring about a temporary suspension of hostilities, does not end a war. A special armistice, or truce, ceases hostilities in a portion of the war theater. A general armistice is a temporary cessation between all parties. While the general armistice might appear to terminate war, it does not do so in a legal sense. Under contemporary practice, however, an armistice is often a prelude to a peace treaty, and it may be followed by the gradual establishment of peaceful relations. To the extent that it indicates an intent of the parties to terminate war, it is inconsistent to deny that the state of war has ended.

Capitulation is an agreement between opposing commanders for the surrender of troops in a prescribed locality or district. It is not a contractual agreement and does not refer to the surrender of the entire state. Unconditional surrender by the state does not terminate war unless the victor indicates that a total termination of hostilities on its part will accompany this submission by the defeated state.

Subjugation is the total military and political conquest of one state by the other. The subjugated state ceases to exist; its government disintegrates and eventually disappears; there is a total absence of resistance to the conqueror. If resistance continues, there may be a military "conquest" by one state of the other, but there is no subjugation.

3. RIGHTS AND RESPONSIBILITIES OF NATIONS NOT INVOLVED IN THE CONFLICT

A neutral nation ostensibly refrains from any participation in a foreign war. This restraint includes the neutral state's responsibility to prevent and regulate acts, whether by its government, its nationals, or by other nations, which are inconsistent with such nonparticipation. Some scholars claim that neutrality is no longer available to nations during an international war, primarily because of provisions of the U.N. Charter such as Art. 2(5), which requires U.N. members to abandon neutrality and assist the U.N. in any military action it undertakes. However, Art. 2(5) applies only to conflicts endangering world peace in which collective U.N. action is initiated. Since such action is obviously not taken with regard to all armed conflicts, the rules of neutrality are still an important facet of the modern international law of war.

a. Neutrality vs. Nonbelligerency

Neutrality necessarily implies impartiality. Although a nation may be technically neutral in a given conflict, total impartiality is rarely maintained. For example, prior to 1941, the United States was officially "neutral" concerning the conflict in Europe. Yet American diplomatic and domestic policy clearly favored the Allied Powers.

Emerging schools of international law label these "partial neutrals" as "nonbelligerents," thereby affording them certain rights and protections. The label is appropriate, for example, in those situations in which the neutral state's preferential treatment of one belligerent over another results from treaty obligations assumed before a war, which the neutral must continue to honor. The status of these nonbelligerents is the specific subject of two treaties, The Hague Conventions V and VIII of 1907 (HC V and VIII), which define the rights and duties of neutral powers and persons during land and naval warfare respectively. Both represent modifications of the customary international law of neutrality, yet the precise substance and scope of application of these rules remain unclear.

b. Rights and Responsibilities of Neutrals

The rights of neutral powers stem from one premise: a belligerent should not interfere with the independence of a neutral state. Accordingly, the neutral power has a right to the inviolability of its territory, to uninterrupted trade, and to the continuance of its status as a neutral.

The right of inviolable territory prohibits belligerent invasion, occupation or other use of neutral land. Corollary rules prohibit a belligerent from establishing communication facilities on the territory of a neutral nation for military purposes (HC V, Art. 3a) or using prewar facilities located on neutral land in the war effort. (HC V, Art. 4). The same rights extend to a neutral state's territorial waters. (HC VIII, Art. I). There are, however, two important exceptions to the general principle of inviolability. First, if neutral territory is invaded and the neutral state cannot or does not prevent the violation of its neutrality, a second belligerent party may attack the invader while it is on neutral land. Second, with regard to territorial waters, a neutral state may at its discretion either forbid all access to its waters or grant 24–hour asylum. (HC VIII, Art. 12).

The right to uninterrupted trade is embodied primarily in The Hague Convention VIII which prohibits interference with neutral commerce on the seas. Neutral goods are immune from seizure even if on an enemy ship, and a neutral flag protects all goods except contraband of war. (Declaration of Dans 1856, the predecessor to HC VIII). Other treaties protect other forms of trade. For example, a neutral power may allow private persons to continue trade with belligerents. (HC V, Art. 7). Only if the government of the neutral state trades with a belligerent is neutral status lost.

The right to continued neutral status permits a neutral state to resort to force to preserve that status without losing its neutrality. (HC V, Art. 10).

The primary duty of the neutral state is to refrain from participation or involvement in a foreign conflict. To this end, neutrals must prevent, by all means at their disposal, provision of military supplies, munitions, or other aid to a belligerent. Incident to this obligation is a duty to prevent violations of their neutrality. (HC V, Art. 5). Hence, a neutral is required to intern belligerent troops found within its territory, unless the forces are merely sick and wounded being transported away from the battle area. (HC V,

Art. 12). These restrictions, however, only pertain to the governments of the neutral state. Although most nations, in an effort to preserve their neutrality, actively attempt to limit the activities and contacts of their nationals with a foreign belligerent, they are not required to do so. Furthermore, the rules of neutrality do not in theory apply to conflicts which are internal to a single nation, so long as the neutral's aid is channeled to the recognized government.

B. SOURCES AND SUBSTANCE

The sources of the rules which govern the conduct of a nation involved in an armed conflict of an international character can be divided into two primary categories: first, "statutory" expressions of the law found in various international agreements and treaties; and second, the "common law" or customary law of armed conflict reflected in decisions of international or domestic courts, the domestic laws and armed forces regulations of the combatants, and simply the consistent behavior of nations over a significant period of time.

1. TREATIES RELATING TO ARMED CONFLICT

a. Treaties on Use of Force

The primary restraint on the use of force by nations in settling their disputes is the Charter of the United Nations. It provides that its members are to refrain from the threat or use of force against other nations in any manner inconsistent with the purposes of the U.N. The Security Council is given primary responsibility for enforcing the peace. However, the Charter left intact in Art. 51 "the inherent right of individual or collective self-defense" if a member is attacked until the Security Council takes some action to restore peace. If the system of collective security does not function effectively, members have recourse to mutual security pacts based on "collective self-defense," or to the use of regional "arrangements" or "agencies" for maintaining peace under Arts. 52–54. For example, Art. 51 furnished a secondary ground for justifying the recourse to force by many U.N. members in 1950 to repel the North Korean attack upon South Korea, despite the fact that South Korea was not a member of the U.N. In addition, Art. 52 was used as the basis for the American "defensive quarantine" of Cuba in 1962, under the auspices of the Organization of American States.

b. Treaties on Conduct of Hostilities

The law of armed conflict is comprised of treaties to which the United States is a signatory or acceding power as well as customary international law. U.S. Const. Art. VI, cl. 2; and The Paquete Habana (S.Ct.1900). This body of law governs the conduct of American armed forces during war. The United States is a party to most major treaties relating to warfare, including The Hague Conventions of 1907, the Geneva Conventions of 1929 and 1949, the Genocide Convention of 1948, and the Geneva Protocol for the Prohibition of the Use in War of Asphyxiating, or Other Gases and Bacteriological Methods of Warfare of 1925.

All of these treaties are based upon three closely related fundamental principles: (1) military necessity—force should be directed only at those targets which are directly related to the enemy's ability to wage war; (2) proportionality—the degree of such force used should be directly related to the importance of the target and should be no more than is necessary to achieve the military objective; and (3) avoidance of unnecessary suffering or the humanitarian principle—those targets and degrees of force should be selected which will result in the least possible suffering, destruction of civilian property, loss of civilian life, and loss of natural resources.

(1) The 1907 Hague Conventions

These treaties represent an early attempt to regulate the conduct of war. Although there are actually five Hague Conventions of 1907 to which the United States is a party, the most important for the purposes of this chapter is the Fourth Hague Convention of 1907 Respecting the Laws and Customs of War on Land, and its Annexed Regulations.

The provisions of The Hague Conventions are now recognized as customary international law. To preserve human lives and rights, military attacks must be strictly necessary to a legitimate military aim. Destruction and loss of life must be minimized and not disproportionately related to the advantages of a particular military engagement. Captured prisoners cannot be killed, captured towns cannot be pillaged, weapons used must not cause unnecessary suffering, and property, rights, and lives of civilians must be respected. This basic Hague law serves as the foundation for subsequent developments in the law of war.

(2) The Geneva Conventions

(a) General

After World War I, the restrictions embodied in the 1907 Hague Conventions were complemented and expanded in the Geneva Conventions of 1929. Similarly, a revision of the 1929 treaties followed World War II. There are four separate Geneva Conventions of 1949 relevant to the protection of war victims: (1) the Convention for the Amelioration of the Condition of the Wounded and Sick in Armed Forces in the Field (GWS); (2) the Convention for the Amelioration of the Condition of the Wounded, Sick and Shipwrecked Members of Armed Forces at Sea (GWS–Sea); (3) the Convention Relative to the Treatment of Prisoners of War (GPW); and (4) the Convention Relative to the Protection of Civilian Prisoners in Time of War (GCC). They were concluded in 1949 and entered into force in 1950. They became binding upon the United States when ratified by the Senate in February, 1956, but were observed prior to that during the Korean War as customary international law.

(b) Scope of Application

Article 2, common to all four Geneva Conventions of 1949, indicates which international conflicts trigger application of the treaties. Parties to a conflict who are also parties to the conventions are bound. Significant portions of the four conventions have acquired the status of customary international law and are binding even on states that are not parties to them. See Meron, "The Geneva Conventions as Customary Law," 81 Am. J. Int'l L. 348 (1987).

The most difficult questions of applicability of these conventions arise where one of the parties to the hostilities is not a recognized "power" or nation. The factors relevant to the determination of whether an entity can legitimately claim the status of statehood or belligerency have been discussed previously. Protocols I and II Additional to the 1949 Geneva Conventions extend humanitarian protections to combatants in conflicts which have not reached the level of a belligerency as well as additional protections to civilians in circumstances not now covered by the four Geneva conventions. Portions of Protocol I incorporate principles which have the status of customary international law. See Hogue, "Identifying Customary International Law in Protocol I: A Proposed Restatement," 13 Loy. L.A. Int'l & Comp. L. J. 279 (1990).

(c) Substance

(i) *General Provisions.* The general, common themes which run throughout these conventions have been described above. In addition, there are a number of more specific principles which are common to all four of the conventions. These are set out below in tabular form:

Convention Articles

Principle	GWS	GWS-Sea	GPW	GCC
To respect and insure respect for Conventions	1	1	1	1
Adherence to Conventions even when opponent is not a party thereto	2	2	2	2
Application of Conventions to any armed conflict, including internal conflicts	2,3	2,3	2,3	2,3
Nondiscrimination by race, sex, language or religion	3,12	3,12	3,16	3,13,27
Rights of parties to enter into special supplementary agreement	6	6	6	7
Inability of protected persons to renounce the benefits of the Conventions	7	7	7	8
Use of neutral "protecting powers" to insure compliance with the Conventions	8,10,11	8,10,11	8,10,11	9,11,12
Private relief organizations permitted to continue activities unimpeded by Conventions	9	9	9	10
Requirement for education of military and civilian populations concerning Conventions	49	48	127	144
Requirement to make violations of Conventions violations of domestic law of party as well	49,50	50,51	127	146

(ii) *Classification of Participants.* The conventions attempt to isolate the effects of warfare as much as possible by distinguishing between military and nonmilitary targets and by categorizing the population of a warring state into combatants (both lawful and unlawful) and noncombatants. A person who engages in the conflict is legally entitled to do so, and can claim the protections of international law, only if certain factors are present. The individual will be a lawful combatant if he or she is a member of the regular armed forces of a party to the hostilities or if he or she is a member of an irregular force that fulfills certain requirements which thereby afford them international legal recognition. These requirements are: (1) command of the force "by a person responsible for his subordinates"; (2) clear designation of the force by "a fixed distinctive sign recognizable at a distance"; (3) establishment of clear combatant status of the force by "carrying arms openly"; and (4) conduct of the operations of the force "in accordance with the laws and customs of war." GPW, Art. 4A(2).

The convention also gives "lawful" status to those persons engaged in what some commentators term a "*levee en masse*," i.e., a spontaneous resort to arms by the inhabitants of a nation being invaded who have not had sufficient time to form themselves into regular armed units. However, to retain the protection of international law, these citizen groups must carry their weapons openly and themselves respect the law of war.

The objective in war is to win, to defeat the enemy. Within the boundaries of the law of war, members of an enemy's armed forces may be injured or killed and property destroyed. Obedience to the laws of war does not interfere with the successful prosecution of the battle.

Hostile forces may always be attacked. By the same token, however, a combatant must be spared when rendered unable to further resist and ceases hostile action. The laws of war, to the extent possible, focus war and its effects on combatants, those engaged in or seeking to engage in hostilities; those on the periphery—civilians, noncombatants, and those out of the fight by injury, sickness or capture—are to be spared.

Upon capture, an enemy who is *hors de combat* (out of action) must be given all the rights of a prisoner of war: (1) guarantee of the basic necessities of life, including adequate food, medical care, shelter, and clothing (GPW, Art. 25–30); (2) notice of capture communicated to the prisoner's home country (GPW, Art. 69); (3) if forced to work, the prisoner must receive compensation, be placed in a decent work environment, and be employed only in specified classes of work (GPW, Art. 49–57); and (4) if suspected of or charged with war crimes, the prisoner must be accorded basic due process of law, such as a fair trial before a competent tribunal, a right to confront witnesses, the right to prepare a defense with the aid of an attorney, and if a sentence is imposed, the prisoner's home country must be notified and execution of the sentence must be delayed until six months after such notification (GPW, Art. 85).

A neutral state can be designated a "protecting power" by agreement between the parties to the conflicts; representatives of this state are permitted to inspect internment facilities whenever circumstances permit to insure compliance with the Convention. GPW, Art. 8.

"Noncombatants" can include both civilians and certain military personnel, such as chaplains and medical personnel. GCC delineates protections to be accorded the noncombatant population in time of war. Specifically: (1) civilians and undefended towns are not to be the object of attack, although noncombatant casualties are permissible as incidental to a legitimate attack on a military target; (2) wounded and sick civilians are to be assisted if at all possible, and civilian hospitals are immune from siege; (3) pillage is prohibited; (4) noncombatants cannot be taken as hostages, and internment of civilians can be justified only by the strictest military necessity; and (5) if interned, the same rights guaranteed combatant prisoners of war are to be accorded noncombatant prisoners. GCC, Art. 13–38.

There is, however, at least one limitation in the definition of "civilian" in GCC which undermines its humanitarian purpose. According to Art. 4, certain noncombatants who will not be protected by the Conventions are (1) citizens of a neutral nation who are present in the territory of a belligerent when their home country has retained normal diplomatic relations with the belligerent; and (2) citizens of a co-belligerent nation who are "in the hands of" the belligerent state when their home country has retained normal diplomatic relations with the belligerent.

The lack of clarity with regard to this second category is particularly troublesome. Does "in the hands of" mean "in the territory of" similar to neutrals? What of citizens forced to cross the border into the territory of the belligerent state?

The German execution of Hungarian Jews, for example, might not have been considered a war crime under GCC since these persons would have been nationals of a co-belligerent of Germany. The only protections afforded such noncombatants are found in the absolute guarantees of GCC, Arts. 13–22 (protection of the wounded, aged, expectant mothers, children under the age of fifteen, etc.).

Some individuals may lack authority under either the domestic law of their home country or the international law of armed conflict to engage in hostilities. These would include the following: (1) combatants, individually or in groups, who do not qualify as a *levee en masse* and fail to observe the requirements of an irregular force (often referred to as "guerrillas" or "partisans"); (2) spies; and 3) mercenaries. When these combatants are captured, their treatment is left to the discretion of the detaining nation. Some nations extend prisoner-of-war protections to all combatants despite their actual or alleged status, although allowed to treat these illegal participants as common criminals. See The Law of Land Warfare, FM 27–10, App. A-21, para. 80. GPW does require that if there is any doubt concerning the status of a prisoner, the protections of the Convention should apply. The Law of Land Warfare requires a determination by a competent tribunal comprised of no fewer than three officers to be convened to determine this issue. FM 27–10, App. A-19, para. 71.

Yet the modern relevance of these rules, which permit the denial of prisoner-of-war status to such groups, is open to question. Given the nature of modern warfare, many combatants fail to qualify for the label "lawful" within the meaning of GPW, Art. 4. Guerrilla warfare, partisan underground movements, spies, and mercenaries frequently exist in modern conflicts and, in fact, are often essential elements of military strategy. Yet the inherently subversive nature of such forces deprives their members of prisoner-of-war status upon capture. Indeed, mercenaries, according to the scant authority in the area, are illegal under both customary international law and the domestic law of many nations. Thus, none of these groups come within the mandate of Art. 4 and are frequently subjected to inhumane treatment or execution upon capture.

Under both international and domestic law, American citizens who fight in the military forces of an enemy belligerent may be tried by military tribunal and held as a prisoner of war until the termination of hostilities. See Ex parte Quirin (S.Ct. 1942) (capture in U.S.) and In re Territo (9th Cir. 1946) (overseas battlefield capture in open conflict).

(3) The Genocide Convention

Another major treaty relevant to armed conflict to which the United States is a party, and which binds all nations as customary law, is the 1948 Convention on the Proceedings and Punishment of the Crime of Genocide. This treaty punishes any "act committed with intent to destroy, in whole or in part, a national, ethnic, racial, or religious group." It thereby plugs any potential loopholes left in the protections afforded civilian populations in Art. 4 of GCC by prohibiting campaigns of annihilation within the belligerent itself, or a co-belligerent, during the conflict. Officials of a state directly involved in the commission, attempt, or encouragement of acts of genocide are held criminally responsible.

Who should enforce the Genocide Convention? A variety of approaches have been followed in recent instances of genocide. For example, the United Nations Security Council created a tribunal to adjudicate war crimes through The Statute of the International Criminal Tribunal for former Yugoslavia in 1993, and a similar tribunal for the trial of war crimes in Rwanda in1994. As a substitute for the ad hoc approach reflected in the instances of the former Yugoslavia and Rwanda (and the post-World War II prosecutions against Germany and Japan), the International Criminal Court was established by treaty (the Rome Statute of the International Criminal Court) in 1998. The United States did not ratify the treaty establishing the court and is not a party to it. The jurisdiction of the court is discussed further below.

(4) Geneva Convention Protocols I and II

Just as World War I and World War II revealed gross inadequacies in then-existing laws of armed conflict, the hostilities in Vietnam, the Mideast, and Africa have exposed gaps in the protections afforded by the Geneva Conventions of 1949. In 1972, the International Committee of the Red Cross sponsored the first session of the Diplomatic Conference on the Reaffirmation and Development of International Humanitarian Law Applicable in Armed Conflict. After four conferences attended by the signatories of the 1949 conventions, two Draft

Protocols were opened for signature on December 12, 1977: the Protocol Additional to the Geneva Conventions of 12 August 1949 and Relating to the Protection of Victims of International Armed Conflicts (Protocol I); and the Protocol Additional to the Geneva Conventions of 12 August 1949 and Relating to the Protection of Victims of Noninternational Armed Conflicts (Protocol II).

Protocol I strengthens the Geneva Conventions by: 1) extending to civilian medical units the protections accorded to military medical units; 2) clarifying the protections accorded medical transport, including aircraft; 3) increasing the responsibilities of parties to search for, report on, and care for the missing and the remains of the dead; 4) providing expanded protection for civilians and civilian objects; and 5) insuring humane treatment for all persons. Despite these virtues, Protocol I weakens the conventions and the convention process itself by politicizing the law of war. This is evident, for example, in Protocol I's treatment of certain types of irregulars who would receive law of war protections notwithstanding their failure to distinguish themselves from civilians or acknowledge their status as combatants. Protocol I, Art. 44. This provision is a substantial disincentive for guerrillas and other combatants to distinguish themselves from civilians. Protocol I thereby reduces civilian protection because civilians will be suspected of harboring concealed guerrillas or combatants in their midst.

With respect to the problem of mercenaries, noted above, Protocol I denies prisoner-of-war status to mercenaries. Protocol I, Art. 47. This further politicizes the law of war by rationing humanitarian protection based on one's motives for joining the conflict.

Protocol II extends the traditional norms of war to a broader class of armed conflicts. Article 1 supplements common Article 3 of the Geneva Conventions by applying protections to non-international or internal conflicts. Article 2 extends "protections to all persons affected by an armed conflict 'without any' adverse distinction based * * * on race, colour, sex, language, religion or belief, political or other opinion, national or social origin, wealth, * * * birth or other status." Article 4 provides that nonparticipants in a conflict subject to the Protocol are entitled to humane treatment. Expressly banned are murder and cruel treatment such as torture, mutilation, or corporal punishment. In addition, collective punishments, hostage-taking, acts of terrorism, outrages on personal dignity (e.g., humiliating and degrading treatment, rape, forced prostitution, and indecent assault), slavery and slave trade, and pillage. Children receive special protection under this article. Under Article 5, special protections must be extended to captives including medical treatment, relief, and special protection for women.

Other articles provide, *inter alia*, protection for medical units and medical transport, protects against making civilians the object of attack, and prohibits attacks designed to starve civilians by destroying water supplies and the agricultural infrastructure. Dams, dikes and nuclear power stations are protected from targeting if civilians would suffer severe casualties from their attack. Protection is also extended to historic monuments, works of art and culturally significant places of worship.

Serious questions remain concerning the application of Protocol II. The Protocol, apparently, is not meant to be applicable to mere "police actions" or "isolated riots," but the distinctions between these and true civil wars will be difficult to determine. This problem may be partially resolved by Prosecutor v. Tadic (ICTY 1995), which established that international humanitarian law applies to all parties in internal conflicts that fall short of belligerency. Also, Protocol II is not specific with respect to appropriate mechanisms to assure compliance with its provisions. Enforcement may prove a serious problem in many instances where the combatants are themselves poorly supplied and therefore unable to extend the sorts of protections envisioned by the Protocol.

(5) International Covenant on Civil and Political Rights

The International Covenant on Civil and Political Rights became binding upon all its signatories as of March 1976, three months after its 35th ratification. Based upon the 1948 Universal Declaration of Human Rights, promulgated as a resolution by the U.N. General Assembly, the covenant seeks to preserve fundamental human rights during both war and peace. The treaty guarantees the right to life and security of any individual (Arts. 6 and 9), the right to freedom from torture and other inhumane treatment (Art. 7), and forbids arbitrary detention (Arts. 9–12). These rights may be derogated in times of "public emergency", but only "to the extent strictly required by the exigencies of the situation" and be preserved without distinction as to "race, colour, sex, language, religion or social origin" (Art. 4). Thus, the covenant would significantly affect treatment of captives and civilians during war.

The United States ratified the Covenant in 1992 with five reservations, four interpretative declarations and five understandings. These qualifications to Articles 6 and 7 of the Covenant sought to preserve the right of the United States to impose the death penalty and limit the meaning of the terms "cruel, inhuman or degrading treatment or punishment" to that prohibited by the U.S. Constitution. But at least some elements of Articles 6 and 7 may reflect customary international law binding on the United States.

2. THE CUSTOMARY LAW OF ARMED CONFLICT

Customary international law is often defined simply as the identified parameters of acceptable conduct which have developed or been discovered from the consistent behavior of nations over a period of time. That behavior is expressed in a number of different forms: acceptance of the decisions of international tribunals (the International Court of Justice, the Nuremberg Tribunal, etc.); reflection of international legal principles in domestic judicial decisions, statutes, and regulations; and the observations and opinions of legal scholars. These elements collectively comprise customary international law, and more narrowly for our purposes, the "common law" of armed conflict, an evolving but nevertheless significant body of international legal obligations. The fact that there is a search for these obligations indicates a commitment to the notion that there are certain universal norms and mores about war. The result is that certain conduct is proscribed because consensus world opinion forbids it. The United States recognizes the obligatory nature of customary international law. In Ex parte Quirin (S.Ct.1942), the Supreme Court upheld the jurisdiction of a military tribunal over German saboteurs for their use of civilian disguises. No codified prohibition of such spying then existed to justify their trial. Yet the Court allowed prosecution on the ground that infiltration by disguise violated the customary law of armed conflict. See also The Paquete Habana (S.Ct.1900).

The heart of customary restrictions upon warfare are the principles of military necessity, proportionality, and humanity (i.e., avoidance of unnecessary suffering) discussed earlier which were first enumerated in The Hague Conventions. Because these principles have been consistently reflected in subsequent treaties, court decisions, and domestic statutes, the world community recognizes the obligatory nature of these norms in all conflicts, despite the possible absence of express regulations on a particular activity. Many nations have enacted specific regulations which stem from these precepts.

One specific portion of the law of armed conflict which is a clear example of customary law is the area of criminal responsibility for acts in violation of the law of war, discussed in more detail below. Theories of such responsibility have been developed almost exclusively by judicial decision, both international and domestic, and by the statements of scholars and statesmen.

Yet, because there are few workable enforcement mechanisms for international obligations embodied either in treaties or in customary law, effectiveness of these norms depends upon the consent of nations to be bound. If a nation specifically rejects a rule of law expressed in a treaty signed by others or embodied in conduct observed by all other nations, it is difficult to argue that such a nation is in any way bound by that rule or can be held responsible for violations thereof. Fortunately, an exception exists to this requirement for consent. The doctrine of *jus cogens* holds that certain fundamental, behavioral norms are absolutely binding upon all nations. Nottebohm case (Liechtenstein v. Guatemala) [1955] I.C.J.Rep. 4. When a norm attains this peremptory status, it takes precedence over all other law, including treaty obligations.

These peremptory norms have significant relevance to the law of armed conflict. For example, prohibition of genocide is a peremptory norm. Thus, any country which exterminates racial, ethnic, or religious groups would be subject to sanction regardless of its status as a signatory to the genocide convention. Attorney General of Israel v. Eichmann (Israel, S.Ct.1968). Other peremptory norms are those crimes considered to be "grave breaches" of the law of armed conflict, including willfully killing, torturing, or inhumanely treating the wounded, prisoners of war, and civilians; compelling service in the armed forces of an enemy; and willfully depriving a captive of the rights of fair trial. GWS, Art. 50; GWS–Sea, Art. 51; GPW, Art. 130; and GCC, Art. 147.

An important part of the law of armed conflict is the Martens Clause, named for the Russian delegate to the 1907 Hague Peace Conference:

> Until a more complete code of the laws of war is issued, the High Contracting Parties think it right to declare that in cases not included in the Regulations adopted by them, populations and belligerents remain under the protection and empire of the principles of international law, as they result from the usages established between civilized nations, from the laws of humanity and the requirements of the public conscience.

"[O]riginally designed to provide residual humanitarian rules for the protection of the population of occupied territories, especially armed resisters in those territories," the clause has been employed to express in particular cases an international moral consensus. See Meron, "The Martens Clause, Principles of Humanity, and Dictates of Public Conscience," 94 Am. J. Int'l L. 78 (2000). The Martens Clause prevents erosion of international humanitarian law by a failure to specify textually all contingencies and thereby default to the judgment of military commanders.

C. THE LAW OF ARMED CONFLICT: MODERN WAR ISSUES

1. AIR WARFARE

a. Attacks Against Enemy Aircraft

The only generally recognized protection for military aircraft is the safety of neutral territory. Enemy aircraft may be attacked, destroyed, or captured by any means anywhere outside the boundaries of nations which have declared their neutrality. The only exceptions to this rule are identified medical aircraft which pose no threat, and any other aircraft specifically protected by agreement between the parties (for example, aircraft carrying negotiators or prisoners of war).

An aircraft which is disabled during combat is not granted any sort of protection. Since it is not possible to verify the fact that the aircraft has lost all means of combat, there are no practical means of enforcing a surrender. Parachutists evacuating a disabled aircraft should not be fired upon assuming they avoid engaging in hostilities. By contrast, paratroops deployed for hostile purposes are lawful targets and may be fired upon. Downed airmen are, of course, subject to capture upon surrender. They, as well as any rescue teams, may be attacked if resistance continues. Upon capture, airmen are entitled to prisoner-of-war status.

The civil aircraft of any enemy are entitled to additional protection. Military aircraft by their very nature constitute a valid military objective for an attack, but civil aircraft do not. The latter, to be a valid subject of attack, must exhibit some military threat, such as flying into a restricted area or failing to properly verify its status as a noncombatant. The rules with regard to attack of civil aircraft while on the ground are even more nebulous and are more directly related to the rules of aerial bombardment discussed in the next section. Clearly, such aircraft could be put to military use as transports at any moment. Thus, "as a practical matter, the degree of protection afforded to civil aviation and the potential military threat represented, varies directly with the intensity of the conflict."   Air Force Pamphlet (AFP) 110–31, ¶ 4–3(b).

b. Aerial Bombardment

The regulation of aerial bombardment follows the same pattern as the rules of air-to-air combat: it is lawful to attack military targets. Civilians and nonmilitary facilities are entitled to a certain degree of immunity from attack. The obvious difficulties in this area relate to the definition of a military target and situations in which military targets and protected civilian entities are placed side by side. When protected persons and facilities exist in close proximity to one another, generally speaking, the military target continues to be lawful and damage to protected persons or facilities is attributable to the enemy's choice as to location. The resulting damage is considered collateral damage and does not violate the law of war. An example of this is the location of anti-aircraft guns next to a hospital clearly marked with a Red Cross. The hospital loses its protection by being used to shield the guns from attack. The violation of the law of war in this instance is the placement of the guns. Damage to the hospital from aerial bombardment would be considered collateral to the lawful targeting of the guns.

A number of international agreements have attempted to set limits on the use of aerial bombardment. The Hague Peace Conference of 1899 adopted the "Hague Balloon Declaration" prohibiting the dropping of bombs from balloons for five years. By the time the Second Hague Conference was convened in 1907, it was clear that powered flight was a military reality; the parties agreed to expand the earlier ban to include these aircraft and to extend the ban until the Third Conference.

World War I prevented the convening of this Conference and also demonstrated that an absolute prohibition of aerial bombardment was unrealistic and unworkable. The result was yet another meeting at the Hague of eminent jurists and scholars who prepared the Draft Hague Rules of Air Warfare of 1923. These Rules have never been adopted by any state, yet they do reflect many of the recognized customary rules in this area which are discussed below.

World War II again evidenced the futility of rules which ignore the modern methods of total war. It is significant that not a single person accused of war crimes after the war was accused of violating the international law of aerial bombardment. Since World War II there have been few attempts to draft specific rules regulating air warfare. Instead, there have been agreements such as the 1949

Geneva Conventions and United Nations General Assembly Resolutions 2444 (XXIII) and 2675 (XXIV) which reemphasize the requirement to give civilian populations the maximum possible protection.

These agreements have incorporated the basic concepts of humanity, proportionality, and military necessity, and have resulted in several generally recognized rules of aerial bombardment.

First, military and civilian targets must be distinguished, and attacks limited to the former. The civilian population should not be the object of attack. "The mass annihilation of enemy people is neither humane, permissible, nor militarily necessary." AFP 110–31, 25–3(b)(2). Civilian casualties and damage incidental to attacks on legitimate military targets are not prohibited and are limited only by "proportionality"; i.e., the loss inflicted should be proportionate to the military advantage gained by the attack. Attacks on targets containing so-called "dangerous forces," such as nuclear reactors or dams, are allowed unless the primary purpose is to inflict suffering on civilians. Protocol II, as discussed above, would modify this.

Second, "undefended" areas should not be attacked. However, "in the U.S. view, it has been recognized by the practice of nations that any place behind enemy lines is a defended place because it is not open to unopposed occupation. Thus, although such a city is incapable of defending itself against aircraft, nonetheless, if it is in enemy-held territory and not open to occupation, military objectives in the city can be attacked." AFP 110–31, ¶ 5–3 (3)(2).

Third, civilian populations should be moved from military target areas and should not be used as a shield for these targets. Of course, civilians who take part in the hostilities may be made objects of attack.

Fourth, warnings of specific impending attacks, although required by The Hague Conventions of 1907 when circumstances permit, are not now recognized as a requirement of international law. Certain facilities which have been extended specific protection from bombardment include fixed and mobile medical and hospital establishments, and related transports; "safety zones" agreed upon by the parties to the conflict; buildings and monuments of religious and cultural significance; and prisoner of war camps.

Use of military aircraft for the purpose of disseminating propaganda is permitted. However, "propaganda which would incite illegal acts of warfare, as for example killing civilians, killing or wounding by treachery or the use of poison or poisonous weapons, is forbidden." AFP 110 31, ¶ 5,6(b).

As technology improves the target accuracy of bombing, for example through the development of laser-guided "smart bombs," the principle of proportionality will limit the degree of acceptable side-effects upon a civilian population.

2. NAVAL WARFARE

The rules of naval and air warfare are very similar. Indeed, the 1907 Hague Convention No. XI Concerning Bombardment by Naval Forces in Time of War forms the basis for several of the general rules applicable to aerial bombardment noted above. Likewise, the rules of naval warfare suffer from the same lack of relevance to modern techniques of armed conflict that plagues the rules of air warfare. However, widespread naval warfare has not been a feature of recent conflicts; consequently, there is currently little impetus to reconsider or redraft these rules.

The law of naval warfare reflects the same requirements for distinction between military and civilian vessels and targets. The basic rules in this area are as follows: (1) enemy warships may be attacked, destroyed, or captured by any means anywhere outside neutral territory; (2) since sea vessels may surrender more easily and effectively than aircraft, they must be permitted to do so without further attack (in addition, persons abandoning such vessels are not subject to attack); (3) certain vessels are specifically protected from attack, including hospital ships, small coastal fishing vessels, and vessels protected by special agreement between the parties to the hostilities.

Enemy merchant ships, although subject to capture and prize proceedings, in theory should be immune from attack because of the legal requirements to avoid injury and damage to civilians. However, the practice of nations has not demonstrated respect for this concept. Earlier in this century, customary international law required at a minimum that the crew of the merchant vessel be permitted to evacuate prior to attack. More modern convoy techniques have rendered such rules impracticable, and the U.S. Navy has adopted the following procedure:

Enemy merchant vessels may be attacked and destroyed, either with or without warning, in any of the following circumstances:

1. Actively resisting visit and search or capture;

2. Refusing to stop upon being duly summoned;

3. Sailing under convoy of enemy warships or enemy military aircraft;

4. If armed, and there is reason to believe that such armament has been used, or is intended for use, offensively against an enemy;

5. If incorporated into, or assisting in any way, the intelligence system of an enemy's armed forces;

6. If acting in any capacity as a naval or military auxiliary to an enemy's armed forces. U.S. Navy, *Law of Naval Warfare* pamphlet, NWIP 10–2, ¶ 503(b)(3).

3. WEAPONS SYSTEMS

A weapon can be illegal according to international law either because of the manner of its use or because of its very nature. The analysis of illegality under either theory is the same: the weapon or its use must meet the requirements of

military necessity, proportionality, and humanity
described and defined above. These requirements
have been translated into rules against
"superfluous injury" and "unnecessary suffering."
Specifically, "the critical factor in the prohibition
against unnecessary suffering is whether the
suffering is needless or disproportionate to the
military advantages secured by the weapon, not
the degree of suffering itself." AFP 110–31, ¶ 6–
3(b)(2). With these general concepts as a
foundation, major weapons types must be analyzed
separately.

a. Conventional Weapons

Several conventional weapons have been
specifically outlawed by international agreement
because their obvious purpose is to increase
suffering. These include barbed weapons, "dum
dum" or exploding bullets, projectiles filled with
glass or materials which tend to inflame or infect
the wound or are difficult to locate through x-ray,
irregularly shaped bullets, and bullets with scored
surfaces or whose ends have been filed off. Other
conventional weapons may be illegal because they
are incapable of being controlled and therefore
inflict their harmful effect indiscriminately. Such
weapons offer no certainty whatsoever that they
will be targeted on military objectives. The Scud
missile developed by the Soviets in the mid-1960s
and still used by many countries is a contemporary
example. The weapon lacks a precision guidance
system and is dangerously erratic.

Several conventional weapons, because of their
effective antipersonnel characteristics, have had

their legality questioned, although the practice of nations clearly indicates a general acceptance by the world community. Generally speaking, they are lawful weapons although they can be used illegally. These include explosive devices filled with fragmentation particles, including cluster bomb units and flachettes; incendiary weapons, such as flame throwers and napalm which can be used in bombs against hardened targets and as fougasse (drums of napalm with an igniter and trip wire) used for perimeter defense; and delayed action explosives including mines. Some weapons in the latter category are generally considered illegal if they are deployed in the form of booby traps attached to objects protected by international law, such as wounded persons, or if in the form of items likely to be used by civilians, such as letters, fountain pens, jewelry, etc.

Weapons issued to American armed forces are required to undergo legal review to assure their conformity with the law of war. DoD Instruction 5500.15 (Review of Legality of Weapons Under International Law). Members of the armed forces may, therefore, assume that their weapons are legal if used in the manner in which they are intended. (Unorthodox use may constitute an illegal use of a legal weapon.) For examples of recent weapons reviews see Overholt, "Memorandum of Law: The Use of Lasers as Antipersonnel Weapons," Army Lawyer 3 (Nov. 1988); and Parks, "Memorandum of Law—Review of Weapons in the Advanced Combat Rifle," Army Lawyer 18 (July 1990).

b. Chemical and Biological Weapons

Due primarily to their indiscriminate and uncontrollable nature, all chemical and biological weapons have been considered illegal to one degree or another since their invention. Some are the subject of specific international agreements, for example: the Geneva Protocol for the Prohibition of the Use in War of Asphyxiating, Poisonous, or Other Gases, and of Bacteriological Methods of Warfare, June 17, 1925; the Convention on the Prohibition of the Development, Production, and Stockpiling of Bacteriological (Biological) and Toxin Weapons and on Their Destruction, 1972; and Art. 23(a) of the 1907 Hague Regulations Respecting the Laws and Customs of War on Land, Annex to Hague Convention No. IV, which specifically prohibits the use of poisons. The gas warfare Protocol was not ratified by the United States Senate until 1975, and then only with the reservation that the United States could use chemical weapons as a reprisal for their first use by an enemy.

Two other chemical weapons, although not presently covered by any international agreement, deserve mention because they are specifically regulated in the United States by Executive Order. E.O. 11850, issued April 8, 1975, prohibits (1) the "first use" of herbicides by U.S. forces (which were in common use during the Vietnam War) except in very limited, defensive circumstances; and (2) the first use of "riot control agents" which temporarily disable rather than permanently injure, except in certain specified situations such as rescue missions and control of prisoners in prisoner of war camps.

c. Nuclear Weapons

No treaty or rule of customary international law presently prohibits the use of nuclear weapons as a means of waging war in all circumstances. However, the International Court of Justice (ICJ) in 1996 issued an advisory opinion on the legality of nuclear weapons in response to a request by the General Assembly of the United Nations, the World Health Organization and other bodies. The ICJ reached the following principal conclusions: (1) international law neither specifically authorized nor prohibited the threat or use of nuclear weapons; (2) any use of nuclear weapons would have to comply with Articles 2(4) and 51 of the U.N. Charter regarding the use of force as well as any specific treaty obligations relating to nuclear weapons; and (3) the threat or use of nuclear weapons might be legal "in an extreme circumstance of self-defense, in which the very survival of a State is at stake." Advisory Opinion on the Legality of the Threat or Use of Nuclear Weapons (United Nations), 1996 I.C.J. 226. The court was narrowly divided on the last issue.

In early 2003, news reports revealed early that the classified version of the National Security Presidential Directive "National Strategy to Combat Weapons of Mass Destruction" (NSPD-17, Sept. 17, 2002 [unclassified version]) included the following provision:

The United States will continue to make clear that it reserves the right to respond with overwhelming force—including potentially nuclear weapons—to the use of [weapons of mass

destruction] against the United States, our forces
abroad, and friends and allies.

To the extent that this proposed use of nuclear
weapons exceeds the requirements of self-defense
in the context of national survival, it would be
inconsistent with the Advisory Opinion.

Unpublished annotations to ¶ 35 of The Law of
Land Warfare, FM 27–10, explain why atomic
weapons, including the atomic bomb, are lawful.
An atomic bomb has three effects—fire, blast, and
radiation. Two of these, fire and blast, are clearly
lawful under the law of war. So long as the
primary effect of the weapon is blast, a use similar
to all high explosives, and fire, like other
incendiary devices, it is legal. Two examples of
illegal use would be a detonation of an atomic
bomb under a harbor for the purpose of drenching
the port in radioactive water, or a high altitude
detonation intended to create a radioactive plume
and attenuated blast and fire effects. Both
instances would arguably violate Article 23(a) of
the Hague Regulations which prohibit the use of
poisoned weapons. Because the destruction
potential of these weapons is so enormous, they are
subject to political restraint and have been
regulated indirectly by a number of treaties. The
subject of nuclear arms reduction and nuclear
nonproliferation is beyond the scope of this book.

d. Convention on Conventional Weapons

The sections immediately following deal with
areas of protection delineated in the United
Nations Convention on Conventional Weapons
(CCW) of 1980. The CCW regulates the use in

armed conflict of certain conventional arms deemed to cause excessive suffering to combatants or indiscriminate harm to civilian populations through four protocols.

- Protocol I (1980) prohibits use of "any weapon the primary effect of which is to injure by fragments which in the human body escape detection by X-rays."

- Protocol II (1980, amended in 1996) regulates mines and booby-traps and is discussed further below.

- Protocol III (1980) treats incendiaries and restricts the uses of any "weapon or munition which is primarily designed to set fire to objects or to cause burn injury to persons through the action of flame, heat, or a combination thereof, produced by a chemical reaction of a substance delivered on the target." Protocol on Prohibitions or Restrictions on the Use of Incendiary Weapons (Protocol III), Oct. 10, 1980, 19 I.L.M. 1534 (1980).

- Protocol IV (1995) prohibits use of "laser weapons specifically designed, as their sole combat function or as one of their combat functions, to cause permanent blindness * * * ." It does not prohibit the battlefield use of laser systems for such purposes as range-finding, jamming, dazzling, communications, weapons guidance, or attack or destruction of materiel even though these uses may produce incidental eye injury.

e. Land Mines

State obligations with respect to sea mines have long been clear. E.g., Corfu Channel case (U.K. v. Albania), 1949 I.C.J. 4 (Albania responsible for the death and destruction caused by anchored automatic mines placed in the Corfu Channel in violation of the right of innocent passage). Land mines have proven more controversial. Land mines are munitions placed under, on or near the ground or other surface area designed to be detonated by the presence of a person or vehicle. A related device is the booby-trap which is a device designed to kill or injure which detonates unexpectedly when a person disturbs or approaches an apparently harmless object or performs an apparently safe act.

Despite suggestions that the use of land mines violates the norms of international humanitarian law, state practice as evidenced by the extensive, ongoing use of land mines suggests that their use is permitted under customary international law. The use of treaties to regulate the types and uses of land mines likewise suggests that they are a legal means of warfare. Two treaties govern the obligation of States with respect to the use and removal of land mines: (1) the Amended Protocol on Prohibitions or Restrictions on the Use of Mines, Booby-Traps and Other Devices, Oct. 10, 1980, 19 I.L.M. 1529 (Protocol II), which is a protocol to the Convention on the Use of Certain Conventional Weapons Which May Be Deemed to be Excessively Injurious or to Have Indiscriminate Effects, 10 Oct. 1980, 19 I.L.M. 1523, and (2) the Convention on the Prohibition of the Use,

Stockpiling, Production and Transfer of Anti-Personnel Mines and on Their Destruction, Sept. 18, 1997, 36 I.L.M. 1507 (APM Convention).

Under Protocol II, State Parties to a conflict are not allowed to use mines and booby traps for non-military objectives and are prohibited from setting booby traps near facially or deceptively safe premises such as hospitals burial sites, monuments or items attractive to children. State Parties are responsible for all mines they deploy and must maintain an inventory record of mines. They are required to clear, remove, or destroy such weapons after the cessation of active hostilities. The United States is a party to this treaty.

The APM Convention mandates a complete ban on the use, development, production, acquisition, stockpiling, retention or transfer of anti-personnel mines and calls for their destruction. Parties are required to destroy mines in their jurisdiction. A provision of this treaty establishes mine awareness and victims' assistance programs. The United States is not a party to this treaty.

The 1996 amendments to Protocol II expand the scope of the Protocol to encompass internal armed conflicts, require remotely delivered anti-personnel land mines to be self-deactivating and non-remotely delivered anti-personnel land mines to be self-destructing or self-neutralizing unless they are in controlled, marked and monitored minefields. There is an exception for claymore mines, including he current U.S. claymore mine [the M18A1], an anti-personnel weapon placed on the ground that delivers round steel shot in a fan-shaped pattern. The restrictions of Amended

Protocol II do not apply to claymores employed in a tripwire mode for up to seventy-two hours, located in the immediate proximity of the military unit that emplaced them, and in an area monitored by military personnel to prevent civilian entry and harm. Another provision requires that anti-personnel land mines must contain the equivalent of eight grams of iron to facilitate detection.

4. OTHER

a. Protection of Cultural Property

Although cultural property is protected by the Hague Convention of 1907, widespread looting of cultural properties during World War II prompted adoptions of the Hague Convention for the Protection of/Cultural Property in the Event of Armed Conflict, May 14, 1954 (249 U.N.T.S. 240). This Convention extends protection to cultural treasures on the theory that cultural property belongs to all mankind. Armed forces are obliged to avoid damage to cultural property including "buildings dedicated to public worship, art, science, or charitable purposes; and historic monuments. [including and] irrespective of origin or ownership: (a) movable or immovable property of great importance to the cultural heritage of every people * * * , (b) buildings whose main * * * purpose is to preserve or exhibit * * * movable cultural property, [and] (c) centers containing a large amount of cultural property * * * to be known as 'centers containing monuments." Parties to the treaty agree "to take, within the framework of their ordinary criminal jurisdiction, all necessary steps to prosecute and impose penal or disciplinary sanctions upon those persons, of whatever nationality, who commit or order" breaches of the Convention. The Second Protocol to the Hague Convention of 1954 for the Protection of Cultural Property in the Event of Armed Conflict, March 26, 1999, provides a framework to protect objects as cultural property from damage and destruction during an armed conflict, including armed conflict not of an international character. The Second Protocol has not entered into force.

b. Protection of Children

One of the emerging issues in international humanitarian law is the use of children in armed conflict. The Optional Protocol to the Convention on the Rights of the Child on the Involvement of Children in Armed Conflict (Optional Protocol), which entered into force on February 12, 2002 (G.A. Res. 54-263, U.N. GAOR, 54th Sess., Agenda Item 116 (a), U.N.Doc. No A/RES/54/263 (2001)) represents a step toward elimination of the use of child soldiers. The Optional Protocol establishes certain limitations on the involvement of children in armed conflict: the minimum age of compulsory recruitment is 18 and those under that age are prohibited from taking direct part in hostilities; state parties must establish the minimum age of voluntary recruitment at 15; voluntary recruitment is generally to be accompanied by the informed consent of a parent or guardian and reliable proof of age.

c. Note on U.N Security Council Resolutions

In recent years, the U.N. Security Council has passed a number of Resolutions dealing with a variety of issues. These include such matters as the protection of civilians in armed conflict, on women and peace and security, the role of the Security Council in the prevention of armed conflict, and children in armed conflict. These Resolutions are framed in precatory rather compulsory terms or condemn practices without requiring States to refrain from them. Thus, they cannot be considered as establishing new rules of international law.

5. STRATAGEMS, TREACHERY, OR PERFIDY

The Hague Regulations, Art. 24, allow for ruses of war and measures to obtain intelligence about an enemy so long as absolute good faith with the enemy is maintained. Good faith is broken when one deliberately lies or misleads when there is a moral obligation to speak the truth. For example, by feigning surrender in order to gain and advantage or falsely broadcasting news of an armistice. These steps would so undermine good faith that troops would be unable to tell when true surrender was intended or a cease fire arranged, and armed forces would fight on rather than cease fighting; casualties and death would thereby be promoted in violation of the principles of humanity, proportionality and military necessity. Legitimate ruses include surprises, feigned attacks, simulations that suggest a larger force than is actually there, false message traffic, and psychological warfare techniques.

It is forbidden to misuse flags of truce and distinctive badges of the Geneva Convention such as the Red Cross. Vehicles and facilities marked with the Red Cross may only be used for humanitarian purposes such as the care of the wounded and sick. Ambulances and medical aircraft may be used for military purposes such as ammunition and troop transport *only* if their Red Cross markings have been removed or obliterated. Use of vehicles or facilities marked with the Red Cross for military purposes is a violation of the law of war.

D. REDRESSING VIOLATIONS OF THE LAW OF ARMED CONFLICT

The term "war crime" encompasses a large number of actions in violation of international law. It includes at least three separate concepts: traditional violations of the law or customs of war (a general war crime), inhumane acts against an enemy's civilian population (a crime against humanity), and the act of initiating an aggressive war (a crime against peace). All three have been the subject of attempts at redress of one form or another, although the third has been difficult to prove due to the evidentiary requirement of direct participation in the decision to initiate hostilities.

The subject matter of redress for war crimes can be examined either on the basis of the object of the sanction (i.e., the nation as a whole or the

offending person individually) or on the basis of
when the sanction can be functionally applied (i.e.,
during the conflict or after the cessation of
hostilities). The following discussion uses the latter
organization.

1. MEASURES DURING THE CONFLICT

Some practical sanctions available to redress
wrongs even as the fighting continues are 1) public
denunciation and informal sanctions; 2) United
Nations action; and 3) reprisals.

The victim of a violation of the law of warfare
does not normally keep the violation secret.
Rather, the wronged party publicizes the violation
as effectively as possible, hoping to accomplish one
of several objectives. First, it may embarrass the
offender sufficiently to cause it to punish the
individual perpetrators for the violation according
to its own domestic procedures. Second, the
publicity may cause neutral states to reevaluate
their neutrality toward the offender, or at least
consider some form of trade embargo or other
informal sanction against the offending nation.
Third, one party's war crimes may excuse the
other's. That is, reprisals, discussed below, may be
legitimated.

The United Nations, through the Security
Council, is authorized to respond to violations of
the law of armed conflict, particularly the crime of
waging an aggressive war, by publicly denouncing
the aggressor, calling for collective economic
sanctions, or by military action. United Nations
involvement in the response to Iraq's invasion of

Kuwait (Operation Desert Storm) and in the Korean War are obvious examples.

A reprisal is an act which otherwise would be prohibited by the law of armed conflict but becomes legal because it is committed in response to an illegal act by the enemy and with the intention of convincing the violator not to repeat its action. The reprisal must be meant to serve a law enforcing function. It cannot be simply an act of revenge. Although the general term "retaliation" is often used to describe responsive behavior, the precise definition of reprisal is limited to the above. Retaliation can also include retorsion, which is a state's response to an enemy's discourteous and objectionable but legal action. Since it is in response to a legal act, the retorsion must likewise be a legal act.

There are a number of additional rules associated with reprisals, some imposed by international agreement and some by customary international law. Reasonable notice must be given that a reprisal will be taken. However, the practice of states indicates that little more than a complaint may serve this purpose. The reprisal should be a last resort. All other reasonably available means to force the offender to cease violating international law and punish the individuals responsible should first be exhausted. It must be intended to damage only the offending state, and not any neutral which may be supplying the offender, and it must be proportional to the violation which caused it.

Certain persons or things protected by the Geneva Conventions are also protected from reprisals in all circumstances.* They include 1) prisoners of war (GPW, Art. 13); 2) wounded and sick (GWS, Art. 46, GWS–Sea, Art. 47); 3) shipwrecked (GWS–Sea, Art. 47); 4) other buildings, vessels, or equipment protected by the Conventions (GWS, Art. 46, and GWS–Sea, Art. 47).

2. MEASURES AFTER THE CONFLICT

Some measures of redress, usually only practical and effective after the cessation of hostilities and the defeat of the offending state, are 1) compensation and 2) trial of individual war criminals.

a. Compensation

Several international agreements confirm the principle that a state itself is liable for violations of the law of warfare committed by citizens acting on behalf of the state. For example, Art. 3 of the 1907 Hague Convention No. IV Respecting the Laws and Customs of War on Land states:

---

* Article 60(5) of the Vienna Convention on the Law of Treaties, itself declared to be a reflection of customary international law by the International Court of Justice in the Namibia case (Advisory Opinion on the Legal Consequences for States of the Continued Presence of South Africa in Namibia (South West Africa) Notwithstanding Security Council Resolution 276 (1970), [1971] I.C.J. 3, 35), prohibits any state from violating provisions of treaties "relating to the protection of the human person contained in treaties of a humanitarian character."

A belligerent party which violates the provisions of said (Hague) Regulations shall, if the case demands, be liable to pay compensation. It shall be responsible for all acts committed by persons forming part of its armed forces.

Similar provisions can be found in GPW, Art. 12, and GCC, Art. 29.

As a practical matter, however, and as a general rule, the state's responsibility to pay compensation will only arise when it can be shown that the violations occurred because its officials were in some way at fault, for example, by providing inadequate supervision or training of its armed forces.

b. Trial of Individual War Criminals

Although individual responsibility is normally not a feature of international law, it is central to the law of armed conflict. Effective enforcement of the rules of war requires that those persons who violate the law be subject to sanctions similar to those imposed on any other criminal found guilty of heinous crimes. Indeed, nations will also seek to impose responsibility on certain individuals to avoid guilt being placed upon an entire populace. Imposition of individual responsibility for war crimes is usually accomplished in one of two ways. First, each nation is required to bring these individuals to justice before its own courts on behalf of all nations. For example, each of the four Geneva Conventions of 1949 requires parties to search for and prosecute any person who violates the provisions of these treaties, and, if necessary, amend or adopt penal codes to satisfy this obligation. Second, the military authorities of victorious powers can establish *ad hoc* international military tribunals. The most recent examples of these courts are those established by the Allies after World War II: the International Military Tribunal for the Trial of German Major War Criminals (the Nuremberg Tribunal) and the International Military Tribunal for the Far East (the Tokyo Trials). As a consequence of the exclusive use of these two methods, until recently the development of the law of individual criminal responsibility for war crimes is contained almost entirely in the opinions of domestic or *ad hoc* international courts.

In the wake of evidence of widespread genocide in parts of the former Yugoslavia and in Rwanda, the United Nations established an International War Crimes Tribunal for the former Yugoslavia based at the Hague and a similar, separate tribunal to deal with Rwanda. These are the first since the Nuremberg and Tokyo tribunals at the end of World War II.

c. The International Criminal Court

A substitute for the ad hoc approach followed in the instances of Nuremburg, Tokyo, Yugoslavia and Rwanda has emerged. The Rome Statute of the International Criminal Court, July 17, 1998, U.N. Doc. A/ CONF. 183/9 (1998) (United Nations Diplomatic Conference of Plenipotentiaries on the Establishment of an International Criminal Court, July 17, 1998), 37 I.L.M. 998 (1998) establishes an international forum, the International Criminal

Court (ICC), to prosecute the most serious crimes concerning the international community.

Under the Rome Statute, the ICC is consists of two independent parts -- a judiciary comprised of the judges and their administrative support personnel under a President and a prosecutorial arm which includes the investigative staff under an independent Prosecutor. The overall supervision of the ICC is accomplished by an Assembly made up of individual representatives appointed by State Parties to the Rome Statute. It is the task of the Assembly to provide management oversight regarding administration of the Court, including budgetary oversight.

The ICC has eighteen judges, a number that can be increased by two-thirds vote of the Assembly. The judges vote among themselves to select the President and the First and Second Vice-Presidents, who, together, comprise the Presidency. The eighteen judges are in turn divided into an Appeals Division made up of the President and four other judges, and Pre-Trial and Trial Divisions made up of at least six judges each.

The ICC has jurisdiction over genocide, crimes against humanity, war crimes and crimes of aggression. Article 6, Genocide, includes any of the following acts committed with the intent to destroy in whole or in part, a national, ethnic, racial or religious group: killings, causing serious bodily or mental harm; deliberately inflicting on a group conditions of life calculated to bring about it physical destruction; imposing measures intended to prevent births; forcibly transferring the children of the group to another group. Article 7, Crimes against humanity, includes any of the following acts when committed as a part of a widespread or systematic attack directed against any civilian population with knowledge of the attack: murder, extermination; enslavement; deportation or forcible transfer; imprisonment or other severe deprivation of physical liberty in violation of fundamental international laws; torture; rape, sexual slavery, enforced prostitution, forced pregnancy, enforced sterilization, or any other form of sexual violence; group persecution; enforced disappearance; apartheid; other inhumane acts of a similar character. Article 8, War crimes, includes when committed as part of a plan or policy: grave breaches of the Geneva Conventions; willful killing; torture or inhumane treatment including experimentation; causing great suffering or serious injury; wanton and unlawful destruction or appropriation of property not justified by military necessity; compelling a prisoner of war or other protected person to serve in the armed forces of a hostile power; willfully depriving a prisoner of war or other protected person of the right to a fair and regular trial; unlawful deportation or transfer or unlawful confinement; hostage taking. Article 8 also proscribes attacks on civilian populations and objects, personnel and related support for humanitarian assistance and peacekeeping missions, attacking a surrendering combatant and similar violations of the Geneva Conventions.

An individual is criminally liable if he or she individually or jointly commits an act in violation of the Statute; orders, solicits or induces the commission of such crime; aides, abets or in any way assists in the commission of a crime. Attempts may also be prosecuted.

The United States is not a party to the Rome Statute. Article 98 of the Statute provides that the ICC may not require a State Party to abide by the Court's request for surrender of individuals charged by the Court if such surrender by the State Party would in any way be contrary to its international obligations with other Parties. The United States has utilized Article 98 by entering into bilateral agreements, notably with Romania and Israel, whereby American citizens would be granted immunity from prosecution and not extraditable to the ICC in those respective States.

d. Issues in the Trial of Accused War Criminals

The following sections consider issues applicable to the trial of accused war criminals: the responsibility of commanders, and of their subordinates, and the responsibility of non-military persons for war crimes.

(1) Responsibility of Superior Officers

Military commanders are necessarily occupied with a wide variety of duties while engaged in war. Although they cannot be expected to know every act of their subordinates, the interests of humanity require placing some responsibility upon superiors to prevent the commission of atrocities.

The cases resulting from World War II created two competing theories of command responsibility for war crimes. The first developed from the leading case of In re Yamashita (S.Ct.1946), in which a Japanese General was accused of a breach of duty in allowing members of his command to commit atrocities against United States and Philippine citizens. Yamashita claimed that these acts were committed by subordinates remote from his command and that he did not knowingly permit the massacres. The Supreme Court rejected this defense and ruled that a commander has an affirmative duty to take measures necessary to protect POW's and civilians. Yamashita represents a strict "constructive knowledge" standard.

A significantly different conclusion was reached in United States v. von Leeb (the High Command Case) (1950). Recognizing that a commanding officer cannot be cognizant of all acts committed by subordinates, the International Military Tribunal at Nuremberg used a more lenient "actual knowledge" standard: the war crime must be directly traceable to the superior or his failure to supervise subordinates must constitute criminal negligence before criminal responsibility is imposed. Von Leeb distinguished Yamashita on the basis that the Japanese General had exclusive command over the entire operation, whereas von Leeb, an occupational commander, was subject to restrictions imposed by his superiors. Thus, the responsibility of these "intermediate," subordinate commanders for acts ordered by their superiors can be described as follows: If the illegal order is not illegal on its face, and if the intermediate commander does not know it is illegal, then the mere administrative function of passing on the order does not make him criminally liable. If he passes the order to the chain of command and it is criminal on its face or he knows it is criminal, he will be held criminally responsible. The same basic reasoning applies to chiefs of staff and other staff officers who are generally not held responsible for the acts of subordinates unless it is shown that they personally had something to do with initiating the criminal order. The basis for their freedom from liability lies in the fact that chiefs of staff generally do not have any command authority. They sign orders for and by order of their commanding officers.

Addressing the charge of "waging aggressive war" upon which many of the Nuremberg defendants were convicted, the von Leeb court held that "international common law, at the time they so acted, had not developed to the point of making the participation of military officers below the policy making or policy influencing level into a criminal offense in and of itself." Since these generals were merely instruments of national policy, they were not held responsible for waging aggressive war.

Current U.S. rules of command responsibility reflect these somewhat inconsistent positions. The Law of Land Warfare adopts the constructive knowledge standard of Yamashita. FM 27–10, App. A0117, para. 501. However, this position was not followed in the court-martial of Captain Ernest L. Medina. The military court trying the commanding officer of the troops involved in the My Lai massacre during the Vietnam War shifted towards the "actual knowledge" standard of von Leeb. The court held that while a commander must take reasonable actions to correct situations existing under his command, responsibility will not be imposed without his actual knowledge that subordinates are committing or are about to commit war crimes. In view of the holding of the Supreme Court in Yamashita, many commentators claim that the Medina standards are clearly wrong. See, e.g., J. Bishop, JUSTICE UNDER FIRE 291–292 (1974). The military court's charge to the jury on this issue is reprinted in full in J. Goldstein, B. Marshall, and J. Schwartz, THE MY LAI MASSACRE AND ITS COVERUP: BEYOND THE REACH OF LAW? 465–468 (1972).

(2) Responsibility of Subordinate Combatants

A soldier's responsibility for the commission of war crimes presents another dilemma. Frequently, an illegal act is committed in carrying out orders from a superior officer. United States v. Schwarz (N.C.M.R.1971). To avoid responsibility for a war crime, a soldier might be forced to disobey an order and subject himself to court martial. The Law of Land Warfare attempts to resolve this conflict by placing clear responsibility on the subordinate: if charged with war crimes, the subordinate cannot use the defense of "superior orders" unless he can prove that he "did not know and could not reasonably have been expected to know that the act ordered was unlawful." FM 27–10, ¶ 509. By the same token, the subordinate cannot be convicted for failure to obey an unlawful order of a superior.

These principles are illustrated in United States v. Calley (A.C.M.R.1973) and Calley v. Callaway (M.D.Ga.1974)(habeas granted), in which the defendant, charged with committing war crimes at My Lai during the Vietnam War, claimed that his commanding officer, Captain Medina, ordered him to massacre the villagers. The court rejected this defense, holding that, even if such an order was given, any soldier of reasonable sense and understanding would under the circumstances realize its unlawfulness and refuse to carry it out.

(3) Responsibility of Nonmilitary Persons

The Nuremberg trials were also significant because they extended individual responsibility beyond military leaders for the first time. Cabinet ministers and other civilian officials constituted the majority of those tried. In addition, many who were tried, such as directors of large industrial concerns using slave labor, had no real governmental connections. The law regarding such individuals is now clear: persons who are not members of the armed forces but who order the initiation of hostilities or employment of specific illegal policy may be held responsible as war criminals. The fact that a civilian is acting in an official capacity is not a defense to prosecution. This imposition of responsibility is based upon the premise that "individuals have international duties which transcend the national obligations of obedience imposed by the individual state. He who violates the laws of war cannot obtain immunity while acting in pursuance of the authority of the state if the state in authorizing action moves outside its competence under international law." I Trial of the Major War Criminals Before the International Tribunal 171 (1947).

The United States customarily punishes offenses as war crimes only when they are committed by enemy nationals or those serving the interests of an enemy. Violations of the law of war by members of the American armed forces are generally also violations of the UCMJ and prosecutions are based on that code and tried by court-martial. Violations of the law of war by enemy nationals or others will usually also be violations of state or federal criminal law and can be prosecuted under those laws in the appropriate court. In some instances, a military tribunal has been used. Ex parte Quirin (S.Ct.1942).

CHAPTER 8

DISCHARGE AND ADMINISTRATIVE SEPARATION

An enlistment in the armed services is a commitment to a definite term of service at the conclusion of which the servicemember is normally granted a discharge. While the majority of enlistments are served for the full period and terminate in discharge without any complications, occasionally the government or the servicemember will desire to terminate the enlistment prior to completion. The servicemember has no right to remain in the service until the expiration of his or her enlistment or fulfillment of a service obligation. Rather, the government, through designated means, may terminate the enlistment contract at any time. Statutory authority allowing early discharge is limited, however: The military must advance specific grounds for the termination, and the government is bound by procedural due process requirements and concepts of basic fairness. Waller v. United States (Ct.Cl.1972). This chapter covers the substantive reasons for, procedures for and consequences of discharge and administrative separation both for enlisted servicemembers and officers.

Three important principles shape discharges and administrative separations. First, the

servicemember's relationship with the government
is more one of status than of contract. Second, the
servicemember's status transcends any contract.
Third, because of the servicemember's interest in
continuing in the military, the armed forces must
adhere to due process restrictions when
discharging personnel.

A formal discharge is necessary to terminate
military service because of the status aspect of
associated with being a part of the military. As the
court said in United States v. Melanson (USCAAF
2000):

> A servicemember will not be considered to have
> been lawfully discharged * * * unless: (1) the
> member received a valid discharge certificate or
> a certificate of release from active duty, such as a
> Department of Defense Form (DD Form) 214; (2)
> the member's "final pay" or "a substantial part of
> that pay" is "ready for delivery" to the member;
> and (3) the member has completed the
> administrative clearance process required by the
> Secretary of the service of which he or she is a
> member.

Actual physical receipt of the discharge certificate
(DD Form 214) is not required. All that the
applicable statute, 10 U.S.C.A. § 1168(a) requires
is that the discharge certificate be "ready for
delivery." Earl v. United States (Ct. Cl. 1992).

The timing of discharge is controlled by
regulation. For example, under AR 635-200, a
discharge takes effect at "2400 [hours] on the date
of notice of discharge to the soldier." The fact that
a discharge certificate is received earlier in the day

will not control, unless discharge was intended upon delivery of the certificate: "Even if a discharge certificate and separation orders are delivered to a member earlier in the day as an administrative convenience for the unit or the servicemember, the discharge is not effective upon such a delivery unless it is clear that it was intended to be effective at the earlier time." United States v. Melanson (USCAAF 2000). Timing issues can, of course, be important since the military generally loses court-martial jurisdiction over persons lawfully discharged even as to offenses allegedly committed prior to discharge. United States ex rel. Toth v. Quarles (S.Ct., 1955).

Similarly, because the status that the servicemember assumes transcends any written agreement, the expiration of one's term of service does not lead automatically to discharge. In an emergency or in time of war, the government may order the extension of an enlistment. 10 U.S.C.A. § 12302. In fact, the military always has a strong interest in the timing, manner, and characterization of any termination of service. Factors that can cause an extension of service beyond the anticipated discharge date include, for example, pending criminal proceedings or medical treatment. Taylor v. Resor (C.M.A.1970). See 10 U.S.C.A. § 802(a)(1).

A. DISCHARGES OF ENLISTED PERSONNEL

1. GRADES OF DISCHARGES

The vast majority of separations issued by the military are discharges which characterize the servicemember's performance in the service. The character of the discharge can have a profound effect on the servicemember's future as a civilian. Eligibility for veteran's and other military benefits is predicated on the character of the discharge, and civilian employers traditionally consider the type of discharge in making employment decisions.

There are five types of discharge issued to enlisted personnel. Three are issued administratively: the honorable discharge; the general discharge "under honorable conditions;" and the discharge "under other than honorable conditions" (formerly called an undesirable discharge). The remaining two—the bad conduct discharge and the dishonorable discharge—are punitive in nature and may result only from conviction by court martial. Congress has authorized each branch of the service to issue and characterize administrative discharges pursuant to regulations promulgated by the Secretary of each department. 10 U.S.C.A. § 1169.

Three factors determine the characterization of a servicemember's administrative discharge: 1) the servicemember's quality of service as governed by the standards of acceptable personal conduct and performance of duty, including conduct in the civilian community; 2) the reason for separation (usually a pattern of conduct although in some instances a single incident may provide the basis for characterization); and 3) the servicemember's age, length of service, grade, aptitude, and physical and mental condition.

Whenever a servicemember's record reflects acceptable military conduct and performance of duty, an honorable discharge is issued. 32 C.F.R. Pt. 41, App. A. An honorable discharge signifies adequate military performance, not distinction or meritorious service, which is generally recognized through medals and awards.

Because an honorable discharge entitles the recipient to both tangible and intangible benefits, such as eligibility for veteran's benefits and favorable consideration by civilian employers, an honorable discharge is a valuable property right which cannot be denied without affording the servicemember due process of law. United States ex rel. Roberson v. Keating (N.D.Ill.1949).

When the servicemember's record does not warrant an honorable discharge, due to such problems as inaptitude, defective attitude, and apathy, a general discharge under honorable conditions may be issued. 32 C.F.R. Pt. 41, App. A. However, as with an honorable discharge, even a general discharge is reviewable. Harmon v. Brucker (S.Ct.1958).

A discharge under other than honorable conditions may be issued in the case of a servicemember whose pattern of behavior or a single instance of behavior represents a significant departure from conduct expected of servicemembers. Examples of such conduct include the use of force or violence to produce serious bodily injury or death, the abuse of a special position of trust, disregard by a superior of customary superior-subordinate relationships, acts or omissions endangering the security of the United States or the health and welfare of other servicemembers, and deliberate acts or omissions that seriously endanger the health and safety of other persons. 32 C.F.R. Pt. 41, App. A, Pt. 2.

A discharge under other than honorable conditions may not be issued unless a servicemember has been notified and afforded an opportunity to request review by an Administrative Board. A discharge under other than honorable conditions may be issued without board action in two circumstances: 1) when the servicemember requests discharge "for the good of the service" in lieu of court martial; and 2) when the servicemember waives the right to board action. Courts have upheld the discharge under other than honorable conditions against due process challenges based on its alleged punitive nature so long as the discharge is not issued as a disguise for punitive actions. Pickell v. Reed (N.D.Cal.1971).

The final two characterized discharges, the bad conduct and dishonorable discharges, are punitive discharges. They may issue only after the full court-martial process. The bad conduct discharge may be given after a special or general court-martial, while the dishonorable discharge, which carries the greatest potential stigma, can be issued only after a general court-martial. Both these discharges will result in loss of veterans' benefits and, in some states, of civil rights if issued by a general court-martial.

In addition to the five characterized discharges, Congress has authorized three uncharacterized separations: entry-level separation, release due to void enlistment or induction, and dropping from the rolls.

2. GROUNDS FOR ADMINISTRATIVE SEPARATION

Congress has provided that no regular enlisted member of the armed services can be discharged prior to his or her expiration of term of service except 1) as prescribed by the Secretary of an armed service; 2) in consequence of a sentence by a general or special court-martial, or 3) as otherwise provided by law.   10 U.S.C.A. § 1169.   The respective service Secretaries have issued regulations governing administrative separation. For example, the Secretary of the Army has promulgated AR 635–200, Personnel Separations– Enlisted Personnel. These regulations are based on the reasons, guidelines and procedures for the administrative separation of enlisted personnel issued by the Department of Defense.   32 C.F.R. Pt. 41, App. A.

The regulation specifies several grounds for separation. For example, separations are permitted for the convenience of the government for the following reasons: 1) to allow a servicemember to pursue educational opportunities; 2) to permit one to accept public office; 3) to alleviate dependency or hardship, so long as it is not normally incident to military service [ordinarily, as a matter of proof, one must have either actual or assured civilian employment secured at the time of application, Rickson v. Ward (S.D.Cal.1973)]; 4) to accommodate pregnancy or childbirth; 5) to deal with the responsibilities of parenthood where the servicemember is "unable satisfactorily to perform his or her duties or is unavailable for worldwide assignment or deployment"; 6) to address the needs of conscientious objectors; 7) to protect a surviving family member; 8) to address physical or mental conditions that do not amount to a disability but nevertheless interfere with assignment to or performance of duty such as chronic seasickness or airsickness, bedwetting (enuresis) and other personality disorders. Several of these reasons require that the servicemember receive counseling regarding a deficiency prior to the initiation of separation and an opportunity to overcome the deficiency. The counseling must be appropriately documented. In addition to these grounds, the Secretary of Defense may specify additional grounds for separation for the convenience of the government.

Separation for disability is provided for by statute. 10 U.S.C.A. § 1203. Under the statute, separation must be based on a "physical disability incurred while entitled to basic pay" and not "the result of * * * intentional misconduct or willful neglect" nor "incurred during a period of unauthorized absence."

Separation for defective enlistments and inductions is allowed in the following circumstances: an enlistment by one under the age of 17 is void and separation is required. A member aged 17 shall be separated unless retained for trial by court-martial. 10 U.S.C.A. § 1170. Separation for erroneous enlistment occurs when the enlistment would not have occurred had the government known relevant facts or followed appropriate directives or was the result of fraudulent conduct on the part of the servicemember. Defective enlistment agreements occur as a result of misconduct by recruiting personnel such as a misrepresentation which induces a servicemember to enlist with a commitment for which the member was not qualified or which, for some reason, cannot be fulfilled by the military. Fraudulent entry occurs when a servicemember enlists or is inducted by concealing or omitting facts which would have resulted in rejection if revealed to the military.

A servicemember who is unqualified for further military service because of unsatisfactory performance or conduct (or both) as evidenced by inability, lack of reasonable effort, failure to adapt to the military environment or minor disciplinary infractions may be separated while in entry level status, i.e. during the first 180 days of active military service for one in active duty status. Instead of a discharge, the servicemember receives an entry level separation.

A servicemember whose performance demonstrates that he or she cannot develop adequately to perform assigned duties or will adversely affect good order, discipline or morale may be separated for unsatisfactory performance.

The regulation providing for the administrative separation of homosexuals echoes the congressional determination that homosexuality is incompatible with military service. 10 U.S.C.A. § 654. Because of the stigma attached to public identification of someone as homosexual, an administrative board proceeding is required for separation in order to provide adequate due process protection. A characterization of discharge as under other than honorable conditions may be used only if there is a finding that a homosexual act was attempted, solicited, or committed under the following circumstances: a) by force, coercion, or intimidation; b) with a person under 16 years of age; c) with a subordinate in violation of customary military superior-subordinate relationships; d) openly in public view; e) for compensation; f) aboard a military vessel or aircraft; or g) in a location under military control under aggravating circumstances noted in the finding that have an adverse impact on discipline, good order, or morale comparable to the impact of homosexual activity aboard a vessel or aircraft.

A servicemember who has been referred to either a drug rehabilitation program or an alcohol rehabilitation program may be separated for inability or refusal to participate in, cooperate in or successfully complete the program. Separation for misconduct is appropriate for a pattern of minor disciplinary infractions; for a pattern of misconduct—either discreditable involvement with civil or military authorities or conduct prejudicial to good order and discipline.

If charges have been preferred with respect to an offense for which a punitive discharge is authorized, and it is determined that the servicemember is unqualified for further military service, separation at the request of the servicemember may occur in lieu of trial by court-martial. The characterization for discharge is normally under other than honorable conditions, but may be general (under honorable conditions) if certain guidelines are met. This is commonly part of a plea bargain.

A servicemember may be discharged for security reasons when retention is clearly inconsistent with national security. Department of Defense Directive 5200.2–R prescribes that the conditions, procedures and characterization for a security discharge be based on the servicemember's record. Pre-induction and personal off-duty associations which have no connection with the person's performance cannot be the basis for a security discharge. Stapp v. Resor (S.D.N.Y.1970).

Members of the Ready Reserve who fail to attend drills within a prescribed period and otherwise neglect their obligations may be separated for unsatisfactory participation. The obligations of reserve members are prescribed in 32 C.F.R. §§ 100.1–100.7 (DoD Directive 1215.13).

The regulation also provides plenary authority to the Secretaries of the various military departments to order separations in the best interests of the service and authorizes the military departments to establish reasons for separation by regulation.

Several of the reasons for separation require prior counseling and an opportunity for rehabilitation prior to initiation of separation. This counseling must be appropriately documented.

3. SEPARATION PROCEDURES

When discharging personnel, the armed forces must adhere to due process restrictions by providing notice and an opportunity to be heard commensurate with the gravity of the reasons upon which the separation is based. Two types of separation procedures are prescribed by the regulations: a notification procedure which provides fewer due process safeguards and is more summary, and an administrative board procedure which incorporates more due process protection. 32 C.F.R. Pt. 41, App. A, Pt. 3. Several of the grounds for separation listed above can be used under either procedure, depending on the type of discharge characterization possible.

a. Notification Procedure

Under the notification procedure, the servicemember is entitled to detailed written notice of the pendency of the action which includes the basis for the proposed separation, the facts upon which separation is based, and a reference to the regulations of the military department undertaking the separation which apply. These regulations, such as AR 635–200, are implementations of 32 C.F.R. Pt. 41, App. A. The servicemember must also be notified of the result of the proposed separation, such as whether it could result in discharge rather than release from active duty to a reserve component, and what is the least favorable characterization of discharge authorized for the proposed separation.

The regulations confer these rights on the servicemember: 1) the right to obtain copies of the documents serving as the basis for the separation decision, including summaries of classified documents; 2) the right to submit statements; 3) the right to consult with a qualified military attorney at no expense or with civilian counsel retained at the servicemember's expense; and 4) the right to request an administrative board instead of the notification procedure if the individual has six or more years of active or reserve military service. These rights can be waived either affirmatively or by failing to respond to the notice given. The servicemember must be given at least two working days to respond to the notice and that time may be extended for good cause.

Actions initiated under the notification procedure must be by a special court-martial convening authority or higher authority; although the departmental secretaries may authorize a commanding officer in the grade of 0–5 or above who has a judge advocate or legal advisor available to act as a separation authority for a specified reason for separation. The separation authority must determine whether the reasons given for the separation are supported by a preponderance of the evidence and must record his or her decision. If the separation authority finds that separation is warranted, one of three actions must be recommended: separation for a specific reason, suspended separation, or retention. Guidelines for deciding on separation and the characterization of a discharge are provided in Part 2 of the administrative regulations. 32 C.F.R. Pt. 41, App. A, Pt. 2.

b. Administrative Board Procedure

The respondent before an administrative board has rights in addition to those applicable to a notification procedure. These include the right to representation by a qualified military counsel either appointed by the convening authority or chosen by the respondent, or by civilian counsel at the respondent's expense. As with the notification procedure, these rights can be waived either formally or by inaction, such as failure to appear at the hearing. The respondent must be given at least two working days to respond to the notice, which may be extended for good cause.

The respondent may testify on his own behalf in accordance with Article 31(a), 10 U.S.C.A. § 831 (protection against self-incrimination), may submit written material for the consideration of the board at any time during the proceedings, may call witnesses on his or her behalf, may cross-examine witnesses and may argue before the board either personally or through counsel.

The court-martial convening authority appoints the administrative board comprised of at least three experienced commissioned, warrant, or noncommissioned officers. Enlisted personnel appointed to the board must be in the grade of E–7 or above and must be senior in rank to the respondent. At least one member of the board must be in the grade of O–4 or higher, and a majority of the board must be commissioned or warrant officers. The senior member of the board serves as the president. In addition, the convening authority can appoint a nonvoting recorder and a legal advisor. If the enlisted respondent is in the reserves, at least one reserve officer must be included as a voting member. Voting members shall be senior in grade to the respondent. Voting members of the administrative board or the legal advisor are subject to challenge for cause.

The president of the board rules on matters of procedure and evidence but can be overruled by a majority of the board. If there is a legal advisor, the advisor rules on all evidentiary matters and challenges. Evidence may be oral or written, and payment of expenses to permit the attendance of witnesses is allowed. Rules of evidence do not apply before administrative boards, but the evidence must be relevant and competent.

The board determines its findings in closed session with only voting members present and recommends retention or separation. The reasons for separation must be supported by a preponderance of the evidence. Suspension of separation may be recommended, but such a recommendation is not binding on the separation authority.

When the board recommends a discharge characterization of other than honorable, review of the board's proceedings is required either by a judge advocate (military lawyer) or civilian attorney employed by the military. Other characterizations of discharge also require this review if the respondent raises specific legal issues for consideration by the separation authority.

If the board recommends separation, the separation authority may approve the board's recommendations, approve the board's recommendations but suspend their executions, change the characterization of service or separation to a more favorable one, change a recommendation, if any, regarding transfer to the Individual Ready Reserve (IRR), or disapprove the board's recommendation and retain the servicemember.

Failure to follow procedural regulations or the violation of minimum concepts of basic fairness may void a discharge issued prior to a servicemember's expiration of term of service. To overturn the underlying basis for a discharge, there must be a demonstrated inconsistency between the evidence in the case and the conclusions of the discharge review board or a violation of due process. Bray v. United States (Ct.Cl.1975).

4. SEPARATION REGULATIONS FOR THE ARMY

AR 635–200 illustrates how administrative separation works within a given branch of service.

The separation process in the Army is referred to as "chaptering out" a soldier because AR 635–200 provides discrete grounds for separation in specific chapters. For example, Chapter 5 provides that when parental responsibilities render the soldier unable to perform prescribed duties or result in repeated absences, or when the soldier has a psychiatric disorder that interferes with performance of duty, or when the soldier fails to meet or maintain the weight standards prescribed in AR 600–9, he or she may be separated from the Army, AR 635–200. Other chapters address, for example, erroneous or fraudulent enlistment (Chapter 7), rehabilitation failure under the Army's Alcohol & Drug Abuse Prevention Control Program (ADAPCP) (Chapter 9), entry level inability to adapt (Chapter 11), unsatisfactory performance (Chapter 13), misconduct (Chapter 14), and homosexuality (Chapter 15).

In addition to these provisions, a soldier *may request separation* under AR 635–200 on these grounds:

1) dependency or hardship (Chapter 6) [death or disability causes a family member to rely on the soldier for support of care and separation from the service will alleviate the hardship];

2) pregnancy (Chapter 8) [a soldier whose pregnancy is verified by medical personnel may request discharge if the pregnancy is not terminated prior to 16 weeks];

3) for the good of the service (Chapter 10) [used by one facing court-martial on charges punishable by a punitive discharge]; and

4) bar to reenlistment (Chapter 16) [soldier subject to an administrative bar to reenlistment who feels unable to overcome the bar may request discharge].

Commanders are required to initiate separation actions (1) for soldiers enrolled in the Army weight control program who fail to make satisfactory progress within 6 months or fail to maintain weight standards within 12 months of completing the program (Chapter 5); (2) for soldiers designated alcohol or drug rehabilitation failures (Chapter 9); (3) for soldiers who twice fail the Army Physical Fitness Test (APFT)(Chapter 13); (4) for first-time drug offenders in grades E–5 through E–9 or any first-time drug offender with more than three years active service and for any second-time drug offender irrespective of rank or time in service (Chapter 14); and (5) for any soldier barred from reenlistment after the second consecutive three-month review, unless the commander decides to lift the bar (Chapter 16). While the commander in these five instances must initiate separation, he or she may recommend retention.

AR 635–200 provides a number of protections for the servicemember. One is the requirement that before the initiation of elimination actions, formal written counseling be given to a soldier by a responsible officer or non-commissioned officer of the possibility and consequences of an administrative discharge. Documented prior counseling is required for these discharges: 1) involuntary separation due to parenthood (¶ 5–8); 2) personality disorder (¶ 5–13); 3) entry-level discharge (Chapter 11); 4) unsatisfactory performance (Chapter 13); and 5) minor disciplinary infractions or pattern of misconduct (Chapter 14). The counseling given must include the reason for counseling, notice that separation may be initiated if the problem continues, notice of the type of discharge that could result and its effects, and written documentation of the counseling (DA Form 4856—General Counseling Form is used for this purpose).

The two procedures discussed earlier are used under AR 635–200 for the administrative separation of enlisted soldiers, a notification procedure and an administrative board procedure. Both procedures begin at the company level and are reviewed and endorsed at each command level above that until they reach the appropriate approval authority. The level for approval depends on the basis or grounds for the discharge. More stigmatizing discharges require higher approval authority. For example, only general officers can approve an other-than-honorable discharge.

The procedures to be followed in an administrative separation are set out in detail for example in AR 635-200. Servicemembers may be separated for a variety of circumstances or conditions: parenthood (which interferes with performance of duty or availability for deployment); overweight (failure to meet weight standards); perceived failure to overcome a bar to enlistment; hardship or dependency (death or disability of a family member which causes hardship for person or persons looking to the servicemember for support); pregnancy; alcohol or drug abuse (rehabilitation not possible); for the good of the service (servicemember pending court-martial for offensive for which administrative discharge is authorized); entry-level separation (inability to adopt to military environment within the first 180 days of service); unsatisfactory performance (cannot participate in training or adopt to the service); civilian misconduct; minor disciplinary infractions; a pattern of misconduct; serious offenses; and homosexuality (servicemember engages in, attempts to engage in, or solicits another for homosexual acts, states he is a homosexual, or enters into a homosexual "marriage).

5. CONSCIENTIOUS OBJECTION

Conscientious objector claims can arise even in an all-volunteer force. After training and deployment, servicemembers can come to understand that the job of the military is to win and that winning entails wounding and killing enemy and destroying property. Thoughtful self-examination may lead them to conclude that they have deeply held moral, ethical or religious objections to involvement in war. More frequent deployments abroad, heavier post-Vietnam reliance on reserve components, family commitments, and a desire to escape from educational obligations requiring service following extensive training at government expense all have prompted a change of heart. E.g., Lipton v. Peters (W.D. Tex. 1999) (contract with the Air Force enabled Lipton, a Baptist, to attend medical school;

facts do not support a claim of conscientious objector status).

Processing of conscientious objector claims is governed by 32 C.F.R. Part 75 and applicable service regulations. To qualify for discharge from military service as a conscientious objector, an applicant must establish that (1) he or she is opposed to war in any form, Gillette v. United States (S.Ct. 1971); (2) his or her objection is grounded in deeply held moral, ethical, or religious beliefs, Welsh v. United States (S.Ct. 1970); and (3) his or her convictions are sincere, Witmer v. United States (S.Ct. 1955). The issues are ones of fact and the scope of judicial review of the findings of the service is among "the narrowest known to the law." DeWalt v. Commanding Officer, Fort Benning, Ga., (5th Cir. 1973).

The Supreme Court has extended the concept of "religious beliefs" beyond traditional notions of organized theology to include purely ethical or moral beliefs which nevertheless function as a religion in the person's life because they are so deeply held. Welsh v. United States (S.Ct.1970). Additionally, the servicemember's objection to participation in war of any kind must have become fixed only after entry into the service. This does not mean that the claimant must have had a change in belief; he or she properly may hold the same beliefs before and after entry into the service. Rather, the critical question is whether objection to participation in war "crystallized," or became manifest, after entry into the service. Czubaroff v. Schlesinger (E.D.Pa.1974).

The servicemember has the burden of establishing a claim for conscientious objector status by clear and convincing evidence. 32 C.F.R. § 75.5. Once the servicemember establishes a prima facie case on the three criteria above, the burden of refutation falls on the service. Ward v. Volpe (9th Cir.1973). Practically, as has been recognized by the courts, this is an onerous burden to overcome. The service must demonstrate hard, reliable, provable facts that the applicant should not be believed. If the request for discharge is subsequently denied, the reasons for denial must be reflected clearly in the record. This effectively enables the servicemember to seek judicial relief and the court to adequately review the decision within the narrow scope permitted. Sanger v. Seamans (9th Cir.1974).

6. HOMOSEXUALITY

Prior to World War I, commanders of military units exercised discretion in maintaining unit order and morale, but there was no official regulation of homosexuality in the military. Homosexual conduct was first generally prohibited when "assault with the intent to commit sodomy" was classified as a felony offense under the Articles of War of 1916. Subsequently, this prohibition on homosexual conduct was gradually broadened and penalties for such conduct were regularized. Sodomy, the "unnatural copulation with another person of the same or opposite sex or with an animal" is punishable by court-martial. UCMJ Art. 125.

Homosexual conduct has likewise long been a basis for separation from the service. Current policy is that members of the armed forces "shall be separated from the armed forces" if "the member has engaged in, attempted to engage in, or solicited another to engage in a homosexual act." 10 U.S.C.A. 654(b)(1). Homosexual acts are defined to include "any bodily contact, actively undertaken or passively permitted, between members of the same sex for the purpose of satisfying sexual desires" or any such contact which a "reasonable person" would understand to be for such a purpose. 10 U.S.C.A. 654(e)(3).

The military has regulated homosexual conduct by service members, even if the conduct takes place before service commences or occurs with civilians away from military facilities. Meinhold v. United States DOD (9th Cir.1994). But Texas v. Lawrence (S.Ct.2003) raises some question whether the military ban on participation in homosexual conduct will remain a valid basis for refusing to enlist an individual or for discharging a service member.

Another controversial issue concerning homosexuals in the military relates to those excluded not for conduct, but for manifesting a homosexual orientation. To fulfill manpower needs during the Vietnam War, the services permitted enlistment of some discreet homosexuals. Moreover, during the 1960's and 1970's, discretionary policies concerning discharge of those having a homosexual orientation were implemented by administrative discharge boards which retained some discreet homosexuals while discharging others. In 1981, discharges for homosexuality without homosexual conduct became mandatory, although "the mere fact of homosexuality" was not a ground for less-than-honorable discharge. Between 1980 and 1991, the military so discharged nearly 17,000 homosexuals.

President Clinton, on January 29, 1993, sent a memorandum to Secretary of Defense Aspin directing him to "draft an Executive Order ending discrimination on the basis of sexual orientation" in the military. Political opposition eventually led to a compromise between those opposed to all discrimination based on sexual orientation and those who desired continuation of the preexisting policy of excluding even "celibate homosexuals" from the military. This compromise, embodied in the National Defense Authorization Act of 1994, requires separation from service of individuals who state that they are "homosexual or bisexual, or words to that effect" or who marry or attempt to marry a person "known to be of the same biological sex." 10 U.S.C.A. 654 (b)(2) and (b)(3). This policy, referred to as "Don't Ask, Don't Tell," generally requires discharge of those who voluntarily declare their homosexuality, but bars military recruiters and other military personnel from inquiring into service members' sexual orientation.

Much controversy surrounds both the previous policy of discharging those having a homosexual orientation from the military and the recent "Don't Ask, Don't Tell" modification of this policy. Compare Meinhold v. United States DOD (9th Cir.1994)(Navy directed to reinstate individual discharged solely on his statement that he is gay) with Steffan v. Aspin (D.C.Cir.1993)(discharge of midshipman by Navy for answering affirmatively the question "Are you a homosexual?" upheld).

The two main constitutional provisions utilized to attack the military's policies are the First Amendment and the Equal Protection component of the Fifth Amendment's Due Process clause. Some courts have found a violation of free speech rights when a service member is discharged for saying that he or she is a homosexual, e.g. Able v. United States (E.D.N.Y.1995), while other courts find no First Amendment violation on comparable facts, e.g. Ben-Shalom v. Marsh (7th Cir.1989). Likewise, the courts are split over whether the military's policy violates Equal Protection doctrine. Compare Able (violation of Equal Protection) with Ben-Shalom (no Equal Protection violation). Until the Supreme Court resolves the divisions among the lower courts, litigation will undoubtedly continue.

B. DISMISSAL OF COMMISSIONED OFFICERS

A commissioned officer has no constitutional right to remain in the service and may be separated from the military through one of several methods. Some merely terminate the officer's status in a particular military component, while others sever all connection with the military.

Officers can be separated by termination in some instances, by operation of law because of expiration of appointment for a designated term, by acceptance of an incompatible office or status, by conviction of certain offenses against the United States, or by appointment of a successor to an office.

The President has the authority to drop from the rolls any commissioned officer in regular service or in the reserves who has been absent without authority for at least three months, or who is finally sentenced to confinement in a federal or state penitentiary after having been found guilty of an offense by a court other than a military court or court-martial. 10 U.S.C.A. § 1161(a); 10 U.S.C.A. § 1163(b). Dropping from the rolls is a complete termination of service status.

Separation can be accomplished by retirement, either voluntary or compulsory. Officers upon termination of active duty are placed on the retired list. There are provisions for early retirement when the needs of the service require it. E.g., 10 U.S.C.A. § 612.

Dismissal is the punitive separation of a commissioned officer convicted of a criminal offense. A commissioned officer may be dismissed from any of the armed forces only (1) by sentence of a general court martial, (2) in a commutation of a sentence of general court martial, and (3) in time of war, by order of the President. 10 U.S.C.A. § 1161(b).

Under UCMJ Art. 4, any commissioned officer dismissed by order of the President may request a court-martial in an attempt to clear his or her name. 10 U.S.C.A. § 804. There is no right to such a trial. The officer must apply in writing, swearing under oath that he or she has been wrongly discharged. The President must convene the court-martial, if at all, within six months of the request. However, if the President fails to do so, or if the court-martial acquits the officer or fails to order dismissal as part of its sentence, the officer gains only a limited victory: the secretary of the service substitutes an administrative discharge in lieu of dismissal. The officer does not regain his military position, because the President has the sole power to appoint officers of the Armed Forces. The officer's limited victory does, however, allow him to seek reappointment by the President with full restoration of rank and benefits.

Officers may be discharged for non-selection for promotion unless there is provision for their selective retention and they are retained. Their periods of retention and eligibility are governed by military departmental regulations and vary among the services.

Each department has specific regulations relevant to the separation, dismissal and elimination of officers. Non-probationary officers have the right to an administrative hearing prior to any involuntary administrative separation. Probationary officers may be involuntarily separated from the service without any formal administrative hearing so long as they receive honorable or general discharges.

An officer may not be eliminated under other than honorable conditions without the opportunity to have a hearing before a board of inquiry. Any such hearing must be fair and impartial, but there need not be a dismissal hearing if a post-dismissal hearing is available. The officer must be notified of all statements which will be considered by the board prior to the hearing and is entitled to counsel. The officer may question witnesses who appear before the board and may request additional witnesses of his own.

An officer may resign a commission. Normally, a resignation will not be accepted unless by the requested date of separation the officer has fulfilled all applicable service obligations. If the officer's resignation is accepted, an honorable or general discharge will be issued depending on the officer's military record.

An officer may submit a resignation for the good of the service when court-martial charges have been preferred against the officer with a view toward trial by general court-martial, when the officer is under suspended sentence of dismissal, or when the officer elects to tender his or her resignation because of homosexuality before general court-martial charges have been preferred or elimination action has been initiated.

C. ADMINISTRATIVE REVIEW

1. DISCHARGE REVIEW BOARDS

Congress has created two administrative bodies to review military discharges. A Discharge Review Board (DRB) is established by the Secretary of each department under the authority of 10 U.S.C.A. § 1552 and 32 C.F.R. § 70.5. It is comprised of members who are usually high ranking active duty officers. The DRB, either on its own motion, the servicemember's motion, or the motion of a surviving spouse or next of kin, may review a discharge or dismissal, provided the action is initiated within 15 years of the issuance of the discharge.

Subject to the review of the Secretary, the DRB can change a discharge or dismissal to a higher one or issue a new discharge. The review is based on the servicemember's military record and any other relevant evidence presented by the petitioner. The petitioner may appear in person, with or without counsel, and offer testimony. Generally, the petitioner must establish that the discharge was improperly or inequitably issued under the standards of law and discipline of the military department, or that new standards have been promulgated which are retroactive in application.

2. BOARD FOR CORRECTION OF MILITARY RECORDS

An application for discharge review may be made to the Board for Correction of Military Records (BCMR) either initially or following an unfavorable decision by the DRB. The BCMR, established under 10 U.S.C.A. § 1552, is composed of civilian employees of the Department of Defense. See e.g., 32 C.F.R. § 581.3. The BCMR has the authority to correct any error in a military record, and, except where procured by fraud, the correction is final and conclusive. Generally, the request for correction must be made within three years of the discovery of the error or injustice in the records, although the board may waive this statute of limitations.

Unlike the DRB, the BCMR is not subject to mandatory procedures. There is no right to a hearing, although the board may in its discretion grant a hearing. If the board rules in favor of the applicant, the board will make its recommendation to the Secretary; if it is accepted, the original discharge is vacated and the new one is made retroactive. The applicant may then file a claim for repayment of any fine paid or benefits withheld as a result of the erroneous discharge.

3. JUDICIAL REVIEW

a. Jurisdiction

Any action against the United States, its officers, and agencies must be brought in federal court. In challenging a discharge action, a servicemember may establish jurisdiction in one of three ways, depending on the nature of the challenge. First, the "federal question" statute, 28 U.S.C.A. § 1331, would permit a Constitutional challenge to discharge statutes or regulations without the necessity for showing an amount in controversy in excess of $75,000 (28 U.S.C.A. § 1332). Second, the servicemember could seek mandamus under 28 U.S.C.A. § 1361 to compel a military official or departmental secretary to comply with a discharge statute or regulation. Third, the servicemember could seek review in the United States Court of Federal Claims under 28 U.S.C.A. § 1491. This statute allows the court to order monetary relief for wrongful discharge, restoration to the appropriate duty or retirement status, and correction of military records.

b. Exhaustion of Administrative Remedies

Generally, the courts require exhaustion of administrative remedies as a prerequisite to judicial review. Seepe v. Department of Navy (6th Cir.1975); Woodrick v. Hungerford (5th Cir.1986). The rationale is that (1) the administrative review may provide an adequate remedy, thereby saving the courts and the parties a great deal of time and money, and (2) development of the record during administrative review facilitates judicial review. The exhaustion requirement is a matter of discretion and will not be imposed where an opportunity for administrative relief is lacking or where irreparable harm caused by the delays inherent in administrative review is likely. Ogden v. Zuckert (D.C.Cir.1961). Likewise, where resort to the administrative reviewing body would provide no real opportunity for adequate relief, but would serve only as an exercise in futility, exhaustion is not required. Hodges v. Callaway (5th Cir.1974).

The federal courts and the military judicial system must be considered as two separate and autonomous judicial systems for exhaustion requirement purposes. Thus a federal court should not postpone adjudication of an independent civil lawsuit within its original jurisdiction which otherwise meets the exhaustion requirements. Under these circumstances, the court should stay its hand only if the relief sought—discharge—also would be available to the petitioner with reasonable promptness and certainty through the military courts. Parisi v. Davidson (S.Ct.1972).

c. Preliminary Injunction

In certain situations where a servicemember wishes to stay in the service pending either administrative review or litigation, or does not wish to continue service pending decision on a claimed entitlement to discharge, the court may grant a preliminary injunction. For example, a person who has been ordered discharged but has not yet been physically separated cannot utilize administrative review. If a court issues a stay of discharge pending administrative review, the BCMR then may review the discharge before it takes effect. The criteria for a preliminary injunction are: (1) a likelihood that the servicemember will prevail on the merits of his claim; (2) a likelihood of irreparable injury to him or her if the injunction is not granted; (3) no substantial harm to the other parties if the injunction is issued; and (4) no harm to the public interest. Covington v. Schwartz (N.D.Cal.1964).

d. Scope of Judicial Review

Consistent with the general policy of non-interference by the judiciary in military affairs, the scope of judicial review of military discharges is limited. The grounds of review are generally confined to determining: (1) whether the Secretary acted within his or her authority; (2) whether the military adhered to its statutes and regulations; (3) whether procedural due process was afforded; (4) whether the grounds for the discharge are constitutional; (5) whether there has been an administrative review; and (6) whether the review decision was arbitrary, capricious or unsupported by substantial evidence. Robinson v. Resor (D.C.Cir.1972).

SUBJECT INDEX

References are to Pages
